MORGAN COMMUNITY
COLLEGE LIBRARY

WITHDRAWN BY
MORGAN COMMUNITY
COLLEGE LIBRARY

I0757887

MILTON: THE CRITICAL HERITAGE

THE CRITICAL HERITAGE SERIES

GENERAL EDITOR: B. C. SOUTHAM, M.A., B.LITT. (OXON.)
Formerly Department of English, Westfield College, University of London

Volumes in the series include

JANE AUSTEN	B. C. Southam
BROWNING	Boyd Litzinger, St Bonaventure University and Donald Smalley, University of Illinois
BYRON	Andrew Rutherford, University of Aberdeen
COLERIDGE	J. R. de J. Jackson, Victoria College, Toronto
DICKENS	Philip Collins, University of Leicester
HENRY FIELDING	Ronald Paulson, The Johns Hopkins University, Baltimore and Thomas Lockwood, University of Washington
THOMAS HARDY	R. G. Cox, University of Manchester
HENRY JAMES	Roger Gard, Queen Mary College, London
JAMES JOYCE (2 vols)	Robert H. Deming, Miami University
D. H. LAWRENCE	R. P. Draper, University of Leicester
SCOTT	John O. Hayden, University of California, Davis
SWIFT	Kathleen Williams, Rice University, Houston
SWINBURNE	Clyde K. Hyder
TENNYSON	J. D. Jump, University of Manchester
THACKERAY	Geoffrey Tillotson and Donald Hawes, Birkbeck College, London
TROLLOPE	Donald Smalley, University of Illinois

MILTON

THE CRITICAL HERITAGE

Edited by

JOHN T. SHAWCROSS

Professor of English, University of Wisconsin

MORGAN COMMUNITY
COLLEGE LIBRARY

800.8942
sha

NEW YORK
BARNES & NOBLE, INC.

First published in Great Britain 1970
Published in the United States of America 1970
by Barnes & Noble, Inc., New York, N.Y.

© John T. Shawcross 1970

SBN 389 01094 4

1. Milton, John - Criticism

Printed in Great Britain

General Editor's Preface

The reception given to a writer by his contemporaries and near-contemporaries is evidence of considerable value to the student of literature. On one side we learn a great deal about the state of criticism at large and in particular about the development of critical attitudes towards a single writer; at the same time, through private comments in letters, journals or marginalia, we gain an insight upon the tastes and literary thought of individual readers of the period. Evidence of this kind helps us to understand the writer's historical situation, the nature of his immediate reading-public, and his response to these pressures.

The separate volumes in the *Critical Heritage Series* present a record of this early criticism. Clearly for many of the highly-productive and lengthily-reviewed nineteenth- and twentieth-century writers, there exists an enormous body of material; and in these cases the volume editors have made a selection of the most important views, significant for their intrinsic critical worth or for their representative quality— perhaps even registering incomprehension!

For earlier writers, notably pre-eighteenth century, the materials are much scarcer and the historical period has been extended, sometimes far beyond the writer's lifetime, in order to show the inception and growth of critical views which were initially slow to appear.

In each volume the documents are headed by an Introduction, discussing the material assembled and relating the early stages of the author's reception to what we have come to identify as the critical tradition. The volumes will make available much material which would otherwise be difficult of access and it is hoped that the modern reader will be thereby helped towards an informed understanding of the ways in which literature has been read and judged.

B.C.S.

Contents

vii

Further Seventeenth-century Comment (1675-1699)

Eighteenth-century Comment to Bentley's Edition of *Paradise Lost* (1700-1731)

CONTENTS

ACKNOWLEDGEMENTS

I wish to thank the following for permission to reprint copyright extracts or complete items from the sources listed below: Constable Publishers (London) and Barnes & Noble Inc. (New York) for Helen Darbishire, *The Early Lives of Milton*; the Clarendon Press, Oxford, for George Sherburn (ed.), *The Correspondence of Alexander Pope*, Vols. I and II; excerpts from *The Prose of John Milton*, edited by J. Max Patrick (copyright © 1967 by Doubleday & Company Inc.; reprinted by permission of the publisher); excerpts from *The Complete Poetry of John Milton*, edited by John T. Shawcross (copyright © 1963 by Doubleday & Company Inc; reprinted by permission of the publisher); the Johns Hopkins Press for E. N. Hooker, *The Critical Works of John Dennis*; Columbia University Press for Frank Patterson, gen. ed., *The Works of John Milton*, Vols. VII, VIII, XIV; the Bodleian Library, Oxford, for a brief life of Milton in MS. Wood D.4, fol. 140.

For use of their holdings of Miltoniana, I thank the Libraries of the University of Wisconsin and Yale University. I am sincerely appreciative of the work of my research assistant, Miss Mary Jane Doherty. Her assembling of texts has been invaluable.

NOTE ON THE TEXT

The materials printed in this volume follow the original texts; any alterations are indicated in the headnotes or by ellipses. Most quotations from Milton's works have been omitted, their presence in the original being shown by a bracketed reference.

Introduction

I

As a man of controversy and as a creative artist attempting new forms and approaches, John Milton has been the subject of much discussion from his own lifetime to the present. The appearance of his name in print before 1800 (apart from his own works) falls into four categories: allusions, incidental and non-critical; argument, political or theological; illustration of points or brief critical statements; and longer biography, essays, or studies. Allusions or brief citations do not always name Milton or his works; and often the work of other writers incorporates Milton's language or subject-matter (almost entirely from the poems), either for praise or satire. The number of longer essays or studies devoted exclusively to Milton are few, and the bulk of material falls into the category of illustration or brief statement. However, the material available does allow a view of Milton's reception and fluctuating reputation, the controversies and adulation, accusations and defence, and changes in attitude and concerns. There is much in the material of a contemporary or near-contemporary nature from which to infer primary critical stands and issues; some of these have continued as viable stands and issues in twentieth-century views.

The definition of contemporary or near-contemporary for Milton, however, poses a problem. His death apparently on Sunday, 8 November 1674, suggests a terminal date around 1700 for this survey; but the period immediately following 1700 developed many of the concepts which readers will find most significant in Milton criticism. Moreover, the lack of a bibliography for the years prior to 1800 encourages one to include as many of the eighteenth-century documents as possible. A terminus of 1731 has therefore been decided upon in order to present most significant materials of a critical nature to that date. These by themselves constitute a full volume; the date immediately precedes the extensive controversy created by Richard Bentley's edition of *Paradise Lost,* which, in a way, marks a new stage in Milton's reputation; and materials after that date are often so long that adequate coverage would be impossible in a volume of this size. Some of the developments of the 1732–1800 and the 1800–1965 periods will be discussed in this Introduction. The few noteworthy items from before 1731 which have been omitted (those in foreign languages and those generally repetitive of statements included) are cited in Appendix C.

The basis for selection has been, simply, critical value. Mere allusions or citations from the works have been omitted. William Riley Parker has given a list of printed allusions to Milton, dated 1641–74, in *Milton's Contemporary Reputation* (Ohio State University Press, 1940); no allusion book exists for the years 1675–1800. A number of books, listed in Appendix B, supply references to poetry directly reflecting Milton's influence in thought, poetic form, allusion, or imitation (see the works of Richmond P. Bond, John W. Good, Raymond D. Havens, and George Sherburn). Much of the argument surrounding Milton concerns his political treatises and his views on divorce; it attacks his thought and character rather than showing interest in literary questions. When, however, allusions or citations or argument also suggest a critical position or point, they have been included. To sum up: the substance of this volume comes from the employment of Milton and his works as illustration for a critical point, from brief critical views, often inserted in discussions of other authors or subjects, and from longer essays or studies (though extracts from the various lives and biographical notices are included only when critical judgement or information useful for evaluation is expressed). The very important criticism that went into the footnotes to editions of the works is mentioned in this Introduction. Milton's frequent remarks about the writing process, his intentions, and his own literary opinions are given wide coverage in the first section.

The present Introduction attempts to give an idea of the publication of Milton's work during 1632–1731. The contemporary printing of his poetry and prose is related in some detail because of its interest to students of Milton and its relationship to the kind of reception available to Milton in his lifetime. In 1688, fourteen years after Milton's death, the fourth edition of *Paradise Lost* was issued, sponsored by Lord Somers, with the first illustrations of the epic by John Baptista de Medina. It is the first edition of a poem to owe its existence to printing by subscription, and the second book so honoured. From this date the literary (as opposed to the politically argumentative) reputation of Milton grew.

The earliest attitude towards Milton results from his prose works treating ecclesiastical, social, and political argument. Literary consideration of these prose works, or of the poetry, is almost totally missing.

But what is significant, as will be indicated throughout this Introduction, is that these negative attitudes towards him, on account of his beliefs, continue to the present time. Milton himself often brought personal and biographical matter into his work—although some readers may see more biography in certain items than Milton may have intended—and this requires some attention to biography. For the most part, however, only Milton's estimate of his own worth, his aims in writing, and his actions to rival literary masters are discussed or illustrated by excerpts from the works. Certainly his decision to win fame as a writer is significant for a full understanding of his accomplishment; and his objectives allow us to compare his hopes for his prose and poetry both with his achievement and with others' evaluation. The critical heritage of Milton has been influenced by such evaluation of the man, his personal statements of his aims and beliefs, and (on the one hand) by his involvement in contemporary issues and (on the other) by the didacticism of his work (poetry included) and its sharp breaks with tradition.

The contradictory attitudes which developed after 1688 have likewise continued to the present day. *First:* Milton is seen either as a great traditionalist who imitated the ancients or the Spenserians, or as a great breaker with tradition who altered the course of poetry in prosody or in form. Under the former attitude Milton is either less successful than Homer and Vergil (the ancients most usually compared) or superior to them; his work is a cento of former authors, too little changed or else greatly improved upon; his poetry succeeds because it is based on classic form and principles, or fails because it does not conform to the classic mould, Milton perhaps not fully understanding Aristotelian poetics. Under the latter attitude Milton is either a great author because he broke with traditional form and prosody, creating his own vehicle, or an unsuccessful author because of inadequate results or misconceived intentions. *Second:* Milton's language and verse are Latinate (and thus either good or bad according to the critic's grinding-axe; though usually bad), or they are sublime (whether Latinate or not). The now more usual twentieth-century view that the language is not strongly Latinate was not current in former times. Discussion of the verse of *Paradise Lost*, originating with Milton's preliminary statement to the poem, has been constant since the seventeenth century, some views approving, some disapproving, most not really understanding its structure or rationale. *Third:* Milton's ideas—particularly in *Paradise Lost*—either obfuscate any literary worth, for they are deplorable, inconsistent, 'dead'; or they provide, in a sense, all knowledge, all necessary philosophy and human-ism. The opposing views here summarized have existed side by side through most of the years since Milton's death. But the modern genera-tion, with its existential tendencies, has found in *Paradise Lost* profound and lasting meaning, for it has looked at the poem rather than at the man. In short, Milton's critical heritage in the years up to 1731 consists of most of the issues and attitudes which were to be viable in succeeding periods.

II

Among the first documents to be examined are those in which Milton expresses his own hopes for writing and the worth of writing. These documents have been of greater significance to nineteenth- and twentieth-century critics than to those critics represented in the main section of this volume. The seventeen items included in the first section, 'Personal Statements and Contemporary Evaluations (1628–1674)', sug-gest a serious student of poetry and an idealist who found himself too often diverted from poetry out of a personal sense of duty. The mention of Milton's ideals for poetry raises the question of the date of his decision to become a poet. The epic themes noted in 'At a Vacation Exercise' (No. 1) and his remarks on the sacred poet and on his writing of 'Ode on the Morning of Christ's Nativity' (No. 2) have generally been taken to indicate his desire to write a great poem, epical in nature and dedic-ated to Christian virtue. Such interpretation would place his decision to be a poet in the middle of 1628; and much of the criticism of the early poetry and of the fulfilment of Milton's ideals with the production of *Paradise Lost* has been based on this interpretation (cf. Nos. 29 and 50). The present editor has challenged this view on the grounds that there is a strong difference between writing poetry (as Milton had done since at least 1624, his English paraphrase of Psalm 114 being the earliest work extant) and deciding to follow a poetic career as a lifework.[1] These early statements, it is urged, should be taken in context when deciding the question of career, but their substance remains unchanged for an understanding of Milton's high artistic ideals. He shows a lack of interest and even a kind of incompatibility with fugitive work— unserious, undirected, facile. Here lies the foundation for his work, prose as well as *Paradise Lost,* according to modern critics, and a main avenue into his use of narrative voice in the epics. The temperament of the vatic poet which was soon to emerge underlies his attitudes and goes a long way towards explaining the didacticism of some of the later works.

We can see him moving in these early poems to the concept he was to formulate later in *An Apology* (p. 16):

And long it was not after, when I was confirm'd in this opinion, that he who would not be frustrate of his hope to write well hereafter in laudable things, ought him selfe to bee a true Poem, that is, a composition, and patterne of the best and honourablest things; not presuming to sing high praises of heroick men, or famous Cities, unlesse he have in himselfe the experience and the practice of all that which is praise-worthy.

A clear statement of his hope for fame, apparently through writing, lies in his letter to his long-time friend, Charles Diodati (No. 4). The letter, now dated November 1637, and 'Lycidas' (with its meditation on immortality and its poetic metaphor), perhaps give additional evidence that this decision about his life had been made only shortly before.

That Milton had faith in his ability as a poet is evident from his statement—written for private ears—in 'Ad Patrem' (No. 5), which is dated variously between 1631 and 1638. The holograph manuscript known as the Trinity MS. (or sometimes as the Cambridge MS.), owned by the Trinity College Library, Cambridge, records his attempts to improve 'Arcades' and 'A Maske' (commonly known as 'Comus'), and also serves as a workbook or repository for such English poems as the three odes, 'Lycidas', and the sonnets. (There are no manuscripts of foreign-language poems or translations.) The dating of this manuscript depends upon the date of a letter to an unknown friend drafted therein and the date of 'Arcades'—for no earlier poem appears. However, the manuscript may have been first used well after the two 'dramatic' poems were written (for both are transcripts), and as a result of Milton's decision to pursue poetry as a career. His intent may have been to make these two poems more appropriate for a reading public.[2] Whatever the date of the manuscript, it reinforces our view of Milton as a young poet seeking to achieve fame through his writing, and as a critic of his own work, altering a word or phrase here and there or replacing or rearranging passages. The revisions recorded for 'At a Solemn Music', the only poem that seems to be actually worked out in the manuscript—the others being transcriptions from some prior version—furnish excellent material for an analysis of the poetic process and Milton's self-criticism.[3] This self-criticism is evident, too, in the note he appended to the fifty-six-line fragment called 'The Passion' in the 1645 edition of his *Poems*: 'This subject the Author finding to be above the yeers he had, when he wrote it, and nothing satisfi'd with what was begun, left it unfinisht'. The poem on Christ's Passion, written in March 1630, was apparently intended as a kind of sequel to the 'Nativity Ode'; perhaps Milton published what is actually only a proem to the main poem because it was a complete unit (whatever was attempted of the main poem being destroyed) and because he wished to present an honest picture of the rising poet. The quotation from Vergil's *Eclogues*, VII, 27–8, which appears on the title-page of the *Poems*, hopes to protect such honesty: 'Baccare frontem/Cingite, ne vati noceat mala lingua futuro' ('Wreathe my forehead with foxglove, lest an evil tongue harm the poet [vates] that is to be'). Perhaps the Commonplace Book of references and quotations from Milton's reading, begun some time during the 1630s but used extensively only from late 1637 onward, also reflects this new writing urge and activity. The Trinity MS. with its authorial revisions and the Commonplace Book with its record of Milton's thoughts on many subjects—these thoughts and quoted subjects frequently appearing verbatim in his later works—have supplied critics with what they consider the essence of Milton's achievements, intentions, and artistic sense.

Prior to 1637/8 the only poem of Milton's in print was 'On Shakespear' in the Second Folio of Shakespeare's Plays, 1632, and the only poems copied into manuscript miscellanies were 'An Epitaph on the Marchioness of Winchester', 'On Time', and his two or three poems on Hobson.[4] (There are also the uncertainly dated Bridgewater MS. of 'A Maske' and two manuscripts of the settings of five songs for the poem, composed by Henry Lawes, one being in Lawes's own hand.) 'An Epitaph on the admirable Dramaticke Poet W. SHAKESPEARE', as its first printing titled it, identified the author by initials only; the poem on the Marchioness and one copy of the Hobson poem beginning 'Here lieth one who did most truly prove' are attributed to 'Jo Milton of Chr: Coll Cambr': and 'Jo: Milton' respectively; but the remaining manuscripts give no indication of the author. In 1637 (or perhaps the very beginning of 1638) 'A Maske' was published anonymously, with a letter from Lawes, who had played Thyrsis, to John, Lord Viscount Braclay, son of the Earl of Bridgewater, the original performer of the role of the Elder Brother. Lawes tells us that 'Although not openly acknowledg'd by the Author, yet it is a legitimate off-spring, so lovely, and so much desired, that the often copying of it hath tir'd my pen to give my severall friends satisfaction, and brought me to a necessitie of producing it to the publick view. . . .' Perhaps it is this 'publick view' to which Milton referred in his poem to his father when he wrote:

Therefore, now that I am a part of the learned company, however humble, I shall sit among the ivy and the laurels of the victor. And now I shall no longer mingle unknown with the indolent rabble and my steps shall shun profane eyes.

Some public comment must have ensued after publication, for Sir Henry Wotton in April 1638 attests to having viewed the poem before Milton presented him with a printed copy apparently bound with an edition of Thomas Randolph's poems (No. 6). This printing is now one of the rarest of Milton's works. Then, some time during 1638, perhaps after Milton went abroad, appeared the first edition of 'Lycidas', printed as the last of the English obsequies in the rare commemorative volume, *Justa Edovardo King naufrago.* . . . The signature assigns the poem to 'J. M.'

Preceding the collected edition of Milton's minor poems in 1645 (entered in the Stationers' Register on 6 October 1645), a few more printings of poems occurred. Two of the three Hobson poems appeared in the 1640 edition of *A Banquet of Jests*, 'Hobson's Epitaph' was included in *Wit's Recreation* in 1640 ,'On Shakespear' was again published, now in Shakespeare's *Poems*, 1640, and 'Epitaphium Damonis' received a private and limited printing also apparently in 1640. This latter volume is known only through the unique copy in the British Museum; it seems to have been produced for Milton's and Diodati's friends and relatives in England and on the Continent. The collected edition reproduces all the previous publications (alterations in all cases indicating Milton's frequent revision of work, even of that already committed to print) with the exception of 'Hobson's Epitaph'. The only other early poems which were not reproduced in the volume are 'On the Death of a Fair Infant Dying of a Cough', 'At a Vacation Exercise', and 'Apologus de Rustico et Hero' (all printed in the second edition of the minor poems in 1673), and two Latin fragments found with an early prolusion when the Commonplace Book was discovered in 1874. *Poems*, 1645, has sometimes been dated 2 January 1646 because the bookseller George Thomason inscribed that date (apparently the purchase date) on his copy. However, the recent holidays probably accounted for the time of purchase or a possible delay in distribution.

The volume was issued in three forms, undoubtedly to appeal to different audiences: English and Latin (and Greek) poems (a copy in the Boston Public Library has these reversed), English poems separately, and Latin poems separately. Such division was effected by separate title-pages and separate paginations. Harris F. Fletcher states that the full volume in sound condition is a great rarity.[5] It does not seem to have created a stir, for allusions to it are generally lacking, or to have been a big seller; copies remained unsold years later. Aside from William Sancroft's manuscript transcriptions of two poems, Joshua Poole's use of the volume in compiling *The English Parnassus* in 1657, and Richard Baron's imitations, we have no evidence of contemporary awareness of the minor poems. In 1656 the edition was advertised for sale in Thomas Blount's *Glossographia*, printed by Milton's frequent printer, Thomas Newcomb, for Humphrey Moseley and George Sawbridge—the first of whom was the publisher of the 1645 *Poems*. Such allusive evidence indicates the general lack of critical knowledge of Milton's poetry. We find this volume listed also by William London in *A Catalogue of the most Vendible Books in England* in 1658, and the Latin poems in *Catalogus Librorum Qui In Bibliopolio Danielis Elsevirii venales extant* (Amsterdam) in 1674.[6] The poetic tributes given here as Nos. 13, 14 and 15 precede the Latin poems and were probably written when Milton was sojourning in Italy, or soon after. The title-page announces the author, 'Mr. John Milton,' and the tributes may have been added, as Parker suggests, to offset the opinions held by the critics of his views on divorce. One of the tributes was by Selvaggi, an Italian acquaintance whose first name we do not know.

To John Milton.
Greece, sound thy Homer's, Rome, thy Virgil's name,
But England's Milton equals both in fame.[7]

As John Dennis and others in the eighteenth century pointed out, Dryden's well-known epigram (No. 37) is basically a translation of this couplet, although Nathaniel Lee (No. 27) knew it, too. The comparison of Milton with Homer and Vergil was to afford the main theme of examination of Milton's sublimity and of Addison's remarks on *Paradise Lost*. Today Milton's indebtedness to these two epic poets is repeatedly assumed, but no full study of his relationship with either exists in print. Only the publisher's (Moseley's) prefatory letter to the reader yields contemporary criticism of the poetry in the volume itself, and it is worth quoting despite its commercial intent:

It is not any private respect of gain, Gentle Reader, . . . but it is the love I have to our own Language that hath made me diligent to collect, and set forth such Peeces both in Prose and Vers, as may renew the wonted honour and esteem of our English tongue: and it's the worth of these both English and Latin Poems, not the flourish of any prefixed *encomions* that can invite thee to buy them, though these are not without the highest Commendations and Applause of the learnedst *Academicks*, both domestick and forrein . . . I know not thy palat how it relishes such dainties, nor how harmonious thy soul is; perhaps more trivial Airs may please thee better. But howsoever thy opinion is spent upon these, that incouragement I have already received . . . hath once more made me adventure into the World, presenting it with these ever-green, and not to be blasted Laurels. The Authors more peculiar excellency in these studies, was too well known to conceal his Papers, or to keep me from attempting to sollicit them from him. Let the event guide it self which way it will, I shall deserve of the age, by bringing into the Light as true a Birth, as the Muses have brought forth since our famouse *Spencer* wrote; whose Poems in these English ones are as rarely imitated, as sweetly excell'd. Reader if thou art Eagle-eied to censure their worth, I am not fearful to expose them to thy exactest perusal.

By the end of 1637, then, Milton had decided upon a poetic career and had begun to dream of writing a great Christian poem. He carried this dream with him to Italy, where he articulated the thought in a verse epistle to Gianbattista Manso, the literary patron of Tasso and Marino. The subject of Milton's verse epic was to be drawn from British history and would revolve around Arthurian contexts—see Nos. 7 and 8, the latter being an expanded restatement in 'Epitaphium Damonis'. Milton includes it there both because it was in his mind while he was abroad and because in 1640 he was engaged in an intensive study of British history and a search for literary topics. These hopes and plans have been examined and re-examined by critics to determine Milton's intentions and formative influences. The influence of Spenser and his followers can be seen in Milton's first thoughts; but the inadequacies of the subject must have become increasingly apparent as the prelatical arguments grew and the Civil War became more imminent. By 1642, at least, the subject had been abandoned. We find him toward the end of 1641 reviewing various topics, genres, aims, and ideas in a long biographical statement encased in *The Reason of Church-Government* (published in February 1642). Whatever he would finally decide to pursue, we know from this statement (No. 9) that it would attempt to inculcate virtue in man and strive to fulfill the function of the wayfaring Christian in this our life. With similar optimism, his humorous sonnet of November 1642 (No. 10) asserts the precedence of the might of the pen to that of the sword.

From 1640 to about 1642 Milton entered in the Trinity MS. various prose outlines for dramas and subjects for literary works drawn from the Bible, British history, and Scottish history. Amongst these plans were drafts for a drama (at first a morality) on 'Paradise Lost' and later 'Adam Unparadis'd'. Some writing was accomplished, for Milton's nephew, Edward Phillips, tells us that he had seen certain lines of Satan's address to the sun in present Book IV in 1642 (see No. 42). However, the intrusion from 1641 to 1645 of religious, political, and social issues deterred Milton from steady pursuit of his poetical writing. The derision that some of his work evoked (as he recorded in the sonnet beginning 'I did but prompt the age') and the inadequacies of common man to understand his teachings (as the sonnet beginning 'A book was writ call'd *Tetrachordon*' suggests) brought a return to intensive attention to his poetical work. The first fruits of that return was the publication of the minor poems, of which Milton himself was to comment, when a replacement was sent to the Bodleian for one lost or stolen (No. 16): 'You at last my labors have not been in vain.'

Whether the years 1645–8 produced more than a few minor poems is a moot question. At least there has been speculation that parts of the three major poems were written during this period, and the beginnings of *Paradise Lost* some years before justify the speculation for that poem. Regardless, the poetic aims and critical attitudes which the youthful Milton and the middle-ageing Milton professed had to wait almost two decades for fulfilment. Had Milton died at forty there would have been only a handful of poems to offer to posterity for judgement: a few great ones, like 'Lycidas' and the 'Nativity Ode' and 'Comus', but insufficient for a poetic fame such as he had envisioned. And indeed there would be no evidence that his poetic work had made any real or lasting impression on the world—whether contemporary or near-contemporary.

The diversion of Milton's energies into public controversy came with the anti-prelatical controversy of 1641, perhaps through the influence of his old teacher Thomas Young, one of the divines whose combined initials make up the odd name SMECTYMNUUS. Milton's polemical writing during this period, and later from 1649 to 1651, is outlined in his *Second Defense of the English People,* written in Latin in 1654 (see No. 17). If we can accept his various statements about why he felt compelled to enter the fray and what his aims were—though we should always remember that he is countering argument, some of it personal and invective—we see a man who has put duty before personal desire, who has championed his Church, his God, and his fellow man despite personal loss, and who has sought freedom and liberty for mankind in all areas of public life. Milton's invective in some of the pamphlets, and his discharging of commissions from the Council of State in *Eikonoklastes* and the *First Defense*, suggest that his statement of justification and purpose were not entirely accurate. Modern critics, however, have taken him at his word and argued for fulfilment of his high ideals through the publication of the prose. The argument in the *Second Defense* that the anti-prelatical tracts constitute an attack on religious enslavement, that the divorce tracts fight for domestic freedom and *Of Education* and *Areopagitica* for other aspects of social freedom, and that the pamphlets of 1649–51 complete a scheme by arguing for political freedom, is a neat plan, but one probably superimposed through hindsight. The break in the late 1640s and the continuing poetic hopes imply that the prose interlude was less planned and philosophical than Milton's later comments would lead one to believe. For the more contemporary aims of his prose works, see Nos. 11, 12, 18, and 19. These suggest didactic purpose, though not an overall plan and philosophy.

The first prose work that Milton published may have been 'A Postscript' to the Smectymnuan volume of March 1641, *An Answer to a Booke entituled, An Humble Remonstrance*. His authorship is questioned and was never acknowledged.[8] By May the full tract *Of Reformation* had been printed, and four more were to follow by April 1642. It would seem that the last two, *The Reason of Church-Government* and *An Apology against a Pamphlet call'd A Modest Confutation*, did not sell well, for in 1654 they were reissued with a new title-page. The pamphlets called forth rebuttals, just as they themselves were often directed by Milton as arguments against an opposing view in print. Some allusions to Milton or these tracts exist; for example, John Bramhall in *The Serpent Salve, or, a Remedie For the Biting of an Aspe* (Dublin [?], 1643) calls Milton 'a young novice' and adds: 'It was truely said by *Seneca*, that the most contemptible Persons ever have the loosest tongues' (p. 212). As we would expect, Milton's reputation depended on which side his critics favoured. There is little in print that can be called literary criticism: there is only agreement or disagreement.

The divorce tracts evoked more numerous and more bitter comments, for to antagonists of divorce anyone who urged it was a fornicator. Witness the comments of Ephraim Pagitt and Robert Baillie, whom Milton refers to in 'I did but prompt' and 'On the Forcers of Conscience' respectively:

These I terme Divorsers, that would be quit of their wives for slight occasions; and to maintaine this opinion, one hath published a Tractate of divorce, in which the bonds of marriage are let loose to inordinate lust, putting away wives for many other causes, besides that which our Saviour onely approveth; namely in case of adulterie, who groundeth his Error upon the words of God, *Gen.* 2.18.[9]

Concerning Divorces, some of them goe farre beyond any of the *Brownists*, not to speak of Mr *Milton*, who in a large Treatise hath pleaded for a full liberty for any man to put away his wife, when ever hee pleaseth, without any fault in her at all, but for any dislike or dyspathy of humour. . . . Mr *Milton* permits any man to put away his wife upon his meer pleasure, without fault and without the cognisance of any Iudge.[10]

The first of the divorce tracts, *The Doctrine and Discipline of Divorce*, appeared in a brief quarto in the middle of 1643, and apparently was so effective that the greatly expanded second edition was called for in February 1644. It was republished in 1645, and an apparently pirated edition came out in the same year. Obviously this pamphlet was in demand and well read. *The Judgement of Martin Bucer* (1644), for which there is not a single allusion, aimed at reinforcement of Milton's position by 'translated' quotation from the work of a well-respected German divine; *Tetrachordon* attempted to counter such scriptural argument as Pagitt's by examining the four places in the Bible which discuss marriage or the nullities of marriage, as Milton put it; and *Colasterion* was written to refute the anonymous *An Answer to a Book, Intituled, The Doctrine and Discipline of Divorce, or, A Plea for Ladies and Gentlewomen, and all other Maried Women against Divorce* (1644).

The reception met by these and later pamphlets is representative of the antagonism that Milton evoked in some late seventeenth- and eighteenth-century critics. Angered by his views, his position in the Cromwellian Government, and his association with the regicides, these later critics, Samuel Johnson among them, heaped negative criticism upon Milton's poetry. While showing a similar personal bias, Sir John Hawkins, in his *Life of Samuel Johnson* (London, 1787), pp. 243-4, comments on this kind of evaluation:

An eulogium on Knolles's History of the Turks, and a severe censure of the 'Samson Agonistes,' of Milton are the only critical essays there [in *The Rambler*] to be found; to the latter he seems to have been prompted by no better a motive, than that hatred of the author for his political principles which he is known to have entertained, and was ever ready to avow. What he has remarked of Milton in his Lives of the Poets is undoubtedly true: he was a political enthusiast, and, as is evident from his panegyric on Cromwell, a base and abject flatterer. His style in controversy was sarcastic and bitter, and not consistent with christian charity. . . . But neither these [certain personal characteristics] nor those other qualities that render him both a bitter enemy and a railing disputant, could justify the severity of Johnson's criticism on the above-mentioned poem, nor apologize for that harsh and groundless censure which closes the first of his discourses on it, that it is 'a tragedy which ignorance has admired, and bigotry applauded'.

Hawkin's interpretation of Sonnet 16 indicates a superficial and pre-conceived reading, and Johnson's position is not unique in the eighteenth century or later. T. S. Eliot's often-quoted comments seem to find their source in like antipathies; disagreement with Milton's beliefs (frequently in *Paradise Lost*) has obscured literary considerations for some—for example, John Peter in *A Critique on Paradise Lost*. Milton as a man of controversy in the prose tract was considered in a climate of dissent and vituperation which has continued up to the present time.

Of Education and *Areopagitica* are alluded to only seldom, the former not until 1670. Milton's plea against censorship (noticed first in 1646) seems to have had little effect, and not to have been judged as it has by modern readers. It was appropriated as the source of Charles Blount's and William Denton's anti-licensing arguments in 1679 and 1681, respectively.

As the end of the Second Civil War came, and movements against the monarchy and for a commonwealth developed rapidly, Milton found himself compelled again to enter public controversy with his calm analysis of the responsibilities of any king or any magistrate. *The Tenure of Kings and Magistrates*, which is not in defence of regicide as uncritical reading has alleged, was published at the beginning of February 1649 and brought Milton to the attention of the Government than being formed. A second, only slightly amplified, edition was called for in the next year. As Secretary for Foreign Tongues to the Council of State, Milton found himself squarely in the midst of opponents to the commonwealth when he produced *Eikonoklastes* in 1649 and again in 1650 (slightly revised), the *First Defense* in 1651 (written in Latin for Continental consumption), the *Second Defense* in 1654, and the *Defense for Himself* in 1655. *Eikonoklastes* and the *First Defense* were to evoke a number of rebuttals and to forge the apparently undying infamy for Milton which has underlain the remarks of Johnson and others. These works are frequently noticed or referred to by Milton's detractors. By parliamentary order the two books were destroyed in a public burning of seditious material in 1660. The latter had also been burned on the

Continent in 1651. The *First Defense* is the most republished and re-issued of all Milton's works in his lifetime; it was immediately translated into Dutch, and then into other languages including English in 1692. Milton's 'noble task' was a work 'Of which all *Europe* talks from side to side' (Sonnet 22). But the other two defences were less known or read. The controversy over regicide and that with Salmasius became the topics for two German dissertations published in 1653 and 1657—a distinction of sorts for a living author.[11] Two passages of verse illustrate the reaction to Milton's political views, as we see here and in No. 23:

> But who appears here with the *Curtain drawn*?
> What *Milton*! are you come to see the sight?
> Oh *Image-breaker*! poor Knave! had he sawn
> That which the fame of, made him crye out-right.
> He'ad taken counsel of *Achitophell*,
> Swung himself weary, and so gone to Hell.
> This is a sure Divorce, and the best way,
> Seek Sir no further, now the trick is found,
> To part a sullen Knave from's Wife, that day,
> He doth repent his Choyce, stab'd, hang'd or drown'd,
> Will make all sure, and further good will bring,
> The wretch will rail no more against his *King*.[12]

Of the four pamphlets of 1659–60 the first two, *A Treatise of Civil Power* and *Considerations touching the likeliest means to remove Hirelings*, received a few advertisements but no notices. *The Readie and Easie Way to Establish a Free Commonwealth* was accorded immediate citation and two lengthy answers; a second edition was called for within a month of its first appearance. The work was read, but had no effect in stemming the Restoration or altering its nature. A passage from one of these answers, the anonymous *The Censure of the Rota*, is given (No. 20) because of its comments on Milton's prose style. The fourth pamphlet, *Brief Notes Upon a Late Sermon*, was attacked immediately by Sir Roger LeStrange in *No Blinde Guides*.

With the Restoration came a general cessation of controversy: Milton had retired to Jewin Street, London, in early 1661 and to Artillery Walk, Bunhill Fields, around 1669. He was engaged in pursuing the dream of achievement which he had reiterated in an epilogue to a revised edition of the *First Defense* in 1658 (No. 18). During this period, though perhaps also in 1655–9, he was writing *Paradise Lost* and compiling *De Doctrina Christiana*. The earlier *Accedence Commenc't Grammar*, *The History of Britain*, the *Art of Logic*, and familiar letters and prolusions were to be published between 1669 and 1674; and, posthumously, *The Character of the Long Parliament, A Brief History of Moscovia,* and letters of state. These works seem to have gone quite unnoticed except for a snide glance at *Grammar,* one or two advertisements, and some manuscript notations of the *History of Britain.*

Only the first of Milton's two late pieces of prose, *Of True Religion, Haeresie, Schism, Toleration* (1673) and an anonymous translation of the *Declaration, or Letters Patents* of the election of John Sobieski as King of Poland (1674), was alluded to in print or manuscript—once each, as far as we know. Richard Leigh launched a long attack on Milton in *The Transposer Rehears'd* (1673) because of his friendship with Andrew Marvell, who had written *The Rehearsal Transpros'd.* Besides references to various pamphlets including *Of True Religion,* Leigh attacked *Paradise Lost* and Milton's use of blank verse (see No. 24). Primarily Leigh opposed Milton's political and religious views, but his strategy was to demean the man and to lampoon the verse and imagery of the epic, an approach which was to be employed often in the future. He used, too, the common quip as to the cause of Milton's blindness which appears, for instance, in a couplet in *A Guild-Hall Elegie, upon the Funerals of that Infernal Saint Iohn Bradshaw, president of the High Court of Iustice* (1659):

> His Justice was as blind as his friend *Milton,*
> Who slandered the *Kings Book* with an ill tongue.

Marvell swiftly came to Milton's defence in the second part of *The Rehearsal Transpros'd* and pointed out the illogicality of Leigh's attacking him through impugning someone else (No. 25). However, the period of critical writing to follow was often to confound poetry and political dissension in the way that Leigh had done, and to debate blank verse and its poetical value.

After 1645 only a few incidental printings of some minor poems occur until the first edition of *Paradise Lost* in 1667, the combined printing of *Paradise Regain'd* and *Samson Agonistes* in 1671, and the second edition of the minor poems in 1673. Milton's sonnet to Henry Lawes appeared in a collection by the Lawes brothers in 1648 called *Choice Psalmes put into Musick for Three Voices*; two Hobson poems were reprinted in the 1657 *Banquet of Jests,* and all three again in *Wit Restor'd* in 1658; 'On Shakespear' re-emerged in the third folio of the plays (1664); and 'Sonnet 17' somehow found its way into George Sykes's *Life and Death of Sir Henry Vane* in 1662. The second edition of the poems, to which was added *Of Education,* contained all the poems in the first edition, a few early poems that had been omitted, and all the minor poems written since the first edition except for four 'political' sonnets. These were to be given in garbled versions by Phillips in his translation of the *Letters of State* (1694): 'Sonnets 15, 16, 17, and 22'. The second edition of the poems is not rare and its printing was large; it was sold originally for two shillings and sixpence according to a catalogue of books in 1673. We might note that William Hog was to begin the translation of these works (and their adaptation) through his Latin version of 'Lycidas 'in 1694 and of 'A Maske' in 1698.

We would like to think of the publication of *Paradise Lost* in 1667 as a great literary event: it was not. In 1668 and 1669 unsold copies were again offered the public, but with new title-pages to give the impression that these were new editions. Apparently to aid the unfit audience and increase the sales, prose arguments (which do not entirely agree with the finished poem) were added in 1668. There are two different title-pages for each year, but only with the second title-page of 1669 do we find a partial resetting of type, perhaps because some sheets of the 1667 printing had run out or were originally more poorly printed than others. Such bibliographic evidence makes clear that *Paradise Lost* did not sell well.

The only printed allusions to the poem before Milton's death seem to be one by his nephew in 1669 and Leigh's comments already mentioned. Yet a new edition was called for in 1674, with alterations. Books VII and X were divided into two each, creating twelve books, and fifteen lines were added here and there, though primarily to effect the two changes at the beginning of the new books VIII and XII. The reasons for these alterations are debated now as in the eighteenth century, many feeling that the change was created to draw a parallel with the structure of the *Aenid* or to emphasize the symmetry of the work. An advertisement tells us that this edition sold for three shillings. Yet if reissues mean anything, this edition was not at first a great seller, for there was a reissue of the 1674 pages with a new title-page in 1675. From the third edition in 1678 onward, however, the work was to be accorded many printings and much commentary, with illustrations by John Baptista de Medina added to the fourth edition of 1688. This edition, commissioned by Lord Somers, inaugurated the widespread interest in Milton and his works that continued through the eighteenth century. Later there were numerous foreign-language translations, beginning with Ernst Gottlieb von Berge into German in 1682, and William Hog's (along with *Paradise Regain'd* and *Samson Agonistes*) into Latin in 1690. The 'fit audience

. . . though few' (*PL, VII*, 31) that Milton beseeched his Muse to find was, in 1674 when he died, small and perhaps not fit, in the sense that it did not understand the poem's thesis and theme. In the ensuing years the barbarous dissonance of the unfit audience, one largely opposed to Milton as a man and to *Paradise Lost* as epic, has often drowned the Harp and Voice.

Milton's note on the verse of *Paradise Lost*, added with the arguments, became a main point of contention as early as the seventeenth century. Dryden's request to 'tag' the lines, that is, turn them into rhyme, is symptomatic of the contemporary attitudes, and was greeted with contempt by Marvell in his commendatory poem printed with the second edition (No. 26). It was praised, however, by Nathaniel Lee in his commendatory poem on Dryden's *The State of Innocence* (No. 27). Others were to attempt wholesale revisions—such as John Hopkins, whose version of Books I and II in rhyming couplets was published in 1699.

Milton's two other major poems, which sold for four shillings, waited until 1680 for a second edition, and this became the erroneous text for the collected editions of Jacob Tonson in the early part of the eighteenth century. Yet it was *Paradise Regain'd* that was given the honour of being the second work to be examined in a full study, Richard Meadowcourt's *A Critical Dissertation on Milton's 'Paradise Regain'd'* in 1732. Milton's ideas about tragedy were elaborated in a preface to *Samson Agonistes* (No. 22), but they were not examined by critics until 1751, when Johnson and Richard Hurd individually explored the drama's Aristotelian elements. The question of catharis in the poem (this is mentioned in the preface and is central to its Aristotelianism) is not yet settled, as we see in several recent articles.

During his lifetime Milton was primarily known through the controversies in which he figured. There is little reputation of any other significance during this period, although soon after his death Milton was to gain a general reputation as a poet. Parker prints 113 allusions, but nineteen are advertisements and sixteen are brief notices. Since only fourteen of the remainder are favourable to Milton, about eighty per cent of the contemporary allusions to Milton arose out of disapproval. However, reference occurs in every year from 1640 to 1664, the greatest number appearing in 1660.[13] Shortly before his death Milton was beginning to be viewed by the Whigs and disgruntled republicans as the representative of a lost cause, and it was largely through the poetry that his growing audience came to seek out his political prose.

III

The period of 1675–99 saw the rise of an interest both scholarly and critical in Milton and his works. Although critics (for example, Voltaire in 1727) remark the neglect of the poet and especially *Paradise Lost*, there was much activity in three areas at this time: editions, biography and biographical notices, and commentary on the epic. Generally Milton and his poem are praised highly. He is viewed as the chief representative of the heroic tradition in England, following a line of comparison with Homer and Vergil. The translation of Longinus into English influenced the analysis of Milton's poetry during this period, and more strongly in the next. Such analysis labelled Milton the most supreme and sublime poet England ever produced. On the Continent Milton's reputation as an advocate of republicanism was also giving way, through the availability of the English, Latin, or German editions of *Paradise Lost* already mentioned, in preparation for his fame in the next century as an epic poet. There was still some antagonism towards Milton's political opinions, and the biographers all touch upon his political position. The attitude often expressed was that his politics were deplorable, but that the epic assured his fame and high opinion.

Among the documents reflecting these general attitudes is the long and rather tedious epitaph by Milton's former student and amanuensis, Thomas Ellwood (No. 29). Here Milton's career is surveyed, and the greatness of his mind, his poetic achievement, and his adherence to his sense of right are clearly expressed. Milton's superior position in the world of poétic greatness is the thesis of a comment in an *Athenian Gazette* in 1692 (No. 38). The comparison with Edmund Waller was frequent in the Restoration, and the answer given (perhaps by Samuel Wesley, one of the editors) is a good reflection of the common attitude. Despite the length of *Paradise Lost*, Milton's corpus of poetry was relatively small when one considered the number of individual poems. Thus Milton was not so much a 'general' poet as a great and sublime one. The comment, it should be noted, indicates a knowledge of the minor poems, which, though consideration of them lags for the most part until Thomas Warton's edition in 1785, are not unknown or so disregarded as Warton charged. We might note also that Milton was often compared with Francis Quarles; but by those, apparently, who wished religious sententiousness in their verse, for Quarles was held to be superior for his thought. Milton's fame is recorded by William Preston

(No. 40), who echoes the epic itself and thus manifests the source of that fame, and by John Hughes (before 1700):

> To the Memory of Milton
> Homer's Description of himself, under the Character of
> Demodochus the Musician at the Feast of King Alcinous.
> *From the Eighth Book of the Odyssey.*
>
> The muse with transport lov'd him; yet, to fill
> His various lot, she blended good with ill;
> Depriv'd him of his eyes, but did impart
> The heavenly gift of song, and all the tuneful art.[14]

Similar is Charles Goodall's vision, the stress upon Milton's blindness indicating the irony that some saw in this fact, and the parallel with Homer:

> *From* A Propitatory Sacrifice, To the Ghost of J——M——,
> in a Dialogue Between Thyrsis and Corydon
>
> His age and fruit together ripe,
> Of which blind Homer only was the type:
> Tiresias like, he mounted up on high,
> And scorn'd the filth of dull mortality;
> Convers'd with gods, and grac'd their royal line,
> All extasie, all rapture, all divine!
> . . . On surer wings, with an immortal flight,
> Taught us how to believe, and how to write![15]

But not all the evaluations were positive. In the midst of the Roman Catholic fears felt by Restoration England and the sustenance that many Whigs received from the views of the republican Milton, Edward Pettit, in a satiric vision of Purgatory, saw the author as one really on the side of the Papal forces because of his arguments against monarchy (see No. 32). In addition there is the disagreement of Charles Leslie (No. 49) concerning Milton's treatment of the angels, God, and the Incarnation. His acceptance of Milton's fiction in *Paradise Lost* as Milton's view of 'truth' makes clear the effect that the poem had upon people at the end of the seventeenth century as well as through all succeeding periods. Part of the antagonism toward Milton in the twentieth century has certainly risen from the critic's reading of the poem and particularly (as in William Empson's view of Milton's God) from the disagreement with the nature of religion presented therein. It is clear that the fiction has been treated as Milton's vision of religious 'truth' and that for some the 'philosophy' of the poem has obliterated consideration of it as a literary creation.

Milton was one of the first English authors subjected to the more of less scholarly treatment of pulling together references to him and his works, and to extensive annotation. In 1694 Sir Thomas Pope Blount, after the following introductory paragraph, assembled and quoted the rather incidental comments of Dryden, Thomas Rymer, and the *Athenian Gazette* (all of which are reproduced in this volume in full):

JOHN MILTON,

Was one whose Natural Parts did deservedly give him a place amongst the Principal of our *English Poets*. He was Author (not to mention his other Works, both in *Latin* and *English*, by which his Fame is sufficiently known to all the Learned of *Europe*) of Two *Heroick* Poems, and a *Tragedy*; namely, *Paradise Lost; Paradise Regain'd*; and *Samson Agonistes*; in which he is generally thought to have very much reviv'd the Majesty, and true *Decorum* of *Heroick Poesie* and *Tragedy*.[16]

A year later Patrick Hume printed extensive learned annotations to *Paradise Lost*, which stressed Biblical, classical, and etymological sources and analogues for the knowledge and language of the poem. Much literary criticism has gone into such notes since that time to the present. A few representative annotations are reproduced in No. 45. The practice of explication in learned texts has become commonplace, but in the seventeenth and earlier eighteenth centuries it was not; what is startling is the amount and nature of the annotations of Milton's work at this time. As the practice continued through the eighteenth century the notes were increasingly devoted to criticism of Milton's use of language, prosody, similes, and meaning. Often the critic tried to justify Milton's writing, sometimes pointing out what he considered failures or lapses in judgement. Thomas Newton's edition of *Paradise Lost* (1749) and of the remainder of the poetry (1751), for example, compiled previous comments from various authors, both published and unpublished, and presented many critical statements and annotations of the editor's own.

The editions of Milton's works are numerous from the 1690s onward. No bibliography exists, and the problems of reprints and slightly altered editions in various sizes or papers pose complexities in determining exactly how many editions, reissues, or reprints came from the presses. In general, the work in demand was *Paradise Lost*; to it were often added the minor poems and the two major poems, or they were printed as a companion volume. Jacob Tonson (1695) and John Toland (1698) attempted to put before the public the whole corpus, including the prose, the latter edition being standard for text for forty years. There is an interesting poem by Thomas Yalden evoked by this latter publication of the prose (No. 51). The poem repeats the dichotomy between Milton's fame as a poet and his reputation as a political figure; it shows a penchant for reading biography and Milton's personality into his works. The penchant has not disappeared. Toland's poetic texts were the source of most later editions until Newton's in 1749 and 1751. The prose collection of the eighteenth century which finally supplanted Toland's and which was not replaced until Charles Symmons's seven-volume edition of 1806 was Thomas Birch's *A Complete Collection of the . . . Works of John Milton* (London, 1738, two vols.), with an important introduction citing the Trinity MS. and its variant readings of some of the poems for the first time. A very few editions of individual prose works also came out during the eighteenth century.

Biography, which had evolved as a form in the seventeenth century, was a major area for discussion and evaluation of Milton and his works. John Aubrey's notes for a life of Milton (No. 30), originally undertaken for Anthony Wood (who included an account in *Fasti Oxonienses*, written around 1674), stressed the usual facts that went into such notes plus those personal characteristics and traits that he could garner from various acquaintances of Milton. The comment reproduced here from Aubrey, coming from Edward Phillips, went into the latter's biography, the source for its constant repetition to the present day. Cyriac Skinner, the so-called 'AnonymousBiographer', a former student and amanuensis, included in his version of the life some critical commentary (No. 35); this biography is significant for its inclusion of material not found elsewhere. It was not printed contemporaneously. To his translation of the letters of state, Edward Phillips prefixed a life of his uncle, one which is fuller than other accounts, though much of what he says is drawn directly from Milton's words in autobiographical sections of his prose. Frequently, however, Phillips errs in dates and similar specific facts. His account of Milton's composition, particularly that of *Paradise Lost*, is an important document for study of the works (No. 42). Finally during this period we have the life written by John Toland for his collection of the works; it was printed separately the next year, apparently because of demand. Again there is literary criticism throughout the biography, of which a representative statement is included here (No. 50). The anathema that the name of Milton the politician evoked caused a flurry of dissension against Toland in 1699. Offspring Blackall anonymously published *Remarks on The Life of Mr. Milton, As publish'd by J. T. With a Character of the Author and his Party* (London, 1699), which was answered by Toland in *Amyntor: or, A Defence of Milton's Life* (London, 1699). This pamphlet comments on Milton and Toland's evaluation of him, but is more concerned with the author's own defence as a person and a scholar. Toland was considered a Socinian by Blackall and others. *Amyntor*, in turn, was rebutted by *Mr. Blackall's Reasons for not Replying To a Book, Lately Published, Entituled, Amyntor* (London, 1699), which did just what its title said it was not going to do, for Blackall was its author.

Biography was to continue through the eighteenth century as vehicle for a continuing evaluation of Milton and his works; for example, see Elijah Fenton's comments (No. 77) and Samuel Johnson's *Life of Milton*, first published in 1779. Biographical dictionaries became popular in the late seventeenth century and Milton was included in many of them, although much of the material was cribbed from various sources such as the lives just mentioned. Many, like the often-quoted Gerard Langbaine or Giles Jacob,[17] simply repeat what appears in other notices. (See Nos. 28, 36, and 48 for Phillips's entry, Winstanley's politically biased one, and Peter Bayle's continental view, respectively.)

Paradise Lost is the work most discussed during this period, although no full essay on it exists. Milton's achievement is praised (as in Nos. 31, 33, 37, 43, 44, 46, and 47), but at times a point of disagreement or criticism is raised as in Dryden's comments (Nos. 34 and 41). Both Gildon in the 'Vindication of *Paradise Lost*' (if he did write it) and Wesley are countering what must have been unpublished attacks on the poem (that it did not conform with classic rules of decorum and heroic verses), and Dennis is objecting to the apparently too frequent inferior imitations of Milton's style and substance. These accounts suggest that the poem was read and discussed among the *literati* quite thoroughly and that many poets were consciously influenced by it, as Sir Richard Blackmore was in *Prince Arthur*. The vogue of writing 'Miltonicks', and even of pillaging his lines, was to hit its peak in the next century (see the discussions of Bond and Havens), but it had its beginnings in the 1690s. The assaults on the poem, besides the question of decorum and epic standards—this criticism was to be resoundingly answered by John Dennis and Joseph Addison a few years later—arose from what some today might still consider viable points and from the argument over rhyme. In 1685 Dryden was bothered by the stretches of verse that he considered dull and harsh of sound; in 1693 he added the criticism that the subject was improper for an heroic poem, that Milton's language is antiquated or neologistic and thus unjustified, and that the blank verse is not defensible; and in 1697 he made an observation that was to become a tradition from Blake and Shelley through the present day:

Spenser has a better plea for his *Fairy Queen*, had his action been finished, or had been one; and Milton, if the devil had not been his hero, instead of Adam. . . .[18]

Some of this sounds strange alongside Dryden's 'Epigram', his comment in the preface to *The State of Innocence* that *Paradise Lost* was 'undoubtedly one of the greatest, most noble, and sublime poems which either this age or nation has produced', and his remark to Lord Buckhurst on the poem that 'this man cuts us all out and the ancients too' (*Diary*, 27 June 1674).

The question of blank verse versus rhyme rears up in many of the opinions on *Paradise Lost* to the end of the eighteenth century. The Earl of Roscommon (No. 33) not only argued for it but wrote his opinion in blank verse; and in 1692 John Dennis first published his conclusion that rhyme was not necessary to verse (No. 39). Yet a part of a sentence from Thomas Rymer (in 1678) was widely cited by adherents of rhyming, though they waited in vain for him to make good his promise of pursuing the subject:

With the remaining *Tragedies* I shall also send you some reflections on that *Paradise lost* of *Miltons*, which some are pleas'd to call a Poem, and assert *Rime* against the slender Sophistry wherewith he attacques it. . . .[19]

IV

The first part of the eighteenth century saw an intensified continuation of the evaluation of Milton and his works which had evolved during the 1690s. The Miltonic tradition of the man, the philosopher, and the artist was established by 1731. Most often Milton's 'sublimity' was asserted: by this commentators meant the capacity of his poetry to enlarge the imagination of his readers. His ideas were 'sublime'; his expression was 'sublime'; and together they indicate the eighteenth-century concern with intention in poetry. Thus Milton's statements of aim in pursuing a poetic career, surveyed before, were examined and quoted. The centre of Miltonic criticism remained *Paradise Lost*. But now it was not just the learned who were reading the poem; ordinary readers were made aware of it through newsheets and magazines, and students were being introduced to it. The increased interest created a demand for numerous and large editions.

On the Continent infrequent vernacular translations and a few references and studies were beginning to put some of the works before a wide audience. We might here look briefly at the Continental reputation. Translations into Latin and Greek were more frequent throughout the century. Paolo Rolli first published an Italian translation of *Paradise Lost* in 1729 and an adaptation of 'Comus' (called 'Sabrina') in 1737, in Italian and English. Handel's adaptation of the companion poems appeared in English in 1739 and in Italian in 1740. The epic appeared in French in 1727, and translations of all the poems were published at The Hague in three volumes in 1730, to which was added a critical dissertation on *Paradise Lost* by Constantin de Magny (a pseudonym), published in Paris the year before, and a discussion of 'The Fall of Man' by M. Durand. 'Critical Letters on Paradise Lost and Regain'd' came out in 1731. Further translations of collected or individual poems continued through the century; and theatrical or musical adaptations of parts of *Paradise Lost* were produced in France by Augustin Nadal (1736), Alexandre Tanevot (1742), Jean-Nicolas Servandoni (1758), and Josse (1763). A German *Paradise Lost* is dated 1740, and a translation of the companion poems into German prose (facing the English text) in 1782 is also recorded. Haydn's setting of *The Creation* was written in 1798.

Indicated by this bibliographic evidence is an increased and increasing interest in Milton and his works. On the Continent as well as in England attention was focused on the poems, and specifically on *Paradise Lost*. The political problems posed by Milton's debates with Salmasius, More, and Du Moulin a half-century before had quite dissipated themselves. A few poems were being refashioned into other metres (e.g. Latin hexameters or rhyme) or into prose or musical adaptations. Ensuing upon this availability and interest were a few critical studies or incidental critical comments, and later in the century a few translations of *Areopagitica* and *Of Education*. However, Milton's influence on Continental writers (except Klopstock) lay mainly in his ideas rather than in his style and technique. His fame stressed his republicanism at first, then his philosophic and artistic achievements in *Paradise Lost*, which were coupled, however, with adverse criticism of the epic as a violator of classic rules. Direct reading of the prose seems to have been negligible. Finally an eye was turned to some of the prose. The reaction was not dissimilar to that in England, only delayed; yet there was less stress on biography and little of the pernicious censure that colours much of the criticism of 1732–1800 in England.

Many people in England seem to have learned their Bible with *Paradise Lost* at hand, for it was considered an exposition of the orthodox creed. This was true for most people during the century, although the charge of Arianism was to rise in mid-century. During the sixty or so years prior to this an affinity with Arianism or Socinianism was sometimes hinted at, although many of the comments were directed against Toland with the epic picking up some guilt by association. Jonathan Richardson alluded to the charge in his *Explanatory Notes on Milton's Paradise Lost* (London, 1734, p. xlix). But the flurry of letters in *Gentleman's Magazine* and the *Daily Gazetteer* in 1738–9 again debated the issue of whether Milton did 'so deliberately and wantonly . . . corrupt our Notions of spiritual things, by gross and sensual Representations; and to blend Heathenism and Christianity together in such an unnatural Medley' (*GM*, VIII, March 1738, p. 125). The charge almost totally disappeared for three-quarters of a century, it seems, for only with the publication of *De Doctrina Christiana* in 1825 do we find scholarly shock at Milton's alleged views. William Ellery Channing and Henry John Todd, Milton's important nineteenth-century editor, individually expressed dismay at the seeming heterodoxy of the poem when each compared the treatise and found what sounded like non-belief in the divinity of the Son. The issue is still current.

During the period 1700–31, in addition to a tacit objection to Milton's politics, there was fault-finding with the ideas and characters, literary devices, language, and prosody of *Paradise Lost*. The results of Milton's art are remarkable and sublime—but the poem does not hold strictly to the rules! The verses are rough and the structure of language not English. Such criticism, often encased in an otherwise commendatory—sometimes almost fulsome—statement, reflects the literary values and tenor of the times much more than it analyses the art and substance of the poem. Addison's papers on the poem (No. 63), for example, indicate on the one hand a careful examination of all facets of *Paradise Lost*, but on the other a blindness to Milton's artistic strategies and complex integration of the poem's elements. Tension, in the modern sense, was not understood. Many of the poem's 'faults' have been echoed in twentieth-century commentary.

Biographical notices, not dissimilar from those of the period immediately preceding, continue (see No. 78), as does general approbation of Milton's genius (see Nos. 52, 70, 72, 73, 80, and 82). Most of the criticism in the early eighteenth century discussed *Paradise Lost*; other works were usually only incidentally mentioned. The minor poems are the concern of Sir William Trumbull in a letter to Pope (No. 55), the divorce tracts are alluded to by Swift in 1708 (No. 58), *Samson Agonistes* is praised by Atterbury in 1722 (No. 75), and *Paradise Regain'd* is specifically discussed by Defoe and Ellwood, although at the same time attention is paid to the major epic (Nos. 62 and 66). Ellwood's remarks are of importance in dating the epics and in suggesting that the inspiration for the brief epic lay in his comments, according to their usual interpretation. One other reference to the prose should be noted, for Samuel Wesley provides evidence that Milton's works were at least surreptitiously being read by students around the turn of the century:

As for what you desire concerning the Books we generally used to read, you may easily believe that the space of almost 20 Years blots many things out of our Minds, but what little Scatterings remain I'll freely give you: We had several of us, *Lucius Junius Brutus* among us, Milton's Apology was in *Deliciis* [in special favour] with most of us, I am apt to believe poor *W. J.* formed his Latine Stile very much by reading him, for he had a very good one. We had also *Eicono-clastes*, . . . and the most lewd abominable Books that ever blasted Christian Eye: There you'll believe our Tutors knew not of, nor did they direct us to the former. All the Reports since spread about the King's Book were then common among us, and Bishop *Gauden*'s Son was quoted as their Author. . . .[20]

But it is *Paradise Lost* that receives most study, including one of the first full examinations of any English literary work. A comment in the first issue of *The True Patriot* (1745) is true enough up to the 1690s, but shows that many during the eighteenth century (as well as later) were unaware of the amount of attention that actually was given the poem:

Of all mankind, there are none whom it so absolutely imports to conform to this golden rule (of fashion) as an author; by neglecting this, *Milton* himself lay long in obscurity, and the world had nearly lost the best poem which perhaps it hath ever seen.[21]

The work of Dennis and Addison summarized and expanded the evaluations of the poem in their age, suggesting avenues for appreciation and investigation which have not always been recognized by modern critics. Later authors, apparently unaware of the work of Dennis, have sometimes presented ideas as if they were new that were, in fact, strongly made by him; too often one meets other concepts in Dennis and Addison that have not been sufficiently examined. Primarily the fault has lain in the lack of easy availability of their work in volumes specifically directed toward students of Milton, with the exception of the first six *Spectator* papers in Thorpe's *Milton Criticism*. The full eighteen papers have been reprinted in such complete editions of the *Spectator* as the Everyman four-volume text, and Dennis's criticism has been made accessible by Edward Hooker's two-volume edition. But few modern Milton critics seem aware of Dennis's work, and the point can be repeated for many commentators and aestheticians of the later eighteenth century, unfortunately passed over in the present collection for lack of space. The criticism of Dennis is given in Nos. 54 and 74, as well as those noted elsewhere (Nos. 39, 46, 53, 72, and 82). Addison's major criticism is given in full in No. 63, but see also Nos. 59 and 64. An interesting reaction to Addison's *Spectator* papers is Lawrence Eusden's poem (No. 67); see also Dennis's comments in No. 74. Other writers on the poem are Defoe (No. 56), John Hughes (No. 68), Elijah Fenton (No. 77), Voltaire (No. 79), Nathaniel Salmon (No. 81), a document using Abdiel as illustration and showing the wide and unexpected influence that the poem had on readers' minds), and John Clarke (No. 83).

Voltaire, while praising the poem, found its inspiring source in the inferior play *Adamo* by Andreini, which he speculated Milton would have seen when in Italy, and then went on to criticize such 'gross defects' as the allegory of Sin and Death. Part of his aim in examining *Paradise Lost* was to argue why great heroic poetry was achieved by some nations, such as England, but not by France. The faults he found proceeded from a view of great literature as that which satisfied certain rules laid down by the ancients and modern interpretations of those rules. The poem is seldom viewed as an integral whole; it is rather examined book by book without regard to its overall plan and integration through verbal reminiscence, the completion of actions, and the interrelationships of subjective elements and characters. The fault-finding is not different from that seen in other critiques throughout the century. Note also Leonard Welsted's strictures on Milton's language (No. 76). The search for sources repeats itself with a vengeance in the charges of plagiarism by William Lauder (and in Samuel Johnson's approval). It continued in subdued form in magazine articles in the last two decades of the century (and into modern times) through the citing of parallel passages alleged either to be Milton's conscious source or unconscious remembrance. Only seldom have such parallels (as in Biblical allusions) been examined to determine the added meaning which Milton implied through the technique of allusion. Paolo Rolli, the author of the operatic adaptation of 'A Maske' called 'Sabrina' in 1737, took Voltaire to task

27

for his suggestion concerning *Adamo*.[22] But the suggestion was repeated in the wake of Lauder's allegations, the Italian scholar Giuseppi Baretti now taking up the cudgels in a 1753 essay originally written in English.[23]

The remarks of John Clarke, inserted in his *Essay Upon Study* (1731), foreshadow the debunking of Milton's genius which was to come with Bentley, Lauder, and Johnson. Clarke was bothered by the religious character of *Paradise Lost*, arguing that it is founded on an absurd supposition, that is, the rebellion of the angels against God, and that the introduction of angelic beings and of God is an unpardonable boldness. Again the art of the poem is ignored.

But more representative are the comments on heroic poetry and Milton's sublimity (for example Nos. 61 and 71, and 53, 65, and 66). One of the strong, but anonymous, statements of Milton's sublimity was provoked by John Philips's imitative poem *Cyder*, along with 'The Splendid Shilling' and a poem on 'Paradise Lost' (London, 1708). (The appropriate sections are given in No. 60.) In this writer's estimate, Milton's genius combines sublimity of ideas with sublimity of expression. The other parts of this poem are taken up with criticism of Philips. The related question of prosody was also being settled during 1700–31, although it flared up at times later. John Mason's approving reference to Milton's blank verse in 1749 reveals the now-usual attitude:

If the antient Poetry was too lax in its Numbers, the modern is certainly too strict. The just Medium between these two Extreams seems to be that which *Milton* hath chosen for his Poem, *viz.* the Penthameter Verse; with the mixt Iambic Measure, free from the Schackle of Rhime; in which the Numbers are neither too free nor too confined; but are musical enough to entertain the Ear, and at the same Time leave Room enough to express the strongest Thought in the best and boldest Languages.[24]

We should observe that *Paradise Lost* need not be named: 'his Poem' has become sufficient identification.

V

The mid-eighteenth century saw a renewed interest in Milton's prose and minor poems, further imitation, musical adaptations (like John Dalton's 'Comus' with music by Thomas Arne in 1738 and N. Hamilton's 'Samson Agonistes' in 1742 with music by Handel in 1743), foreign translations, continued analyses and annotations of *Paradise Lost*, and controversies over the text of the epic, its alleged plagiarism, and the lack of popular appeal in many of Milton's poems. The latter part of the century expanded the developments and attitudes already discussed. Milton's verse became a standard of excellence, an expression of authority, a pattern for imitation, as well as a sanction for poetical licence.

In 1732 Richard Bentley, assuming that the blind Milton could not have produced the excrescences and faults he found in *Paradise Lost*, postulated an editor altering the poem and inserting passages into the text. His main charge, typical of the age, was that the received text offended classic taste. The counter-attacks were numerous in magazines, pamphlets, and poems. Bentley's approach to Milton is understandable, given the climate of antagonism which has always surrounded the poet. But in a way Bentley was attempting to save Milton from faults that should not be charged to him, and the unintended result was to send scholars back to a study of the text and a closer examination of Milton's language, style, and imagery.

The effect of William Lauder's criticism was similarly to bring about closer examination of *Paradise Lost*, primarily through source-searching in classical literature. He alleged that Milton had plagiarized from such works as Jacobus Masenius's Latin version of the fall in 1650 and Hugo Grotius's *Adam Exul* (1601) among others. John Douglas soon discovered that the former parallels were taken from William Hog's Latin translation of the epic in 1690. Lauder's avowed purpose for manufacturing evidence was to correct the excesses of Miltonic idolatry. However, he alleged this purpose only after Douglas had exposed his fabrications. Whether this purpose was true or not, it indicates the popularity of Milton at this time.

Samuel Johnson's championship of Lauder did him no credit even in his own times, as Sir John Hawkins's digression on the matter, in his *Life of Dr. Johnson*, makes clear. Johnson's comments in the *Life* and on 'Lycidas' suggest that it was Milton's political views that awakened his prejudice. In Johnson's opinion, Milton could not have popular appeal (a difficult point to accept when one considers the number of editions of the works) because his form and language were archaic and defective.

Perhaps a more representative view of Milton's reputation in the eighteenth century can be gathered from the opening lines of Sneyd Davies's 'Rhapsody to Milton', written in February 1740; it is certainly a more appropriate transition into a brief consideration of nineteenth- and twentieth-century criticism than the spectre which the names of Bentley, Lauder, and Johnson call forth:

Soul of the Muses! Thou supreme of Verse!
Unskill'd and Novice in the sacred Art
May I unblam'd approach thee? May I crave
Thy Blessing, Sire harmonious! amply pleas'd
Shou'd'st thou vouchsafe to own me for thy Son;
Thy Son, tho' dwindled from the mighty Size,
And Stature; much more from the Parent's Mind.
Content and blest enough, if but some Line,
If but some distant Feature, half express'd,
Tell whence I spring.[25]

Davies represents the meaning of Milton and *Paradise Lost* for writing
in the eighteenth century; he also adds to the continuing debate over
blank verse and rhyme his vote for Miltonic form.

The Romantic period saw the rise of the so-called Satanic school of
Milton criticism. While the activities of the immediate past continue—
numerous editions, much annotation, frequent imitation, discussions of
epic style and prosody and sources—the most influential critical position
was that advanced by Blake and Shelley. The centrality of *Paradise Lost*
to Milton studies and the revolutionary attitudes of the age combined
to re-examine the figure of Satan as hero. The stress given the reading
of the first books of the epic, the magnificence of Satan in person and
speech in those sections, the concepts of freedom from the tyrant and of
leadership out of bondage, all helped formulate the attitude that Milton
was of the Devil's party, as Blake expressed it. The view that Satan was
the hero of the poem had first been offered by Dryden in terms of epic
structure (and note Dennis's comment in No. 54), but twentieth-century
commentators have usually assigned this interpretation to the early nineteenth century because Satan's rebellion was, to Blake, Milton's
inspiration. The influence on Blake can be seen in the almost hundred
paintings and engravings of Miltonic subjects, as well as in the poetry itself.

Coupled with the discovery of *The Christian Doctrine* and its alleged
heterodoxy, this attitude toward Satan called in doubt the theological
and moral system predicated by the poem. Critical examination in the
last two centuries, until most recently, has discredited the poem and poet
often because of this non-acceptance of its basis and because of the
assumption that the poem did not represent Milton's own views. Accordingly the work has been fragmented into successful books and excrescences, and not viewed as a single, coherent work. As Satan became
hero, God became cruel tyrant; as Satan showed a splendid figure, God
appeared a kind of puppet representing Biblical or Christian belief. The

line of dissent can be traced from Blake, Shelley, and Byron, to Matthew Arnold, Water Bagehot, and Sir Walter Raleigh, to A. J. A. Waldock, William Empson, J. B. Broadbent, and John Peter. More recently, however, the poem has been critically reassembled: Books V and VI, XI and XII are deemed essential to the total structure and meaning; the question of obedience to God has been placed in relation to the fuller subject of God's Providence, which implies also Man's regaining of Paradise; Satan and the infernal beings are seen as false advisers and self-deceivers against the Truth, Mercy, and Justice of God; and the patterns of imagery and antithesis have reintegrated the poem to a strong moral statement for today's world.

Arguments, too, have raged in the present century over the effect of Milton's verse on succeeding generations. Ezra Pound, T. S. Eliot, and F. R. Leavis have deplored Milton's supposed Latinate language and form, his lack of dramatic statement, the lack of tension and ambiguity, and the inflexibility of language and verse. But more recent readers have turned against such strictures and have even sometimes rejected writers contrasted with Milton, like Donne and Dryden.

The nineteenth century saw the continued (and still continuing) sweep of editions, the scholarship of sources and allusions and of bio-graphical studies, and the setting in of a kind of stultification, which led Sir Walter Raleigh to classify *Paradise Lost* as a monument to dead ideas. Other works, poetry and prose, were published and studied, but it was *Paradise Lost* and biography that received most attention. The still indis-pensable six-volume biography produced by David Masson in the second half of the century pulled together every piece of information known about the man, his works, and his times. And a vibrancy went out of Miltonic study. Not until Edwin Greenlaw's two studies of 1917 and 1920 did the twentieth-century approach develop: Milton, the Renais-sance humanist, a reassessment particularly advanced by the work of James Holly Hanford. While controversies have clouded the scene, and while academic scholarship and various critical approaches have ex-amined the well-known works of the past, a number of other items—e.g. *Paradise Regain'd*, *Reason of Church-Government*—have taken their rightful place among his significant literary contributions, and others—e.g. the *Nativity Ode*, *Comus*—have been viewed as literary works rather than only historical or philosophic compositions. The decline in popular interest in the 'classics' of Milton seems now to have turned to a feeling that they constitute a vital core of poetry and idea, peculiarly modern in their philosophic probings and involvement.

There are still those who disparage Milton the man—a reaction common since the seventeenth century—and those who find fault with the works—the language, the form, the verse, the ideas, and the intention, the alleged artistry and the biographical element—views also re-echoed since the seventeenth century. But the most prevailing mood in the last three hundred years has been one of approbation. Many would seem to concur with W.S. in 'An Epistle to Mr. W——, Fellow of Trinity College, Cambridge':

> But when sometimes we would unbend our care
> From studies too abstracted and severe,
> Then Poetry we read.
> The lofty Milton was our usual choice,
> Whose elevated, more than human voice,
> Is tun'd to Angels' ears, is tun'd too high
> For any theme but immortality.[26]

NOTES

[1] See John T. Shawcross, 'Milton's Decision to Become a Poet', *Modern Language Quarterly*, XXIV (1963), 21–30.

[2] See John T. Shawcross, 'The Manuscript of "Arcades" ', *Notes and Queries*, VI (1959), 359–64; 'Speculations on the Dating of the Trinity MS. of Milton's Poems', *Modern Language Notes*, LXXV (1960), 11–7; 'Certain Relationships of the Manuscripts of "Comus" ', *Papers of the Bibliographical Society of America*, LIV (1960), 38–56; and 'The Manuscripts of "Comus": An Addendum', ibid., 293–4.

[3] See P. L. Heyworth, 'The Composition of Milton's "At a Solemn Musick" ', *Bulletin of the New York Public Library*, LXX (1966), 450–8.

[4] See the textual notes in my edition of *The Complete English Poetry of John Milton* (New York, 1963) and 'A Note on Milton's Hobson Poems', *Review of English Studies*, XVIII (1967), 433–7, for a full listing of manuscript copies. The poem 'Hobson's Epitaph' may not be Milton's; see William Riley Parker's discussion of authorship in the Columbia Edition of the *Works*, XVIII, 590–2.

[5] Harris F. Fletcher, ed., *John Milton's Complete Poetical Works* (Urbana, 1943), i, 149.

[6] I owe these references, and many others in this Introduction, to Parker's *Milton's Contemporary Reputation*.

[7] Translated by William Cowper, *Latin and Italian Poems of Milton*, ed. William Hayley (London, 1808), 3.

[8] See the discussions of Don M. Wolfe in *The Complete Prose Works of John Milton* (Columbia University Press, 1953), i, 961–5, and John T. Shawcross in *Notes and Queries*, XIII (1966), 378–9.

[9] Ephraim Pagitt, *Heresiography* (London, 1645), ed. 2, 142.

[10] Robert Baillie, *A Dissuasive from the Errours Of the Time Wherein the Tenets of the principall Sects, especially of the Independents, are drawn together in one Map* . . . (London, 1645), 116 (i.e. 112).

[11] *Caspari Ziegleri Lipsiensis Circa Regicidium Anglorum Exercitationes. Accedit Jacobi Schalleri Dissertatio ad Loca Quaedam Miltoni* (1653), and *Dissertationis ad quaedam loca Miltoni pars prior et posterior, quas Adspirante Deo praeside Dn. Iacobo Schallero,* . . . *Solenniter defenderunt Erhardus Kiesser et Christophorus Güntzer* (1657). Apparently Kiesser defended Schaller's dissertation and Güntzer his own.

[12] G. S., *Britains Triumph, for her Imparallel'd Deliverance* (London, 1660), 15.

[13] See *Milton's Contemporary Reputation*, 70.

[14] From Robert Anderson, ed., *The Works of the British Poets* (London, 1795), vii, 314.

[15] [Charles Goodall], *Poems and Translations.* . . . *By a late scholar of Eaton* (London, 1689), 115.

[16] Sir Thomas Pope Blount, 'Characters and Censures: Milton', *De Re Poetica: or, Remarks upon Poetry* (London, 1694), 135.

[17] Gerard Langbaine, *An Account of the English Dramaticke Poets* (Oxford, 1691), 375–7; Giles Jacob, *The Poetical Register: or, The Lives and Characters of All the English Poets* (London, 1723), i, 100–6; ii ('The English Dramatick Poets'), 183–4.

[18] John Dryden, 'Dedication of the Aeneis' (1697), quoted from *The Works of John Dryden*, ed. George Saintsbury (London, 1889), xiv, 144.

[19] Thomas Rymer, *The Tragedies of the Last Age* (1678), quoted from *The Critical Works of Thomas Rymer*, ed. Curt A. Zimansky (Yale University Press, 1956), 76.

[20] [Samuel Wesley], *A Letter from a Country Divine to his Friend in London* (London, 1703), 14.

[21] Cited from *Gentleman's Magazine*, XVI (January 1746), 9.

[22] See Paolo Rolli, *Remarks upon M. Voltaire's Essay on the Epick Poetry of the European Nations* (London, 1728).

[23] Giuseppi Baretti *A Dissertation upon the Italian Poetry in which are interspersed some remarks on Mr. Voltaire's 'Essay on Epic Poets'* (London, 1753); see *Prefazione e Polemiche*, ed. Luigi Piccioni (Bari, 1911), 109–11.

[24] John Mason, *An Essay on the Power and Harmony of Prosaic Numbers* (London, 1749), 47.

[25] From John Whalley, *A Collection of Original Poems and Translations* (London, 1745), 182–6.

[26] Lines 29–33, from *A New Miscellany of Original Poems, on Several Occasions* (London, 1701).

PERSONAL STATEMENTS AND CONTEMPORARY EVALUATIONS

1628–1674

1. Early writing preferences

1628

Extract from 'At a Vacation Exercise' (June 1628), ll. 1–58. John
Milton, *Poems* (1673), 64–6.

Anno Aetatis 19. *At a Vacation Exercise in the Colledge, part* Latin, *part*
English. *The* Latin *speeches ended, the* English *thus began.*

> Hail native Language, that by sinews weak
> Didst move my first endeavouring tongue to speak,
> And mad'st imperfect words with childish tripps,
> Half unpronounc't, slide through my infant-lipps,
> Driving dum silence from the portal dore,
> Where he had mutely sate two years before:
> Here I salute thee and thy pardon ask,
> That now I use thee in my latter task:
> Small loss it is that thence can come unto thee,
> I know my tongue but little Grace can do thee.
> Thou needst not be ambitious to be first,
> Believe me I have thither packt the worst:
> And, if it happen as I did forecast,
> The daintest dishes shall be serv'd up last.
> I pray thee then deny me not thy aide
> For this same small neglect that I have made:
> But haste thee strait to do me once a Pleasure,
> And from thy wardrope bring thy chiefest treasure;

35

Not those new fangled toys, and trimming slight
Which takes our late fantasticks with delight,
But call those richest Robes, and gay'st attire
Which deepest Spirits, and choicest Wits desire:
I have some naked thoughts that rove about
And loudly knock to have their passage out;
And wearie of their place do only stay
Till thou hast deck't them in thy best array;
That so they may without suspect or fears
Fly swiftly to this fair Assembly's ears;
Yet I had rather, if I were to chuse,
Thy service in some graver subject use,
Such as may make thee search thy coffers round,
Before thou cloath my fancy in fit sound:
Such where the deep transported mind may soare
Above the wheeling poles, and at Heav'ns dore
Look in, and see each blissful Deitie
How he before the thunderous throne doth lie,
Listening to what unshorn *Apollo* sings
To th' touch of golden wires, while *Hebe* brings
Immortal Nectar to her Kingly Sire:
Then passing through the Spherse of watchful fire,
And mistie Regions of wide air next under,
And hills of Snow and lofts of piled Thunder,
May tell at length how green-ey'd *Neptune* raves,
In Heav'ns defiance mustering all his waves;
Then sing of secret things that came to pass
When Beldam Nature in her cradle was;
And last of Kings and Queens and *Hero's* old,
Such as the wise *Demodocus* once told
In solemn Songs at King *Alcinous* feast,
While sad *Ulisses* soul and all the rest
Are held with his melodious harmonie
In willing chains and sweet captivitie.
But fie my wandring Muse how thou dost stray!
Expectance calls thee now another way,
Thou know'st it must be now thy only bent
To keep in compass of thy Predicament:
Then quick about thy purpos'd business come,
That to the next I may resign my Roome.

2. The sacred poet and the 'Ode on the Morning of Christ's Nativity'

1629

Extract from *Elegia sexta* (December 1629), ll. 55–90. John Milton, *Poems* (1645), 33–4. Translated by the editor, *Complete English Poetry of John Milton* (1963), 51–2.

But who records wars and heaven under mature Jove,
and pious heroes and half-divine leaders,
and now who sings the sacred counsels of the supreme gods,
now the infernal realms bayed by the fierce dog,
let him live indeed frugally in the fashion
of the Samian teacher, and let herbage furnish his harmless food.
Let the clear water near at hand stand in its bowl of beech wood,
and let him drink nonintoxicating potions from the pure spring.
His youth void of crime and chaste is joined to this
by stern morals and without stain of hand.
With like nature, shining with sacred vestment and lustral waters,
does the priest rise to go to the hostile gods.
By this rule it is said wise Tiresias lived
after his eyes were put out, and Ogygian Linus,
and Calchas fugitive from his appointed house, and old
Orpheus with the vanquished beasts among the forsaken caves.
Thus the one poor of feast, thus Homer, drinker of water,
carried the man of Ithaca through the vast seas
and through the monster-making palace of the daughter of
    Perseis and Apollo,
and shallows dangerous with Siren songs,
and through your mansions, infernal king, where by dark blood
he is said to have engaged the trooping shades.
For truly the poet is sacred to the gods, and priest of the gods,
and his hidden heart and lips breathe Jove.
But if you will know what I am doing (if only at least

you consider it to be important to know whether I am doing
   anything)
I am singing the King, bringer of peace by his divine origin,
and the blessed times promised in the sacred books,
and the crying of our God and his stabling under the meagre roof,
who with his Father inhabits the heavenly realms;
and the heavens insufficient of stars and the hosts singing in the air,
and the gods suddenly destroyed in their temples.
I dedicate these gifts in truth to the birthday of Christ,
gifts which the first light of dawn brought to me.
For you these thoughts formed on my native pipes are also
   waiting;
you, when I recite them, will be the judge for me of their worth.

3. Translation of Psalm 114 into Greek

1634

Letter to Alexander Gill (4 December 1634). Letter V, *Joannis Miltonii Angli, Epistolarum Familiarium Liber Unus* (1674), 13–14. Translated by the editor, *The Prose of John Milton*, ed. J. Max Patrick (1967), 603–4.

Alexander Gill (1597?–1644?) was a tutor at his father's St. Paul's School, which Milton attended from *c.* 1620 to *c.* 1624. The letter, describing Milton's Greek translation of Psalm 114, was evoked by receipt of unknown verses from Gill.

If to me you had presented gold, or preciously embossed vases, or whatever of that sort mortals admire, it would certainly shame me never to have repaid you in return, as much as it might be equated by my abilities. Since you have bestowed upon me such charming and graceful hendecasyllabics the day before yesterday, how much more precious is that indeed than deserved gold, you have made me so much the more troubled by what costly item I should repay the kindness of such a pleasant favor. At hand, indeed, were some things of my own of this kind, but which I should in no way rate worthy of sending in a contest of equality of gift with yours. I send, therefore, what is not exactly mine, but also that truly divine poet's, this ode of whom, only last week, with no deliberate intention certainly, but from I know not what sudden impulse before daybreak, I was rendering, almost in bed, to the rule of Greek heroic verse: so that, it is clear, relying on this assistant, who surpasses you no less in theme than you excel me in art, I should have something that might appear to approach a balancing of accounts. If anything should occur which should satisfy your opinion of my verses less than you are used to, understand that, since I left your school, this is the first and only thing I have composed in Greek—occupied, as you know, more willingly in Latin and English matters. For whoever spends study and labor in this age on Greek writing runs a risk that he sings for the most part to the deaf. . . .

From our suburban residence, 4 December 1634

4. Hope for immortality

1637

Extract from Letter VII to Charles Diodati (23 November 1637), *Joannis Miltonii Angli, Epistolarum Familiarium Liber Unus* (1674), 19. Translated by the editor, *The Prose of John Milton*, ed. J. Max Patrick (1967), 611.

Diodati (1609?–38) was a close boyhood friend whom Milton had not seen for some time when he wrote this letter. The comment here may be the earliest explicit confession of Milton's literary hopes. He lamented Diodati's death in 'Epitaphium Damonis', which is also concerned with Milton's plans.

But now I know you wish to have your curiosity satisfied. You anxiously ask many questions, even as to what I am thinking of. Listen, Theodotus, but let it be in your ear, lest I blush; and allow me for a little while to talk more loftily with you. You ask what I am thinking of? So may the good God help me, of immortality! And in fact what am I doing? Growing my wings and meditating flight; but as yet our Pegasus raises himself on very tender pinions. Let me be lowly wise!

5. Faith in literary ability
1638(?)

Extract from 'Ad Patrem' (c. March 1638), ll. 1–16, 61–6, 101–4, 115–20. John Milton, *Poems* (1645), 63–8. Translated by the editor, *The Complete English Poetry of John Milton* (1963), 125–9.

Milton's father was a composer who had contributed to various song collections.

Now I long for the Pierian fountains
to whirl their watery paths through my breast and to roll
through my mouth the entire stream released from the twinpeaks
so that my Muse, her trifling songs forgotten, might rise
on spirited wings in courtesy of my reverend father.
However, this grateful song she is meditating for you, dear father,
is a poor attempt; yet I do not know myself
what gifts from me could more aptly
repay your gifts, although my greatest ones could never
repay yours, for by no means can barren gratitude which is paid
with empty words be equal to your gifts.
But notwithstanding, this page exhibits mine,
and I have reckoned up on this paper whatever I possess of abilities,
which to me are insignificant, save those which golden Clio has
    given,
those which to me slumbers have begotten in the remote cave
and the laurel groves of the sacred wood, Parnassian shadows.
. . . Now since it has fallen to me to have been born a poet,
why is it strange to you that we, so closely joined by dear blood,
should follow related arts and kindred endeavor?
Apollo, wishing to disperse himself between the two,
gave to me certain gifts, to my father others,
and father and son, we possess the divided god.
. . . Therefore, now that I am a part of the learned company,
    however humble,

I shall sit among the ivy and the laurels of the victor.
And now I shall no longer mingle unknown with the indolent
   rabble
and my steps shall shun profane eyes.
. . . And you, O my juvenile songs and amusements,
if only you dare to hope for immortality
and to remain after your master's death, and to gaze upon the light,
and if dark oblivion does not carry you beneath dense Orcus,
perhaps you will preserve these praises and the name of the father
sung again and again, as an example to a future generation.

6. Wotton on 'Comus'

1638

Extract from Sir Henry Wotton, Letter to Milton (13 April 1638). John Milton, *Poems* (1645), 71–2.

'Mr. *R.*' remains unidentified; 'the late *R*'s Poems' is Thomas Randolph's *The Muses Looking-Glasse* (Oxford, 1638). No copy of Milton's *Mask* bound to Randolph's poems has been found.

A poet and friend of John Donne, Wotton (1568–1639) had been King James's ambassador to Venice and Provost of Eton College when Milton discussed his impending trip to the Continent with him. This statement is one of the earliest evaluations of a Milton poem.

Since your going, you have charg'd me with new Obligations, both for a very kinde Letter from you dated the sixth of this Month, and for a dainty peece of entertainment which came therwith. Wherin I should much commend the Tragical part, if the Lyrical did not ravish me with a certain Dorique delicacy in your Songs and Odes, whereunto I must plainly confess to have seen yet nothing parallel in our Language: *Ipsa mollities* [it is tenderness itself]. But I must not omit to tell you, that I now onely owe you Thanks for intimating unto me (how modestly soever) the true Artificer. For the work it self, I had view'd som good while before, with singular delight, having receiv'd it from our common Friend Mr. *R.* in the very close of the late *R*'s Poems, Printed at *Oxford*, whereunto it was added (as I now suppose) that the Accessory might help out the Principal, according to the Art of *Stationers*, and to leave the Reader *Con la bocca dolce* [with a sweet taste].

7. Subject for poetic work

1638

Extract from 'Mansus' (1638), ll. 78–84. John Milton, *Poems* (1645) 77–8. Translated by the editor, *The Complete English Poetry of John Milton* (1963), 133.

O if my lot might grant me such a friend,
one who so well knows how to honor the devotees of Apollo,
if ever I shall recall our native kings in songs,
and likewise Arthur waging wars under the earth;
or proclaim the magnanimous heroes of the invincible table
with their covenant of companionship, and (O only let the spirit
    be present)
shatter the Saxon phalanxes under British Mars.

8. Subject for poetic work

1639

Extract from 'Epitaphium Damonis' (1639), ll. 162–8. John Milton, *Poems* (1645), 85. Translated by the editor, *The Complete English Poetry of John Milton* (1963), 141–2.

I myself shall celebrate the Dardanian ships through the
Rutupian sea, and the ancient kingdom of Inogene, daughter of
    Pandrasus,
the chieftains Brennus and Arviragus, and old Belinus,
and the Armorican colonists at last under the law of the Britons;
then Igraine pregnant with Arthur by fatal deception,
Gorlois' counterfeit features and assumed arms,
the guile of Merlin.

9. Poetic plans

1642

Extract from Milton's *Reason of Church-Government* (1642) 36–41.
This is one of the most often-quoted prose excerpts. The high
ideals of the vatic poet expressed here are central to Milton's
poetic hopes and achievements, subject-matter and literary forms.

So lest it should be still imputed to me, as I have found it hath bin, that
some self-pleasing humor of vain-glory hath incited me to contest with
men of high estimation, now while green yeers are upon my head, from
this needlesse surmisall I shall hope to disswade the intelligent and equal
auditor, if I can but say succesfully that which in this exigent behoovs
me, although I would be heard only, if it might be, by the elegant &
learned reader, to whom principally for a while I shal beg leav I may
addresse my selfe. To him it will be no new thing though I tell him that
if I hunted after praise by the ostentation of wit and learning, I should
not write thus out of mine own season, when I have neither yet compleated to my minde the full circle of my private studies, although I
complain not of any insufficiency to the matter in hand, or were I ready
to my wishes, it were a folly to commit any thing elaborately compos'd
to the carelesse and interrupted listening of these tumultuous times. Next
if I were wise only to mine own ends, I would certainly take such a
subject as of it self might catch applause, whereas this hath all the disadvantages on the contrary, and such a subject as the publishing whereof
might be delayd at pleasure, and time enough to pencill it over with all
the curious touches of art, even to the perfection of a faultlesse picture,
whenas in this argument the not deferring is of great moment to the
good speeding, that if solidity have leisure to doe her office, art cannot
have much. Lastly, I should not chuse this manner of writing wherein
knowing my self inferior to my self, led by the genial power of nature
to another task, I have the use, as I may account it, but of my left hand.
And though I shall be foolish in saying more to this purpose, yet since
it will be such a folly, as wisest men going about to commit, have only
confest and so committed, I may trust with more reason, because with

more folly to have courteous pardon. For although a Poet soaring in the high region of his fancies with his garland and singing robes about him might without apology speak more of himself then I mean to do, yet for me sitting here below in the cool element of prose, a mortall thing among many readers of no Empyreall conceit, to venture and divulge unusual things of my selfe, I shall petition to the gentler sort, it may not be envy to me. I must say therefore that after I had from my first yeeres by the ceaselesse diligence and care of my father, whom God recompence, bin exercis'd to the tongues, and some sciences, as my age would suffer, by sundry masters and teachers both at home and at the schools, it was found that whether ought was impos'd me by them that had the overlooking, or betak'n to of mine own choise in English, or other tongue, prosing or versing, but chiefly this latter, the stile by certain vital signes it had, was likely to live. But much latelier in the privat Academies of *Italy*, whither I was favor'd to resort, perceiving that some trifles which I had in memory, compos'd at under twenty or thereabout (for the manner is that every one must give some proof of his wit and reading there) met with acceptance above what was lookt for, and other things which I had shifted in scarsity of books and conveniences to patch up amongst them, were receiv'd with written Encomiums, which the Italian is not forward to bestow on men of this side the *Alps*, I began thus farre to assent both to them and divers of my friends here at home, and not lesse to an inward prompting which now grew daily upon me, that by labour and intent study (which I take to be my portion in this life) joyn'd with the strong propensity of nature, I might perhaps leave something so written to aftertimes, as they should not willingly let it die. These thoughts at once possest me, and these other. That if I were certain to write as men buy Leases, for three lives and downward, there ought no regard be sooner had, then to Gods glory by the honour and instruction of my country. For which cause, and not only for that I knew it would be hard to arrive at the second rank among the Latines, I apply'd my selfe to that resolution which *Ariosto* follow'd against the perswasions of *Bembo*, to fix all the industry and art I could unite to the adorning of my native tongue; not to make verbal curiosities the end, that were a toylsom vanity, but to be an interpreter & relater of the best and sagest things among mine own Citizens throughout this Iland in the mother dialect. That what the greatest and choycest wits of *Athens*, *Rome*, or modern *Italy*, and those Hebrews of old did for their country, I in my proportion with this over and above of being a Christian, might doe for mine: not caring to be once nam'd abroad, though perhaps I could attaine to that, but content with these British Ilands as my world, whose fortune hath hitherto bin, that if the Athenians, as some say, made their small deeds great and renowned by their eloquent writers, *England* hath had her noble atchievments made small by the unskilfull handling of monks and mechanicks.

Time servs not now, and perhaps I might seem too profuse to give any certain account of what the mind at home in the spacious circuits of her musing hath liberty to propose to her self, though of highest hope, and hardest attempting, whether that Epick form whereof the two poems of *Homer*, and those other two of *Virgil* and *Tasso* are a diffuse, and the book of *Job* a brief model: or whether the rules of *Aristotle* herein are strictly to be kept, or nature to be follow'd, which in them that know art, and use judgement is no transgression, but an inriching of art. And lastly what K. or Knight before the conquest might be chosen in whom to lay the pattern of a Christian *Heroe*. And as *Tasso* gave to a Prince of *Italy* his chois whether he would command him to write of *Godfreys* expedition against the infidels, or *Belisarius* against the Gothes, or *Charlemain* against the Lombards; if to the instinct of nature and the inboldning of art ought may be trusted, and that there be nothing advers in our climat, or the fate of this age, it haply would be no rashnesse from an equal diligence and inclination to present the like offer in our own ancient stories. Or whether those Dramatick constitutions, wherin *Sophocles* and *Euripides* raigne shall be found more doctrinal and exemplary to a Nation, the Scripture also affords us a divine pastoral Drama in the Song of *Salomon* consisting of two persons and a double *Chorus*, as *Origen* rightly judges. And the Apocalyps of Saint *John* is the majestick image of a high and stately Tragedy, shutting up and intermingling her solemn Scenes and Acts with a sevenfold *Chorus* of halleluja's and harping symphonies: and this my opinion the grave autority of *Pareus* commenting that booke is sufficient to confirm. Or if occasion shall lead to imitat those magnifick Odes and Hymns wherein *Pindarus* and *Callimachus* are in most things worthy, some others in their frame judicious, in their matter most an end faulty: But those frequent songs throughout the law and prophets beyond all these, not in their divine argument alone, but in the very critical art of composition may be easily made appear over all the kinds of Lyrick poesy, to be incomparable. These abilities, wheresoever they be found, are the inspired guift of God rarely bestow'd, but yet to some (though most abuse) in every Nation: and are of power beside the office of a pulpit, to inbreed and cherish in a great people the seeds of vertu, and publick civility, to allay the pertubations of the mind, and set the affections in right tune, to celebrate in glorious and lofty Hymns the throne and equipage of Gods Almightinesse, and what he works, and what he suffers to be wrought with high providence in his Church, to sing the victorious agonies of Martyrs and Saints, the deeds and triumphs of just and pious Nations doing valiantly through faith against the enemies of Christ, to deplore the general relapses of Kingdoms and States from justice and Gods true worship. Lastly, whatsoever in religion is holy and sublime, in vertu amiable, or grave, whatsoever hath passion or admiration in all the changes of that which is call'd fortune from without, or the wily suttleties and refluxes of mans thoughts from within, all these things with a solid and treatable smoothnesse to paint out and describe. Teaching over the whole book of sanctity and vertu through all the instances of example with such delight to those especially of soft and delicious temper who will not so much as look upon Truth herselfe, unlesse they see her elegantly drest, that whereas the paths of honesty and good life appear now rugged and difficult, though they be indeed easy and pleasant, they would then appeare to all men both easy and pleasant though they were rugged and difficult indeed. And what a benefit this would be to our youth and gentry, may be soon guest by what we know of the corruption and bane which they suck in dayly from the writings and interludes of libidinous and ignorant Poetasters, who having scars ever heard of that which is the main consistence of a true poem, the choys of such persons as they ought to introduce, and what is morall and decent to each one, doe for the most part lap up vitious principles in sweet pils to be swallow'd down, and make the tast of vertuous documents harsh and sowr. But because the spirit of man cannot demean it selfe lively in this body without some recreating intermission of labour, and serious things, it were happy for the Common wealth, if our Magistrates, as in those famous governments of old, would take into their care, not only the deciding of our contentious Law cases and brauls, but the managing of our publick sports, and festival pastimes, that they might be, not such as were autoriz'd a while since, the provocations of drunkennesse and lust, but such as may inure and harden our bodies by martial exercises to all warlike skil and performance, and may civilize, adorn and make discreet our minds by the learned and affable meeting of frequent Academies, and the procurement of wise and artfull recitations sweetned with eloquent and gracefull inticements to the love and practice of justice, temperance and fortitude, instructing and bettering the Nation at all opportunities, that the call of wisdom and vertu may be heard every where, as *Salomon* saith, *She crieth without, she uttereth her voice in the streets, in the top of high places, in the chief concours, and in the openings of the Gates.* Whether this may not be not only in Pulpits, but after another persuasive method, at set and solemn Paneguries, in Theaters, porches, or what other place, or way may win most upon the people to receiv at once both recreation, & instruction, let them in authority consult. The thing which I had to say, and those intentions which have liv'd within me ever since I could conceiv my self any thing worth to my Countrie, I return to crave excuse that urgent reason hath pluckt from me by an abortive and fore-dated discovery. And the accomplishment of them lies not but in a power above mans to promise; but that none hath by more studious ways endeavour'd, and with more unwearied spirit that none shall, that I dare almost averre to my self, as farre as life and free leasure will extend, and that the Land had once infranchis'd her self from this im-pertinent yoke of prelaty, under whose inquisitorious and tyrannical duncery no free and splendid wit can flourish. Neither doe I think it shame to covnant with any knowing reader, that for some few yeers yet I may go on trust with him toward the payment of what I am now indebted, as being a work not to be rays'd from the heat of youth, or the vapours of wine, like that which flows at wast from the pen of some vulgar Amorist, or the trencher fury of a riming parasite, nor to be obtain'd by the invocation of Dame Memory and her Siren daughters, but by devout prayer to that eternall Spirit who can enrich with all utterance and knowledge, and sends out his Seraphim with the hallow'd fire of his Altar to touch and purify the lips of whom he pleases: to this must be added industrious and select reading, steddy observation, insight into all seemly and generous arts and affaires, till which in some measure be compast, at mine own peril and cost I refuse not to sustain this expectation from as many as are not loath to hazzard so much credulity upon the best pledges that I can give them. Although it noth-ing content me to have disclos'd thus much before hand, but that I trust hereby to make it manifest with what small willingnesse I endure to interrupt the pursuit of no lesse hopes then these, and leave a calme and pleasing solitarynes fed with cherful and confident thoughts, to imbark in a troubl'd sea of noises and hoars disputes, put from behold-ing the bright countenance of truth in the quiet and still air of delightfull studies to come into the dim reflexion of hollow antiquities sold by the seeming bulk, and there be fain to club quotations with men whose learning and beleif lies in marginal stuffings, who when they have like good sumpters laid ye down their hors load of citations and fathers at your dore, with a rapsody of who and who were bishops here or there, ye may take off their packsaddles, their days work is don, and episcopacy, as they think, stoutly vindicated. Let any gentle apprehension that can distinguish learned pains from unlearned drudgery, imagin what pleasure or profoundnesse can be in this, or what honour to deal against such adversaries. But were it the meanest under-service, if God by his Secretary conscience injoyn it, it were sad for me if I should draw back, for me especially, now when all men offer their aid to help ease and lighten the difficult labours of the Church, to whose service by the intentions of my parents and friends I was destin'd of a child, and in mine own resolutions, till comming to some maturity of yeers and perceaving what tyranny had invaded the Church, that he who would take Orders must subscribe slave, and take an oath withall, which unlesse he took with a conscience that would retch, he must either strait perjure, or split his faith, I thought it better to preferre a blamelesse silence before the sacred office of speaking bought, and begun with servitude and forswearing. Howsoever thus Church-outed by the Prelats, hence may appear the right I have to meddle in these matters, as before, the necessity and constraint appear'd.

10. The might of the pen
1642

'Sonnet 8' (November 1642). John Milton, *Poems* (1645), 49–50.

Captain or Colonel, or Knight in Arms,
    Whose chance on these defenceless dores may sease,
    If ever deed of honour did thee please,
    Guard them, and him within protect from harms.
He can requite thee, for he knows the charms
    That call Fame on such gentle acts as these,
    And he can spread thy name o're lands and seas,
    What ever clime the suns bright circle warms.
Lift not thy spear against the Muses bowr:
    The great *Emathian* Conqueror bidd spare
    The house of *Pindarus*, when temple and towr
Went to the ground: and the repeated air
    Of sad *Electra*'s poet had the power
    To save th' *Athenian* walls from ruin bare.

11. *Of Education* and the place of writing in its plan

1644

Extract from John Milton, *Of Education* (1644), 1, 5–6. To Mr. Samuel Hartlib.

'Janua's' and 'Didactics' refer to *Janua Linguarum Reserata* and *Didactica Magna* by John Comenius (1592–1670), a Bohemian reformer of educational practices. He proposed, like Milton, such reforms as practical language training and a programme in which difficulty would increase.

I am long since perswaded, that to say, or do ought worth memory and imitation, no purpose or respect should sooner move us, then simply the love of God, and of mankind. Nevertheless to write now the reforming of Education, though it be one of the greatest and noblest designs that can be thought on, and for the want whereof this Nation perishes, I had not yet at this time been induc't, but by your earnest entreaties, and serious conjurements; as having my mind for the present half diverted in the pursuance of some other assertions, the knowledge and the use of which, cannot but be a great furtherance both to the enlargement of truth, and honest living, with much more peace. Nor should the laws of any private friendship have prevail'd with me to divide thus, or transpose my former thoughts, but that I see those aims, those actions which have won you with me the esteem of a person sent hither by some good providence from a far country to be the occasion and the incitement of great good to this Island. And, as I hear, you have obtain'd the same repute with men of most approved wisdom, and some of highest authority among us. Not to mention the learned correspondence which you hold in forreign parts, and the extraordinary pains and diligence which you have us'd in this matter both here, and beyond the Seas; either by the definite will of God so ruling, or the peculiar sway of nature, which also is Gods working. Neither can I think that so reputed, and so valu'd as you are, you would to the forfeit of your own discerning ability, impose upon me an unfit and over-ponderous argument, but that the satisfaction which you profess to have receiv'd from those incidental Discourses which we have wander'd into, hath prest and almost constrain'd you into a perswasion, that what you require from me in this point, I neither ought, nor can in conscience deferre beyond this time both of so much need at once, and so much opportunity to try what God hath determin'd. I will not resist therefore, whatever it is either of divine, or humane obligement that you lay upon me; but will forthwith set down in writing, as you request me, that voluntary *Idea*, which hath long in silence presented it self to me, of a better Education, in extent and comprehension far more large, and yet of time far shorter, and of attainment far more certain, then hath been yet in practice. Brief I shall endeavour to be; for that which I have to say, assuredly this Nation hath extream need should be done sooner then spoken. To tell you therefore what I have benefited herein among old renowned Authors, I shall spare; and to search what many modern *Janua's* and *Didactics* more than ever I shall read, have projected, my inclination leads me not. But if you can accept of these few observations which have flowr'd off, and are, as it were, the burnishing of many studious and contemplative years altogether spent in the search of religious and civil knowledge, and such as pleas'd you so well in the relating, I here give you them to dispose of. . . .

And now lastly will be the time to read with them those organic arts which inable men to discourse and write perspicuously, elegantly, and according to the fitted stile of lofty, mean, or lowly. Logic therefore so much as is useful, is to be referr'd to this due place withall her well couch't Heads and Topics, untill it be time to open her contracted palm into a gracefull and ornate Rhetorick taught out of the rule of *Plato, Aristotle, Phalereus, Cicero, Hermogenes, Longinus.* To which Poetry would be made subsequent, or indeed rather precedent, as being less suttle and fine, but more simple, sensuous and passionate. I mean not here the prosody of a verse, which they could not but have hit on before among the rudiments of Grammar; but that sublime Art which in *Aristotles Poetics,* in *Horace,* and the *Italian* Commentaries of *Castelvetro, Tasso, Mazzoni,* and others, teaches what the laws are of a true *Epic* Poem, what of a *Dramatic,* what of a *Lyric,* what Decorum is, which is the grand master-peece to observe. This would make them soon perceive what despicable creatures our common Rimers and

Playwriters be, and shew them, what religious, what glorious and magnificent use might be made of Poetry both in divine and humane things. From hence and not till now will be the right season of forming them to be able Writers and Composers in every excellent matter, when they shall be thus fraught with an universal insight into things.

12. Aim of *Doctrine and Discipline of Divorce*
1644

Extract from Milton's *Doctrine and Discipline of Divorce*, second ed. (1644), A3.

Yet if the wisdome, the justice, the purity of God be to be cleer'd from foulest imputations which are not yet avoided, if charity be not to be degraded and trodd'n down under a civil Ordinance, if Matrimony be not to be advanc't like that exalted perdition, writt'n of to the *Thessalonians, above all that is called God,* or goodnesse, nay, against them both, then I dare affirm there will be found in the Contents of this Booke, that which may concern us all. You it concerns chiefly, Worthies in Parlament, on whom, as on our deliverers, all our grievances and cares, by the merit of your eminence and fortitude are devolv'd: Me it concerns next, having with much labour and faithfull diligence first found out, or at least with a fearlesse and communicative candor first publisht to the manifest good of Christendome, that which calling to witnesse every thing mortall and immortall, I beleeve unfainedly to be true. Let not other men thinke their conscience bound to search continually after truth, to pray for enlightning from above, to publish what they think they have so obtaind, & debarr me from conceiving my self ty'd by the same duties. Yee have now, doubtlesse by the favour and appointment of God, yee have now in your hands a great and populous Nation to Reform; from what corruption, what blindnes in Religion yee know well; in what a degenerat and fal'n spirit from the apprehension of native liberty, and true manlines, I am sure ye find: with what unbounded licence rushing to whordoms and adulteries needs not long enquiry: insomuch that the fears which men have of too strict a discipline, perhaps exceed the hopes that can bee in others, of ever introducing it with any great successe.

13. Salsilli on Milton

1645

Giovanni Salsilli, 'Epigram'. John Milton, *Poems* (1645), 4. Translated by William Cowper, *Latin and Italian Poems of Milton*, ed. William Hayley (1808), 2–3.

This epigram and the two following items were probably tributes to Milton written when he was in Italy; he had read some of his poetry before the Svogliati Academy, an important literary group in Florence. Giovanni Salsilli was a minor poet to whom Milton addressed a Latin poem, 'To Salsilli, the Roman poet, in his illness'.

An Epigram
Addressed to the Englishman JOHN MILTON
A Poet Worthy of Three Laurels,
The Grecian, Latin, and Etruscan,
By John Salsillo of Rome.

Meles and Mincio, both your urns depress,
Sebetus boast henceforth thy Tasso less,
But let the Thames o'er-peer all floods, since he
For Milton famed shall, single, match the three.

14. Manso on Milton

1645

Gianbattista Manso, 'Epigram.' John Milton, *Poems* (1645), 4. Translated by William Cowper, *Latin and Italian Poems of Milton,* ed. William Hayley (1808), 2.

Gianbattista Manso (1560?–1645), poet and leading literary figure, became friendly with Milton when he was in Naples.

The Neapolitan John Baptist Manso, Marquis of Villa,
To the Englishman JOHN MILTON

What features, form, mien, manners, with a mind
Oh how intelligent! and how refined!
Were but thy piety from fault as free,
Thou would'st no Angle but an Angel be.

15. Dati on Milton
1645

Carlo Dati's tribute to Milton. John Milton, *Poems* (1645), 10. Translated by William Cowper, *Latin and Italian Poems of Milton*, ed. William Hayley (1808), 7–8.

Dati (1619–76), another writer whom Milton met in Italy, was a member of two intellectual groups in Florence, the Academia del Cimento and the Academia della Crusca.

To Mr. John Milton of London,

A Youth eminent from his Country and his Virtues,

Who in his travels has made himself acquainted with many nations, and in his studies, with all; that, like another Ulysses, he might learn all that all could teach him;

Skilful in many tongues, on whose lips languages now mute so live again, that the idioms of all are insufficient to his praise; happy acquisition by which he understands the universal admiration, and applause, his talents have excited;

Whose endowments of mind, and person, move us to wonder, but at the same time fix us immoveable; whose works prompt us to extol him, but by their beauty strike us mute;

In whose memory the whole world is treasured; in whose intellect, wisdom; in whose heart, the ardent desire of glory; and in whose mouth, eloquence. Who with Astronomy for his conductor, hears the music of the spheres; with Philosophy for his teacher, decyphers the hand writing of God, in those wonders of creation, which proclaim his greatness; and with the most unwearied literary Industry for his associate,

Examines, restores, penetrates with ease the obscurities of antiquity, the desolations of ages, and the labyrinths of learning;

59

'But wherefore toil to reach these arduous heights?'

To him, in short, whose virtues the mouths of Fame are too few to celebrate, and whom astonishment forbids us to praise as he deserves, this tribute due to his merits, and the offering of reverence and affection, is paid by

CAROL DATI,
A Patrician Florentine,
This great man's servant and this good man's friend.

16. His *Poems*

1647

Extract from 'Ode to Rouse' (January 1647), ll. 73–87. John Milton, *Poems* (1673), 94. Translation by the editor from *The Complete English Poetry of John Milton* (1963), 198.

The Bodleian copy of Milton's *Poems* (1645) was stolen; John Rouse, Librarian of Oxford University, requested a replacement, which was sent with this ode.

You at last my labors have not been in vain,
whatever that sterile genius has brought forth.
Now I bid you hope for placid rest
discharged from envy in a later age, in the blessed abodes
which the good Hermes gives
and the expert protection of Rouse,
where never shall penetrate the insolent speech of the multitude
    and even
the vicious throng of readers shall retire far off;
but our distant descendants,
and a more prudent age
will perhaps exercise a fairer judgment
of things from its unbiassed breast.
Then with envy entombed,
a rational posterity will know if I deserve any merit,
thanks to Rouse.

17. Writing activities in the 1640s
1654

Extract from *The Second Defense* (1654). Translated by George Burnett, Columbia Edition of the *Works* (1933), viii, 129, 131, 133, 135, 137, 139, 253.

No sooner did liberty of speech begin to be allowed, than every mouth was open against the bishops. Some complained of their personal vices, others of the vice of the order itself. It was wrong, they said, that they should differ from all other reformed churches; that it was expedient the church should be governed by the example of the brethren, and above all by the word of God. I became perfectly awake to these things; and perceiving that men were in the right way to liberty; that, if discipline originating in religion continued its course to the morals and institutions of the commonwealth, they were proceeding in a direct line from such beginnings, from such steps, to the deliverance of the whole life of mortal man from slavery—moreover, as I had endeavoured from my youth, before all things, not to be ignorant of what was law, whether divine or human; as I had considered, whether I could ever be of use, should I now be wanting to my country, to the church, and to such multitudes of the brethren who were exposing themselves to danger for the gospel's sake—I resolved, though my thoughts were then employed upon other subjects, to transfer to these the whole force of my mind and industry. Accordingly, I first wrote *Of the Reformation of the English Church*, in two books, to a friend. Next, as there were two bishops of reputation above the rest, who maintained their own cause against certain leading ministers; and as I had the persuasion, that on a subject which I had studied solely for the love of truth and from a regard to Christian duty, I should not write worse than those who contended for their own lucre and most iniquitous domination; to one of them I replied in two books, of which one was entitled *Of Prelatical Episcopacy*, the other *Of the Reason of Church Government*; to the other, in some *Animadversions,* and soon after, in an *Apology*; and thus, as was said, brought timely succour to those ministers, who had some difficulty in maintaining their ground against the bishops' eloquence: from this time too, I held myself ready, should they thenceforward make any reply. When the bishops, at whom every man aimed his arrow, had at length fallen, and we were now at leisure, as far as they were concerned, I began to turn my thoughts to other subjects; to consider in what way I could contribute to the progress of real and substantial liberty; which is to be sought for not from without, but within, and is to be obtained principally not by fighting, but by the just regulation and by the proper conduct of life. Reflecting, therefore, that there are in all three species of liberty, without which it is scarcely possible to pass any life with comfort, namely, ecclesiastical, domestic or private, and civil; that I had already written on the first species, and saw the magistrate diligently employed about the third, I undertook the domestic, which was the one that remained. But as this also appeared to be three-fold, namely, whether the affair of marriage was rightly managed; whether the education of children was properly conducted; whether, lastly, we were to be allowed freedom of opinion—I explained my sentiments not only on the proper mode of contracting marriage, but also of dissolving it, should that be found necessary: and this I did according to the divine law which Christ has never abrogated; and much less has he given a civil sanction to any other, that should be of higher authority than the whole law of Moses. In like manner I delivered my own opinion and the opinion of others concerning what was to be thought of the single exception of fornication—a question which has been also copiously elucidated by our celebrated Selden, in his *Hebrew Wife*, published some two years after. Again, it is to little purpose for him to make a noise about liberty in the legislative assemblies, and in the courts of justice, who is in bondage to an inferior at home,—a species of bondage of all others the most degrading to a man. On this point, therefore, I published some books, and at that particular time, when man and wife were often the fiercest enemies, he being at home with his children, while she, the mother of the family, was in the camp of the enemy, threatening slaughter and destruction to her husband. I next treated, in one little work, of the education of children, briefly it is true, but a sufficient length, I conceived, for those, who apply themselves to the subject with all that earnestness and diligence which it demands—a subject than which there can be none of greater moment to imbue the minds of men with virtue, from which springs that true liberty which is felt within; none for the wise administration of a commonwealth, and for giving it its utmost possible duration. Lastly,

I wrote, after the model of a regular speech, *Areopagitica*, on the liberty of printing, that the determination of true and false, of what ought to be published and what suppressed, might not be in the hands of the few who may be charged with the inspection of books, men commonly without learning and of vulgar judgment, and by whose licence and pleasure, no one is suffered to publish any thing which may be above vulgar apprehension. The civil species of liberty, the last which remained, I had not touched, as I perceived it drew sufficient attention from the magistrate. Nor did I write any thing on the right of kings, till the king, pronounced an enemy by the parliament, and vanquished in war, was arraigned as a captive before judges, and condemned to lose his head. But, when certain presbyterian ministers, at first the bitterest foes to Charles, unable to endure that the independent party should now be preferred to them, and that it should have greater influence in the senate, began to clamour against the sentence which the parliament had pronounced upon the king (though in no wise angry at the deed, but only that themselves had not the execution of it) and tried to their utmost to raise a tumult, having the assurance to affirm that the doctrine of protestants, that all the reformed churches shrunk with horror from the atrocity of such a sentence against kings—then indeed, I thought it behoved me openly to oppose so barefaced a falsehood. Yet even then, I neither wrote nor advised any thing concerning Charles; but simply showed, in general, what may be lawfully done against tyrants; adducing, in confirmation, the authorities of no small number of the most eminent divines; inveighing, at the same time, almost with the zeal of a preacher against the egregious ignorance or impudence of those men, who had promised better things. This book was not published till after the death of the king, being intended rather to compose the minds of men, than to settle any thing relating to Charles; that being the business of the magistrates instead of mine, and which, at the time I speak of, had been already done. These services of mine, which were performed within private walls, I gratuitously bestowed at one time upon the church, at another, upon the commonwealth; while neither the commonwealth nor the church bestowed upon me in return any thing beyond security. It is true, that I gained a good conscience, a fair repute among good men, and that the deeds themselves rendered this freedom of speech honorable to me. Some men however gained advantages, others honours, for doing nothing; but no man ever saw me canvassing for preferment, no man ever saw me in quest of any thing through the medium of friends, fixed, with supplicatory look to the doors of the parliament, or clung to the vestibules of lower assemblies. I kept myself commonly at home, and supported myself, however frugally, upon my own fortune, though, in this civil broil, a great part was often detained, and an assessment rather disproportionate, imposed upon me. Having dispatched these things, and thinking that, for the future, I should now have abundance of leisure, I understook a history of the nation from its remotest origin; intending to bring it down, if I could, in one unbroken thread to our own times. I had already finished four books, when lo! (Charles's kingdom being reduced to a commonwealth) the council of state, as it is called, now first constituted by authority of parliament, invited me to lend them my services in the department more particularly of foreign affairs—an event which had never entered my thoughts! Not long after, the book which was attributed to the king made its appearance, written certainly with the bitterest malice against the parliament. Being ordered to prepare an answer to it, I opposed the *Iconoclast* to the *Icon*; not, as is pretended, 'in insult to the departed spirit of the king,' but in the persuasion, that queen truth ought to be preferred to king Charles; and as I foresaw that some reviler would be ready with this slander, I endeavoured in the introduction, and in other places as far as it was proper, to ward off the reproach. Next came forward Salmasius; and no long time, as More reports, was lost in looking about for some person to answer him, so that all, of their own accord, instantly nominated me, who was then present in the council.—It is chiefly, More, for the sake of those good men, who have otherwise no knowledge of me, that, to stop your mouth and to confound your lies, I have so far given an account of myself. . . .

As for myself, to whatever state things may return, I have performed, and certainly with a good will, I hope not in vain, the service which I thought would be of most use to the commonwealth. It is not before our own doors alone that I have borne my arms in defence of liberty; I have wielded them on a field so wide, that the justice and reason of these which are no vulgar deeds, shall be explained and vindicated alike to foreign nations and to our own countrymen; and by all good men shall no doubt be approved; and shall remain to the matchless renown of my fellow-citizens, and as the brightest example for after-ages. If our last actions should not be sufficiently answerable to the first, it is for themselves to see to it. I have celebrated, as a testimony to them, I had almost said, a monument, which will not speedily perish, actions which were glorious, lofty, which were almost above all praise; and if I have done nothing else, I have assuredly discharged my trust. But as the poet, who is styled epic, if he adhere strictly to established rules, undertakes to embellish not the whole life of the hero whom he proposes to celebrate in song, but, usually, one particular action of his life, as for example, that of Achilles at Troy, or the return of Ulysses, or the arrival of Æneas in Italy, and leaves alone the rest; so likewise will it suffice for my duty and excuse, that I have at least embellished one of the heroic actions of my countrymen. The rest I pass by: for who could do justice to all the great actions of an entire people?

18. *The First Defense*

1658

Extract from the addendum to *The First Defense*, 1658. Translated by S. L. Wolff, Columbia edition of *Works* (1932), vii, 555, 557, 559.

An important epilogue to the prose work which Milton considered his great contribution to republicanism, the following suggests an equation between his ideals to be attained through poetry and his achievements in the prose. The final reference to 'yet greater things' has generally suggested *Paradise Lost*.

It is now several years since I published the foregoing, in haste, as reason of state then required, for I kept thinking that if ever I might take it in hand again at leisure, as occasionally happens, I might thereupon smooth out, or remove, maybe, or add somewhat. This I now judge that I have accomplished, though more briefly than I used to count upon doing it: a memorial which, such as it is, I see will not easily perish. Though someone may be found who may have defended civil freedom more freely than here it is defended, yet there shall hardly be found anyone who hath defended it in a greater and more glorious example. If, then, an action of example so high and illustrious is believed to have been as successfully accomplished as not without God's prompting undertaken, let this be reason good for thinking that in these my praises too it hath even by the same Might and Inspiration been glorified and defended. Indeed I had much rather all men thought so, than that any other success, whether of wit or judgment or industry, were allowed me. Yet as that famous Roman Consul, upon retiring from office, swore in the popular assembly that the state and the city owed their safety to his single efforts, even so, as I now put the last touches to this work, so much only I dare assert, calling God and man to witness: that in this book I have indicated and brought to light, from the highest authors of wisdom both divine and human, matters whereby, I trust, not only the English people has been adequately defended in this cause, to the everlasting reputation of its posterity, but numerous other human beings as well, hitherto deluded by foul ignorance of their right and by false show of religion,—multitudes of men, I say, except such as themselves prefer and deserve to be slaves—have been quite set free. Now the oath of that Consul, great as were its claims, was in that same assembly ratified by oath of the whole Roman people with one mind and one voice; this conviction of mine, I have long understood, is fully ratified by the most excellent not only of my fellow-citizens, but of foreigners too, with the loud voice of nations everywhere.

This my zealous labor's fruit—the highest that I for my part have set before me in this life—I gratefully enjoy; yet therewith too consider chief how I may bear best witness—not only to my own country, to which I have paid the highest I possessed, but even to men of whatever nation, and to the cause of Christendom above all—that I am pursuing after yet greater things if my strength suffice (nay, it will if God grant), and for their sake meanwhile am taking thought, and studying to make ready.

19. Aim in *De Doctrina Christiana*

before 1660(?)

Extract from John Milton, *De Doctrina Christiana*. Translated by Charles R. Sumner, Columbia edition of *Works* (1933), xiv, 7, 9, 11, 13.

According to my judgment, therefore, neither my creed nor my hope of salvation could be safely trusted to such guides; and yet it appeared highly requisite to possess some methodical tractate of Christian doctrine, or at least to attempt such a disquisition as might be useful in establishing my faith or assisting my memory. I deemed it therefore safest and most advisable to compile for myself, by my own labor and study, some original treatise which should be always at hand, derived solely from the word of God itself, and executed with all possible fidelity, seeing that I could have no wish to practice any imposition on myself in such a matter.

After a diligent perseverance in this plan for several years, I perceived that the strongholds of the reformed religion were sufficiently fortified, as far as it was in danger from the Papists, but neglected in many other quarters; neither competently strengthened with works of defence, nor adequately provided with champions. It was also evident to me, that, in religion as in other things, the offers of God were all directed, not to indolent credulity, but to constant diligence, and to an unwearied search after truth; and that more than I was aware of still remained, which required to be more rigidly examined by the rule of Scripture, and reformed after a more accurate model. I so far satisfied myself in the prosecution of this plan as at length to trust that I had discovered, with regard to religion, what was matter of belief, and what only matter of opinion. It was also a great solace to me to have compiled, by God's assistance, a precious aid for my faith; or rather to have laid up for myself a treasure which would be a provision for my future life, and would remove from my mind all grounds for hesitation, as often as it behoved me to render an account of the principles of my belief.

If I communicate the result of my inquiries to the world at large; if, as God is my witness, it be with a friendly and benignant feeling towards mankind, that I readily give as wide a circulation as possible to what I esteem my best and richest possession, I hope to meet with a candid reception from all parties, and that none at least will take unjust offence, even though many things should be brought to light which will at once be seen to differ from certain received opinions. I earnestly beseech all lovers of truth, not to cry out that the Church is thrown into confusion by that freedom of discussion and inquiry which is granted to the schools, and ought certainly to be refused to no believer, since we are ordered 'to prove all thing,' and since the daily progress of the light of truth is productive far less of disturbance to the Church, than of illumination and edification. Nor do I see how the Church can be more disturbed by the investigation of truth, than were the Gentiles by the first promulgation of the gospel; since so far from recommending or imposing anything on my own authority, it is my particular advice that every one should suspend his opinion on whatever points he may not feel himself fully satisfied, till the evidence of Scripture prevail, and persuade his reason into assent and faith. Concealment is not my object; it is to the learned that I address myself, or if it be thought that the learned are not the best umpires and judges of such things, I should at least wish to submit my opinions to men of a mature and manly understanding, possessing a thorough knowledge of the doctrines of the gospel; on whose judgments I should rely with far more confidence, than on those of novices in these matters. And whereas the greater part of those who have written most largely on these subjects have been wont to fill whole pages with explanations of their own opinions, thrusting into the margin the texts in support of their doctrine with a summary reference to the chapter and verse, I have chosen, on the contrary, to fill my pages even to redundance with quotations from Scripture, that so as little space as possible might be left for my own words, even when they arise from the context of revelation itself.

It has also been my object to make it appear from the opinions I shall be found to have advanced, whether new or old, of how much consequence to the Christian religion is the liberty not only of winnowing and sifting every doctrine, but also of thinking and even writing respecting it, according to our individual faith and persuasion; an inference which will be stronger in proportion to the weight and importance of those opinions, or rather in proportion to the authority of Scripture, on the abundant testimony of which they rest. Without this liberty there is neither religion nor gospel—force alone prevails—by which it is disgraceful for the Christian religion to be supported. Without this liberty we are still enslaved, not indeed, as formerly, under the divine law, but, what is worst of all, under the law of man, or to speak more truly, under a barbarous tyranny.

20. Anonymous attack on
The Readie and Easie Way
1660

Extract from *The Censure of the Rota Upon Mr Miltons Book, Entituled, The Ready and Easie Way to Establish A Free Commonwealth* (1660), 12–13.

The image of the flat hand of Milton's exposition as opposed to the fist of logical argument is a withering comment on his ineffectual pamphleteering to stem the Restoration.

By this time they began to grow weary of your perpe[t]uall falshoods and mistakes, and a Worthy Knight of this Assembly stood up and said that if we meant to examin all the particular fallacies and flawes in your writing we should never have done, he would therefore (with leave) deliver his judgement upon the whole, which in briefe was thus. That it is all windy foppery from the beginning to the end, written to the elevation of that Rabble and meant to cheat the Ignorant. That you fight always with the flat of your hand like a Retorician, and never Contract the Logicall fist. That you trade altogether in universals the Region of Deceits and falacie, but never come so near particulars, as to let us know which among diverse things of the same kind you would be at. For you admire Common-wealths in generall, and cry down Kingship as much at large. . . .

21. Verse of *Paradise Lost*

1668

Prefatory note to *Paradise Lost,* 1668(?). John Milton, *Paradise Lost,* ed. 1, second issue (1668).

The Verse.

The Measure is *English* Heroic Verse without Rime, as that of *Homer* in *Greek*, and of *Virgil* in *Latin*; Rime being no necessary Adjunct or true Ornament of Poem or good Verse, in longer Works especially, but the Invention of a barbarous Age, to set off wretched matter and lame Meeter; grac't indeed since by the use of some famous modern Poets, carried away by Custom, but must to thir own vexation, hindrance, and constraint to express many things otherwise, and for the most part worse then else they would have exprest them. Not without cause therefore some both *Italian* and *Spanish* Poets of prime note have rejected Rime both in longer and shorter Works, as have also long since our best *English* Tragedies, as a thing of it self, to all judicious ears, triveal and of no true musical delight; which consists onely in apt Numbers, fit quantity of Syllables, and the sense variously drawn out from one Verse into another, not in the jingling sound of like endings, a fault avoyded by the learned Ancients both in Poetry and all good Oratory. This neglect then of Rime so little is to be taken for a defect, though it may seem so perhaps to vulgar Readers, that it rather is to be esteem'd an example set, the first in *English*, of ancient liberty recover'd to Heroic Poem from the troublesom and modern bondage of Rimeing.

22. The nature of tragedy
1671(?)

Prefatory note to *Samson Agonistes*. John Milton, *Paradise Regain'd . . . To which is added Samson Agonistes* (1671), 3–5, second pagination. The beginning of the last paragraph has been revised as in standard editions.

Of that sort of Dramatic Poem which is call'd Tragedy.

Tragedy, as it was antiently compos'd, hath been ever held the gravest, moralest, and most profitable of all other Poems: therefore said by *Aristotle* to be of power by raising pity and fear, or terror, to purge the mind of those and such like passions, that is to temper and reduce them to just measure with a kind of delight, stirr'd up by reading or seeing those passions well imitated. Nor is Nature wanting in her own effects to make good his assertion: for so in Physic things of melancholic hue and quality are us'd against melancholy, sowr against sowr, salt to remove salt humours. Hence Philosophers and other gravest Writers, as *Cicero, Plutarch* and others, frequently cite out of Tragic Poets, both to adorn and illustrate thir discourse. The Apostle *Paul* himself thought it not unworthy to insert a verse of *Euripides* into the Text of Holy Scripture, 1 Cor. 15.33. and *Paraeus* commenting on the *Revelation*, divides the whole Books as a Tragedy, into Acts distinguisht each by a Chorus of Heavenly Harpings and Song between. Heretofore Men in highest dignity have labour'd not a little to be thought able to compose a Tragedy. Of that honour *Dionysius* the elder was no less ambitious, then before of his attaining to the Tyranny. *Augustus Caesar* also had begun his *Ajax*, but unable to please his own judgment with what he had begun, left it unfinisht. *Seneca* the Philosopher is by some thought the Author of those Tragedies (at lest the best of them) that go under that name. *Gregory Nazianzen* a Father of the Church, thought it not unbeseeming the sanctity of his person to write a Tragedy, which he entitl'd, *Christ suffering*. This is mention'd to vindicate Tragedy from the small esteem, or rather infamy, which in the account of many it undergoes at this day with other common Inter-

74

ludes; hap'ning through the Poets error of intermixing Comic stuff with Tragic sadness and gravity; or introducing trivial and vulgar persons, which by all judicious hath bin counted absurd; and brought in without discretion, corruptly to gratifie the people. And though antient Tragedy use no Prologue, yet using sometimes, in case of self defence, or explanation, that which *Martial* calls an Epistle; in behalf of this Tragedy coming forth after the antient manner, much different from what among us passes for best, thus much before-hand may be Epistl'd; that *Chorus* is here introduc'd after the Greek manner, not antient only but modern, and still in use among the *Italians*. In the modelling therefore of this Poem, with good reason, the Antients and *Italians* are rather follow'd, as of much more authority and fame. The measure of Verse us'd in the Chorus is of all sorts, call'd by the Greeks *Monostrophic*, or rather *Apolelymenon*, without regard had to *Strophe*, *Antistrophe* or *Epod*, which were a kind of Stanza's fram'd only for the Music, then us'd with the Chorus that sung; not essential to the Poem, and therefore not material; or being divided into Stanza's or Pauses, they may be call'd *Allæostropha*. Division into Act and Scene referring chiefly to the Stage (to which this work never was intended) is here omitted. It suffices if the whole Drama be found not produc't beyond the fift Act.

Of the style and uniformitie, and that commonly call'd the Plot, whether intricate or explicit, which is nothing indeed but such œconomy, or disposition of the fable as may stand best with verisimilitude and decorum; they only will best judge who are not unacquainted with *Æschulus, Sophocles,* and *Euripides,* the three Tragic Poets unequall'd yet by any, and the best rule to all who endeavour to write Tragedy. The circumscription of time wherein the whole Drama begins and ends, is according to antient rule, and best example, within the space of 24 hours.

23. Butler on Milton

early 1670s (?)

Extract from Samuel Butler, 'Fragments of an Intended Second Part of the Foregoing Satire', ll. 141–52. George Gilfallen, ed., *Poetical Works* (1854), II, 235.

Samuel Butler (1612–80) was the well-known author of *Hudibras*. Milton had criticized Salmasius in the *First Defense* for errors in his Latin prose and for his lack of understanding of English. Butler lampoons Milton's writing by making him attend to insignificant detail and overlook the momentous issue.

'The Foregoing Satire' is 'Satire Upon the Imperfection and Abuse of Human Learning'. 'He' in l. 143 is Milton: 'breaking Priscian's head', l. 149, means 'violating the rules of grammar'.

So some polemics use to draw their swords
Against the language only and the words:
As he who fought at barriers with Salmasius,
Engaged with nothing but his style and phrases;
Waived to assert the murder of a prince,
The author of false Latin to convince;
But laid the merits of the cause aside,
By those that understood them to be try'd;
And counted *breaking Priscian's head* a thing
More capital than to behead a king:
For which h' has been admired by all the learn'd,
Of knaves concern'd, and pedants unconcern'd.

24. Leigh on the antiprelatical tracts

1673

Extract from Richard Leigh (?), *The Transproser Rehears'd: of the Fifth Act of Mr. Bayes's Play* (1673), 41–3.

The pamphlet is a reply to Marvell's *The Rehearsal Transprosed,* Part One (1672). The author refers to Milton's attack upon Bishop Joseph Hall's *A Defence of the Humble Remonstrance, Against the frivolous and false exceptions of Smectymnuus* (1641) in *Animadversions* (1641), a counter pamphlet thought erroneously to be by Hall and entitled *A Modest Confutation of A Slanderous and Scurrilous Libell, Entituled, Animadversions* (1642), and Milton's answer in *An Apology Against a Pamphlet call'd A Modest Confutation* (1642). Hall had written *Virgidemiarum, Sixe Bookes. First three Bookes. Of Tooth-lesse Satyrs. 1. Poeticall. 2. Academicall. 3. Morall* (1598).

[E]ven timerous Minds are Couragious and bold enough to shape prodigious Forms and Images of Battels; & dark Souls may be illuminated with *bright* and shining thoughts. As, to seek no farther for an instance; the *blind* Author of *Paradise lost* (the odds betwixt a *Transproser* and a *Blank Verse Poet,* is not great) begins his third Book thus, groping for a beam of *Light* [III, 1–2]. And a little after, [III, 21–26]. No doubt but the thoughts of this *Vital Lamp* lighted a *Christmas* Candle in his brain. What dark meaning he may have in calling this *thick drop Serene,* I am not able to say; but for his *Eternal Coeternal,* besides the absurdity of his inventive Divinity, in making *Light* contemporary with it's Creator, that jingling in the middle of his Verse, is more notoriously ridiculous, because the *blind Bard* (as he tell[s] us himself in his Apology for writing in blank Verse) studiously declin'd Rhyme as a *jingling sound of like endings.* Nay, what is more observable, it is the very same fault, which he was so quick-sighted, as to discover in this Verse of *Halls Toothless Satyrs.*

> *To teach each hollow Grove and shrubby-Hill.*

This *teach each*, he has upbraided the Bishop with in his *Apology* for his *Animadversions on the Remonstrants Defence against Smectymnuus*. You see Sir, that I am improved too with reading the Poets, and though you may be better read in *Bishop Dav'nants Gondibert;* yet I think this *Schismatick* in *Poetry,* though nonconformable in point of Rhyme, as authentick ev'ry jot, as any *Bishop Laureat* of them all.

25. Marvell in defence of Milton

1673

Extract from Andrew Marvell, *The Rehearsall Transpros'd: The Second Part*, (1674), 339–42.

Andrew Marvell (1621–78) was a friend of Milton, became assistant Secretary for Foreign Tongues to the Council of State in 1657 through Milton's earlier recommendation, and was M.P. for Hull after the Restoration. He charges Leigh with unjustifiedly injecting Milton into their political argument because the author of *The Transproser Rehears'd* must erroneously suspect Milton's hand in Marvell's work. Nos. 24 and 25 point up a frequent bias against Milton's work (particularly the poetry): it was criticized adversely because his politics were disliked. *A Reproof to the Rehearsal Transprosed* (1673) was written by Samuel Parker; *Common Places* refers to the anonymous *A Common-place-Book out of the Rehearsal Transpros'd* (1673).

You do three times at least in your *Reproof*, and in your *Transproser Rehears'd* well nigh half the book thorow, run upon an Author *J. M.* which does not a little offend me. For why should any other mans reputation suffer in a contest betwixt you and me? But it is because you resolved to suspect that he had an hand in my former book, wherein, whether you deceive your self or no, you deceive others extreamly. For by chance I had not seen him of two years before; but after I undertook writing, I did more carefully avoid either visiting or sending to him, least I should any way involve him in my consequences. And you might have understood, or I am sure your Friend the Author of the *Common Places* could have told you, (he too had a slash at *J. M.* upon my account) that had he took you in hand, you would have had cause to repent the occasion, and not escap'd so easily as you did under my *Transprosal*. But I take it moreover very ill that you should have so mean an opinion of me, as not to think me competent to write such a simple book as that without any assistance. It is a sign (however you upbraid me

79

often as your old acquaintance) that you did not know me well, and that we had not much conversation together. But because in your 115 *p.* you are so particular *you know a friend of ours,* &c. intending that *J. M.* and his answer to *Salmasius,* I think it here seasonable to acquit my promise to you in giving the Reader a short trouble concerning my first acquaintance with you. *J. M.* was, and is, a man of great Learning and Sharpness of wit as any man. It was his misfortune, living in a tumultuous time, to be toss'd on the wrong side, and he writ *Flagrante bello* certain dangerous Treatises. His Books *of Divorce* I know not whether you may have use of; but those upon which you take him at advantage were of no other nature then that which I mentioned to you, writ by your own father; only with this difference, that your Fathers, which I have by me, was written with the same design, but with much less Wit or Judgment, for which there was no remedy: unless you will supply his Judgment with his High Court of Justice. At His Majesties happy Return, *J. M.* did partake, even as you your self did for all your huffing, of his Regal Clemency, and has ever since expiated himself in a retired silence. It was after that, I well remember it, that being one day at his house, I there first met you and accidentally. Since that I have been scarce four or five times in your Company, but, whether it were my foresight or my good fortune, I never contracted any friendship or confidence with you. But then it was, when you, as I told you, wander'd up and down *Moor-Fields* Astrologizing upon the duration of His Majesties Government, that you frequented *J. M.* incessantly and haunted his house day by day. What discourses you there used he is too generous to remember. But he never having in the least provoked you, for you to insult thus over his old age, to traduce him by your *Scaramuccios,* and in your own person, as a School-Master, who was born and hath lived much more ingenuously and Liberally then your self; to have done all this, and lay at last my simple book to his charge, without ever taking care to inform your self better, which you had so easie opportunity to do; nay, when you your self too have said, to my knowledge, that you saw no such great matter in it but that I might be the Author: it is inhumanely and inhospitably done, and will I hope be a warning to all others, as it is to me, to avoid (I will not say such a *Judas,*) but a man that creeps into all companies, to jeer, trepan, and betray them.

26. Marvell on *Paradise Lost*

1674

Andrew Marvell, 'On Paradise Lost', *Paradise Lost* (1674).

Marvell's is one of the earliest indications of the controversy that was to be waged over rhyme and blank verse. His appreciation of the scope of the poem is noteworthy for the time.

The last verse paragraph refers to John Dryden's 'tagging' Milton's epic in 'The State of Innocence'. Dryden had been satirized as John Bayes (since he was the poet-laureate) in Buckingham's play *The Rehearsal* (1672).

On Paradise Lost

> When I beheld the Poet blind, yet bold,
> In slender Book his vast Design unfold,
> *Messiah* Crown'd, Gods Reconcil'd Decree,
> Rebelling Angels, the Forbidden Tree,
> Heav'n, Hell, Earth, Chaos, All; the Argument
> Held me a while misdoubting his Intent,
> That he would ruine (for I saw him strong)
> The sacred Truths to Fable and old Song
> (So *Sampson* groap'd the Temples Posts in spight)
> The World o'rewhelming to revenge his sight.
>
> Yet as I read, soon growing less severe,
> I lik'd his Project, the success did fear;
> Through that wide Field how he his way should find
> O're which lame Faith leads Understanding blind;
> Lest he perplex'd the things he would explain,
> And what was easie he should render vain.
>
> Or if a Worke so infinite he spann'd,
> Jealous I was that some less skilful hand
> (Such as disquiet always what is well,
> And by ill imitating would excell)

Might hence presume the whole Creations day
To change in Scenes, and show it in a Play.
    Pardon me, Mighty Poet, nor despise
My causeless, yet not impious, surmise.
But I am now convinc'd, and none will dare
Within thy Labours to pretend a share.
Thou hast not miss'd one thought that could be fit,
And all that was improper dost omit:
So that no room is here for Writers left,
But to detect their Ignorance or Theft.
    That Majesty which through thy Work doth Reign
Draws the Devout, deterring the Profane.
And things divine thou treatst of in such state
As them preserves, and thee, inviolate.
At once delight and horrour on us seise,
Thou singst with so much gravity and ease;
And above humane flight dost soar aloft
With Plume so strong, so equal, and so soft,
The Bird nam'd from that Paradise you sing
So never flaggs, but always keeps on Wing.
    Where couldst thou words of such a compass find?
Whence furnish such a vast expence of mind?
Just Heav'n thee like *Tiresias* to requite
Rewards with Prophesie thy loss of sight.
    Well mightst thou scorn thy Readers to allure
With tinkling Rhime, of thy own sense secure;
While the *Town-Bayes* writes all the while and spells,
And like a Pack-horse tires without his Bells:
Their Fancies like our Bushy-points appear,
The Poets tag them, we for fashion wear.
I too transported by the Mode offend,
And while I meant to Praise thee must Commend.
Thy Verse created like thy Theme sublime,
In Number, Weight, and Measure, needs not Rhime.

27. Lee on *Paradise Lost*

1674 (?)

Extract from Nathaniel Lee, 'To Mr. Dryden, on his Poem of Paradise' (*c.* 1674), ll. 11–26. John Dryden, *The State of Innocence and Fall of Man: An Opera* (1677).

Nathaniel Lee (1653?–92) was a popular playwright, who wrote blank verse as well as rhyme, although he here calls the former 'rude' and 'rough'. *The Rival Queens*, his first blank verse venture, was written significantly in 1677, some while after he had made the present comment.

To the dead Bard your Fame a little owes,
For *Milton* did the wealthy Mine disclose,
And rudely cast what you could well dispose:
He roughly drew on an old Fashion'd Ground,
A Chaos; for no perfect World was found,
Till through the Heap your mighty Genius shin'd;
His was the Golden Ore which you refin'd.
He first beheld the Beauteous rustick Maid,
And to a Place of Strength the Prize convey'd;
You took her thence, to Court this Virgin brought,
Drest her with Gems, new weav'd her hard spun thought,
And softest Language, sweetest Manners taught.
Till from a Comet she a Star did rise,
Not to affright, but please our wond'ring Eyes.
Betwixt ye both is fram'd a Nobler Piece,
Than e're was drawn in *Italy* or *Greece*.

FURTHER SEVENTEENTH-CENTURY COMMENT

1675–1699

---

28. Phillips's notice of his uncle

1675

Edward Phillips, *Theatrum Poetarum* (1675), 113–14.

Edward Phillips (1630–96?) was Milton's nephew and lived with him. A student of his uncle's, Phillips acted as his amanuensis from time to time, professing to have corrected the accidentals of *Paradise Lost* during its composition. He wrote an important life (see No. 42), prefaced to his translation of Milton's *Letters of State*. His accuracy, particularly in dates, is sometimes unreliable.

Iohn Milton, the Author (not to mention his other Works, both in Latin and English, both in strict and solute Oration, by which his Fame is sufficiently known to all the Learned of Europe) of two Heroic Poems, and a Tragedy; namely *Paradice lost, Paradice Regain'd*, and *Sampson Agonista*; in which how far he hath reviv'd the Majesty and true *Decorum* of Heroic Poesy and Tragedy: it will better become a person less related then my self, to deliver his judgement.

29. Ellwood's 'Epitaph on Milton'
1675(?)

Thomas Ellwood, 'Epitaph on Milton' (1675?), from 'Rhapsodia',
holograph manuscript, Friends' Library, London, pp. 145-6.
Ellwood, a founder of the Society of Friends, studied with Milton,
apparently did scribal work for him from time to time, and
acquired the house at Chalfont St. Giles, Bucks., in which Milton
stayed during the Great Fire of 1666-7.

Upon the excellently-learned John Milton, An Epitaph

> Within this Arch embalm'd doth lie
> One, whose high fame can never die;
> *Milton*, whose most ingenious pen
> Obliged has all learned men.
> Great his undertakings were
> (None greater of this kind)
> Which sufficiently declare
> The worth and greatness of his mind;
> Mean Adversaries he declin'd,
> And battel with the Chiefest joyn'd.
> Not e'en the Royal Pourtraicture
> Proudly could before him stand,
> But fell and broke,
> Not able (as it seems) t' indure
> The heavy stroke
> Of His Iconoclastes hand.
> Thus the so fam'd *Eikon Basilike*
> Became the Trophy of his victory.
> On his triumphant Chariot too did wait,
> One who had long the Crown of Learning wore,
> And of Renown had treasur'd up good store,
> But never found an equal Match before,
> Which puff't him up, and made him too elate.

This was the great *Salmasius*, he whose name
Had tower'd so high upon the wing of fame,
And never knew till now
What 'twas (alas!) to bow.
(For many a gallant Captive, by the heel,
Had He in Triumph, dragg'd at's Chariot-wheel)
But now is fain to stoop, and see the Bough
Torn from his own, to deck another's brow.
This broke his heart: for (having lost his fame)
He died, 'tis hard to say whether through grief or shame.
Thus great *Salmasius*, in his winding-sheet,
Lies prostrate at far greater *Milton's* feet;
Milton, in whom all brave endowments meet!
    The Majesty of Poesy he reviv'd,
The common Road forsaking,
And, unto Helicon a new track making,
To write in Measures without Rime, contriv'd.
He knew the beauty of a Verse well-made
Doth in a just and due proportion lie
Of Parts, true feet, right Cadence, Symphony
(A thing by vulgar Poets, lightly weigh'd)
Not in the tinkling Chime
Of an harsh and far-fetch't Rime.
    Two great Examples of this kind he left
(The natural Issue of his teeming Brain),
Th' one shews how man of Eden was bereft;
In t' other man doth Paradise regain,
So far as naked Notion can attain.
    Nature in him a large Foundation laid,
And he had also super-built thereon
A Structure great indeed, and fair enough,
Of well-prepar'd and finely polish't stuff,
Admir'd by all, but equalled by none.
So that of him it might be said
(And that most truly too)
Nature and Art,
Had plaid their part,
As if they had a wager laid,
Which of them most for him should do.
His natural Abilities

Were doubtless of the largest size;
And thereunto he surely had acquir'd
Learning, as much as could be well desir'd:
More known his learning was not than admir'd.
    Profound his Judgment was, and clear;
His Apprehension of the highest strain:
His Reason all before it down did bear,
So forcible, demonstrative and plain
It did appear.
Lofty Fancy, deep Conceit,
Style concise and Language great
Rendered his Discourse compleat,
On whatsoever Subject he did treat.
Invention never high rose
In Poetic strains, or Prose.
In Tongues he so much skill had got,
He might be call'd the Polyglot.
Even they 'gainst whom he writ
Could not but admire his Wit;
And were forced to confess
(For indeed it was in vain
To deny a thing so plain)
That their Parts than his were less.
    Unto him the Muses sent,
And that, too, not in compliment
(For doubtless 'twas his due,
As all that knew him knew)
The Title of Most Excellent,
    Of which Title may he rest
    Now, and evermore, possest.

30. Aubrey's notes for a *Life*

late 1670s

Extract from John Aubrey, 'Minutes of the Life of Mr. John Milton'. Helen Darbishire, ed., *The Early Lives of Milton* (1932), 13.

John Aubrey (1626–1697), an antiquarian, collected notes for a life of Milton for Anthony Wood, whose biographical account is found in *Fasti Oxonienses*. The anecdote reappears in Phillips's Life, from which it was frequently repeated in later years.

from Mr E. Philips.

₊His Invention was much more free and easie in the Æquinoxes than at the Solstices; as he more particularly found in writing his Paradise lost. Mr Edw. Philip his, [his Nephew and ᵗʰᵉⁿ Amanuensis] hath₊ All the time of writing his *Paradise lost*, his veine began at the Autumnall Æquinoctiall and ceased at the Vernall or thereabouts (I believe about May) and this was 4 or 5 yeares of his doeing it. He began about 2 yeares before the K. came-in, and finished about 3 yeares after the K's Restauracõn.

31. F.C. on *Paradise Lost*

1680

F.[rancis] C.[raddock], 'To Mr. John Milton, On His Poem Entitled Paradise Lost' (1680). Francis Fawkes and William Woty, eds., *The Poetical Calendar* (1753), viii, 69.

Francis Craddock's poem praising *Paradise Lost* was allegedly discovered in a copy of the work. It was often reprinted in magazines and miscellanies.

> O thou! the wonder of the present age!
> An age immerst in luxury and vice;
> A race of triflers; who can relish naught,
> But the gay issue of an idle brain:
> How could'st thou hope to please this tinsel race?
> Tho' blind, yet with the penetrating eye
> Of intellectual light thou dost survey
> The labyrinth perplex'd of heaven's decrees;
> And with a quill, pluck'd from an angel's wing,
> Dipt in the fount that laves th' eternal throne,
> Trace the dark paths of providence divine,
> 'And justify the ways of God to Man'.

32. Pettit on Milton's advancement
of papal aims

1680

[Edward Pettit], *The Vision of Purgatory* (1680), 99–101.

The vision of Milton as a papist seems ludicrous to us today, but Pettit was merely capitalizing upon Milton's notoriety as a governmental antagonist in the midst of the fears of the Popish Plot. Pettit's knowledge of Milton and his works seems lacking, but papal subversion is more startlingly underscored by his choosing one who was identified with the Puritanic state.

We went with him to a Back-gate, where stood a Guard to keep out a number of men, who were very desirous to get in; as soon as we came up to them, I was amased to find *Milton* at the head of a company in short Cloaks, short hair, and with white Caps turn'd up under black ones: but before I could take particular notice of any one man, I was diverted by *Milton*, whom I observed to be very earnest with a Provincial of the Jesuits (who stood there to give orders) and because he was a man of singular Eloquence, I took a great deal of pains to hear what he said, which was to this effect: 'May it please you Reverence to consider how I am injured, who am denied the honour which is so easily granted to men vastly beneath my Merits, and Deserts; for what can any man do for the promotion of your Interests that I have not done? Did not I constantly attend your Consults, and observe your Orders? Did not I promote the late Rebellion in *England* by all the Artifices Imaginable; by siding with the Malecontents and seditious Rabble, who wanted a man of my Parts and Learning to gild their Treasons, with pompous pretences of Justice, and Reformation; and to urge them to greater Excesses? Did not I bestow the best Flowers of Rhetorick for Garlands to adorn the heads of victorious Traytors, and triumphant Usurpers? and gave them a Counterfeit Majesty with the Roabs of Eloquence? Were not the people gull'd to part with their

Religion, and Property to those to whom I had given the glorious Titles of *Preservers of the Commonwealth, and Redeemers of their Liberty?* Have not I shaken the Crowns of Princes in that unparallel'd Book of mine against *Salmasius?* Have any of you Thundred against Monarchy at that rate? No, not any of you; not *Barionus* himself, who called it an *Adulterine Name,* and *A Tower of* Babel; Well then do not I deserve?'

He would have gone on, but that the Jesuit interrupted him, by telling him, That if he did still really wish the welfare of their Order, he would not desire such unreasonable Honours. . . .

33. Roscommon on *Paradise Lost*

1685

Extract from Wentworth Dillon, Earl of Roscommon, *An Essay on Translated Verse*, ll. 377–403, second ed. (1685).

Wentworth Dillon, the fourth Earl of Roscommon (1633?–85), was the first publicly to praise *Paradise Lost*. His imitation of its blank verse further indicates his admiration. Roscommon was known in the eighteenth century as one who, in Johnson's words, improved taste.

An Essay on blanc verse out of the 6th Book of *Paradise Lost* [marginal note]

   Have we forgot how *Raphaels* Num'rous Prose
Led out exalted Souls through heavenly Camps,
And mark'd the ground where proud Apostate Thrones
Defy'd *Jehovah*? Here, 'twixt Host and Host,
(A narrow but a dreadful Interval)
Portentous sight! before the Cloudy van
Satan with vast and haughty Strides advanc'd,
Came tow'ring arm'd in Adamant and Gold.
There Bellowing Engines, with their fiery Tubes,
Dispers'd Æthereal forms, and down they fell
By thousands, Angels on Arch-Angels rowl'd;
Recover'd, to the hills they ran, they flew,
Which (with their pond'rous load, Rocks, Waters, Woods)
From their firm Seats torn by the Shaggy Tops,
They bore like shields before them through the Air,
Till more incens'd they hurl'd them at their Foes.
All was confusion; Heavens Foundations Shook,
Threatning no less than Universal Wrack,
For *Michael's* arm main Promontories flung,
And over prest whole Legions weak with Sin;
For they Blasphem'd and struggled as they lay,
Till the great Ensign of *Messiah* blaz'd,

And, arm'd with vengeance, Gods Victorious Son
(Effulgence of Eternal Deity),
Grasping ten thousand Thunders in his hand,
Drove th' old Original Rebels headlong down,
And sent them flameing to the vast Abysse.

34. Dryden on *Paradise Lost*

1685

Extract from John Dryden, 'Preface to the Second Miscellany' (1685). George Saintsbury, ed., *The Works of John Dryden* (1885), xii, 300–1.

The various scattered comments of John Dryden (1631–1700) indicate a sharp difference between him and Milton on literary matters. Dryden's adherence to 'rules' contrasts with Milton's repeated breaks with tradition while remaining within a formal framework.

Imitation is a nice point, and there are few poets who deserve to be models in all they write. Milton's *Paradise Lost* is admirable; but am I therefore bound to maintain, that there are no flats amongst his elevations, when it is evident he creeps along sometimes for above an hundred lines together? Cannot I admire the height of his invention, and the strength of his expression, without defending his antiquated words, and the perpetual harshness of their sound? It is as much commendation as a man can bear, to own him excellent; all beyond it is idolatry.

35. Skinner on Milton

1686 (?)

Extract from *Anonymous Life* (written by Cyriac Skinner), 1686?.
The Life of Mr. John Milton, Bodleian MS. Wood, D4.

Skinner was a student of Milton's at Aldersgate Street, and later
occasionally acted as amanuensis. Perhaps through him Milton
met Marvell. The biography of Milton formerly known as the
Anonymous Life has been assigned to Skinner on the basis of hand-
writing.

He had naturally a Sharp Witt, and steddy Judgment; which helps
toward attaining Learning hee improv'd by an indefatigable attention
to his Study; and was supported in that by a Temperance, allways
observ'd by him, but in his Youth even with great Nicety. Yet did hee
not reckon this Talent but as intrusted with him; and therefore dedicated all his labours to the glory of God, & some public Good; Neither
binding himselfe to any of the gainfull Professions, nor having any
worldly Interest for aim in what he taught. Hee made no address or
Court for the emploiment of Latin Secretary, though his eminent fitt-
ness for it appeer by his printed Letters of that time. And hee was so
farr from beeing concern'd in the corrupt designs of his Masters, that
whilst in his first and second *Defensio pro populo Anglicano* he was an
Advocate of Liberty against Tyranny & Oppression (which to him
seem'd the case, as well by the public Declarations on the one side as
by the Arguments on the other side, which run mainly upon the
justifying of exorbitant & lawless power) hee took care all along
strictly to define, and persuade to true Liberty, and especially in very
solemn Perorations at the close of those Books; where hee also, little
less than Prophetically, denounc'd the Punishments due to the abusers
of that Specious name. . . .
Hee rendered his Studies and various Works more easy & pleasant by
allotting them thir several portions of the day. Of these the time friendly
to the Muses fell to his Poetry; And hee waking early (as is the use of

temperate men) had commonly a good Stock of Verses ready against his Amanuensis came; which if it happened to bee later than ordinary, hee would complain, Saying *hee wanted to bee milkd*. The Evenings hee likewise spent in reading some choice Poets, by way of refreshment after the days toyl, and to store his Fancy against Morning. Besides his ordinary lectures out of the Bible and the best Commentators on the week day, That was his sole subject on Sundays. And Davids Psalms were in esteem with him above all Poetry.

36. Winstanley's notice

1687

William Winstanley, 'Milton', *The Lives Of the Most Famous English Poets* (1687), 195.

One of the most important compilers of early biographical dictionaries, William Winstanley (1628?–98) gave himself up to ridicule by this biased comment on Milton.

John Milton was one, whose natural parts might deservedly give him a place amongst the principal of our English Poets, having written two Heroick Poems and a Tragedy; namely, *Paradice Lost, Paradice Regain'd*, and *Sampson Agonista*; But his Fame is gone out like a Candle in a Snuff, and his Memory will always stink, which might have ever lived in honourable Repute, had not he been a notorious Traytor, and most impiously and villanously bely'd that blessed King *Charles* the First.

37. Dryden's 'Epigram'

1688

John Dryden, 'Epigram' (1688), printed beneath Milton's portrait in *Paradise Lost*, ed. Jacob Tonson (1688).

Three poets, in three distant ages born,
Greece, Italy, and England, did adorn.
The first, in loftiness of thought surpassed;
The next, in majesty; in both, the last.
The force of nature could no further go;
To make a third, she joined the former two.

38. Comment on Milton

1692

Question and Answer from *Athenian Mercury* (i.e. *Athenian Gazette: or Casuistical Mercury*), Vol. V, No. 14 (16 January 1692).

Quest. 3. Whether Milton *and* Waller *were not the best English Poets? and which the better of the two?*

Answ. We shall answer this double Question together: They were both excellent in their kind, and exceeded each other, and all besides. *Milton* was the *fullest* and *loftiest, Waller* the *neatest* and most *correct* Poet we ever had. But yet we think *Milton* wrote too little in Verse, and too much in Prose, to carry the Name of *Best* from all others; and Mr. *Waller,* tho' a full and noble Writer, yet comes not up in our Judgments to that,—*Mens divinior atque os—Magna Sonaturum* [the more divine mind and mouth—great are they of sound], as *Horace* calls it, which *Milton* has, and wherein we think he was never equalled—His Description of the *Pandaemonium,* his Battles of the Angels, his Creation of the World, his Digression of *Light,* in his Paradice lost, are all inimitable pieces, and even that antique Style which he uses, seems to become the Subject, like the strange dresses wherein we represent the old Heroes. The Description of *Samson*'s Death, the artificial and delicate preparation of the Incidents and Narrations, the turn of the whole, and more than all, the terrible *Satyr* on *Woman,* in his Discourse with *Dalilah,* are undoubtedly of a piece with his other Writings; and to say nothing of his Paradice regain'd, whereof he had only finish'd the most barren part, in his Juvenile Poems, those on Mirth and Melancholly, an Elegy on his Friend that was drown'd, and especially a Fragment of the Passion, are incomparable: However, we think him not so *general* a Poet as some we have formerly had, and others still surviving.

39. Dennis on rhyme

1692

Extract from John Dennis, 'The Preface to *The Passion of Byblis*' (1692). E. N. Hooker, ed., *The Critical Works of John Dennis* (1939), i, 3–4.

A major critic, but lampooned by Swift and Pope, John Dennis (1657–1734) spoke out strongly for Milton's use of blank verse, his sublimity of style and subject, and his strategies of characterization in *Paradise Lost*. Dennis's criticism has generally been overlooked by students of Milton.

I must beg Pardon for the Liberty which I have taken in the numbers, which is so great that it may well be entitled License. But then the Reader will have the greater Variety, and if those Numbers are not harmonious, it is not for want of care about them: I have particularly taken care to be exact in the Rhimes, in which the former Translators of this passage have been very defective. I am not so miserably mistaken, as to think rhiming essential to our *English* Poetry. I am far better acquainted with *Milton*, than that comes to. Who without the assistance of Rhime, is one of the most sublime of our *English* Pocts. Nay, there is something so transcendently sublime in his first, second, and sixth Books, that were the Language as pure as the Images are vast and daring, I do not believe it could be equall'd, no, not in all Antiquity. But tho' I know that Rhiming is not absolutely necessary to our Versification, yet I am for having a Man do throughly what he has once pretended to do. Writing in blank Verse looks like a contempt of Rhime, and a generous disdain of a barbarous Custom; but Writing in such Rhimes as a Boy may laugh at, at *Crambo*, looks at the best like a fruitless Attempt, and an impotent Affectation.

40. Preston on Milton's fame

1693(?)

Extract from William Preston, 'Epistle to a Young Gentleman'
(c. 1693). *The Poetical Works of William Preston* (1793), i, 178–9.

Preston was a minor eighteenth-century poet. His appreciation of
Paradise Lost reflects the prestige which the epic held among other
poets.

> And thou, with age oppress'd, beset with wrongs,
> And fall'n on evil days, and evil tongues,
> In darkness and with dangers compass'd round;
> What stars of joy thy night of anguish crown'd?
> What breath of vernal airs, or sound of rill,
> Or haunt by Siloa's brook, or Sion's hill,
> Or light of cherubim, th' empyreal throne,
> Th' effulgent car and inexpressive ONE?
> Alas, not thine the foretaste of thy praise;
> A dull oblivion wrapt thy mighty lays.
> Awhile thy glory sunk, in dread repose,
> Then, with fresh vigour, like a giant rose,
> And strode sublime, and pass'd, with gen'rous rage,
> The feeble minions of a puny age.

41. Dryden on *Paradise Lost*

1693

Extract from John Dryden, 'Original and Progress of Satire' (1693). George Sainstbury, ed., *The Works of John Dryden* (1887), xiii, 18–20, 117.

The following summarizes Dryden's view of Milton, the problem of rhyme, his language, and questions of genre.

As for Mr. Milton, whom we all admire with so much justice, his subject is not that of an heroic poem, properly so called. His design is the losing of our happiness; his event is not prosperous, like that of all other epic works; his heavenly machines are many, and his human persons are but two. But I will not take Mr. Rymer's work out of his hands: he has promised the world a critique on that author; wherein, though he will not allow his poem for heroic, I hope he will grant us, that his thoughts are elevated, his words sounding, and that no man has so happily copied the manner of Homer, or so copiously translated his Grecisms, and the Latin elegances of Virgil. It is true, he runs into a flat of thought, sometimes for a hundred lines together, but it is when he is got into a track of Scripture. His antiquated words were his choice, not his necessity; for therein he imitated Spenser, as Spenser did Chaucer. And though, perhaps, the love of their masters may have transported both too far, in the frequent use of them, yet, in my opinion, obsolete words may then be laudably revived, when either they are more sounding, or more significant, than those in practice; and when their obscurity is taken away, by joining other words to them, which clear the sense; according to the rule of Horace, for the admission of new words. But in both cases a moderation is to be observed in the use of them: for unnecessary coinage, as well as unnecessary revival, runs into affection; a fault to be avoided on either hand. Neither will I justify Milton for his blank verse, though I may excuse him, by the example of Hannibal Caro, and other Italians, who have used it; for whatever causes he alleges for the abolishing of rhyme, (which I have not now the leisure to examine,) his own particular reason is plainly this, that rhyme was not his talent; he had neither the ease of doing it, nor the graces of it; which is manifest in his *Juvenilia*, or verses written in his youth, where his rhyme is always constrained and forced, and comes hardly from him, at an age when the soul is most pliant, and the passion of love makes almost every man a rhymer, though not a poet. . . .

Then I consulted a greater genius, (without offence to the manes of that noble author,) I mean Milton; but as he endeavours everywhere to express Homer, whose age had not arrived to that fineness, I found in him a true sublimity, lofty thoughts, which were clothed with admirable Grecisms, and ancient words, which he had been digging from the mines of Chaucer and Spenser, and which, with all their rusticity, had somewhat of venerable in them. But I found not there neither that for which I looked. At last I had recourse to his master, Spenser, the author of that immortal poem called the *Fairy Queen*; and there I met with that which I had been looking for so long in vain. Spenser had studied Virgil to as much advantage as Milton had done Homer; and amongst the rest of his excellences had copied that.

42. Phillips on various works

1694

Extract from Edward Phillips, 'The life of Mr. John Milton'.
Edward Phillips, ed., *Letters of State, written by Mr. John Milton*
(1694), xxiv–xxv, xxxiv–xxxv, xxxviii–xxxix.

Phillips's quotation from the early tragedy differs in one point
from the recorded text; the editions give 'Matchless King' rather
than 'Glorious King' in IV, 41.

[S]o that he forthwith prepared to Fortify himself with Arguments for
such a Resolution [of his marital difficulties], and accordingly wrote
two Treatises, by which he undertook to maintain, That it was against
Reason, (and the enjoyment of it not proveable by Scripture), for any
Married Couple disagreeable in Humour and Temper, or having an
aversion to each other, to be forc'd to live yok'd together all their
Days. The first was, his *Doctrine and Discipline of Divorce*; of which
there was Printed a Second Edition, with some Additions. The other in
prosecution of the first, was styled *Tetrachordon*. Then the better to
confirm his own Opinion by the attestation of others, he set out a
Piece called *the Judgement of Martin Bucer*, a Protestant Minister, being a
Translation, out of that Reverend Divine, of some part of his Works,
exactly agreeing with him in Sentiment. Lastly, he wrote in answer
to a Pragmatical Clerk, who would needs give himself the Honour of
Writing against so great a Man, his *Colasterion*, or Rod of Correction
for a Sawcy Impertinent. . . .

But the Heighth of his Noble Fancy and Invention began now to be
seriously and mainly imployed in a Subject worthy of such a Muse, *viz.*
A Heroick Poem, Entituled, *Paradise Lost*; the Noblest in the general
Esteem of Learned and Judicious Persons, of any yet written by any
either Ancient or Modern: This Subject was first designed a Tragedy,
and in the Fourth Book of the Poem there are Ten Verses, which several
Years before the Poem was begun, were shewn to me, and some others,

as designed for the very beginning of the said Tragedy. The Verses are these; [IV, 32–41].

There is another very remarkable Passage in the Composure of this Poem, which I have a particular occasion to remember; for whereas I had the perusal of it from the very beginning; for some years, as I went from time to time, to Visit him, in a Parcel of Ten, Twenty, or Thirty Verses at a Time, which being Written by whatever hand came next, might possibly want Correction as to the Orthography and Pointing; having as the Summer came on, not been shewed any for a considerable while, and desiring the reason thereof, was answered, That his Vein never happily flow'd, but from the *Autumnal Equinoctial* to the *Vernal*, and that whatever he attempted was never to his satisfaction, though he courted his fancy never so much; so that in all the years he was about this Poem, he may be said to have spent but half his time therein. . . .

And this was his last Stage in this World, but it was of many years continuance, more perhaps than he had had in any other place [Artillery Walk] besides. Here he finisht his noble Poem, and publisht it in the year 1666 [error for 1667]. The first Edition was Printed in Quarto by one *Simons*, a Printer in *Aldersgate-Street*; the other in a large Octavo, by *Starky* near *Temple-Bar*, amended, enlarg'd, and differently dispos'd as to the Number of Books, by his own Hand, that is by his own appointment; the last set forth, many years since his death, in a large Folio with Cuts added by *Jacob Tonson*. Here it was also that he finisht and publisht his History of our Nation till the Conquest, all compleat so far as he went, some Passages only excepted, which being thought too sharp against the Clergy, could not pass the Hand of the Licencer, were in the Hands of the late Earl of *Anglesey* while he liv'd; where at present is uncertain.

It cannot certainly be concluded when he wrote his excellent Tragedy entitled *Samson Agonistes*, but sure enough it is that it came forth after his publication of *Paradice lost*, together with his other Poem call'd *Paradice regain'd*, which doubtless was begun and finisht and Printed after the other was publisht, and that in a wonderful short space considering the sublimeness of it; however it is generally censur'd to be much inferiour to the other, though he could not hear with patience any such thing when related to him; possibly the Subject may not afford such variety of Invention, but it is thought by the most judicious to be little or nothing inferiour to the other for stile and decorum.

43. Addison on *Paradise Lost*

1694

Extract from Joseph Addison, 'An Account of the Greatest English Poets' (3 April 1694), *Works*, ed. 2 (1730), i, 36–7.

This is the earliest tribute to Milton's greatness which Joseph Addison (1672–1719) published. It forecasts his frequent quotation, imitation and analysis of Milton and his works.

> But *Milton* next, with high and haughty stalks,
> Unfetter'd in majestick numbers walks;
> No vulgar heroe can his Muse ingage;
> Nor earth's wide scene confine his hallow'd rage,
> See! see, he upward springs, and tow'ring high
> Spurns the dull province of mortality,
> Shakes heav'ns eternal throne with dire alarms,
> And sets th' Almighty thunderer in arms.
> What-e'er his pen describes I more than see,
> Whilst ev'ry verse, array'd in majesty,
> Bold, and sublime, my whole attention draws,
> And seems above the critick's nicer laws.
> How are you struck with terror and delight,
> When angel with arch-angel copes in fight!
> When great Messiah's out-spread banner shines,
> How does the chariot rattle in his lines!
> What sounds of brazen wheels, what thunder, scare,
> And stun the reader with the din of war!
> With fear my spirits and my blood retire,
> To see the Seraphs sunk in clouds of fire;
> But when, with eager step, from hence I rise,
> And view the first gay scenes of *Paradise*;
> What tongue, what words of rapture can express
> A vision so profuse of pleasantness.
> Oh had the Poet ne'er profan'd his pen,

To vernish o'er the guilt of faithless men;
His other works might have deserv'd applause!
But now the language can't support the case;
While the clean current, tho' serene and bright,
Betrays a bottom odious to the sight.

44. Gildon's vindication of *Paradise Lost*

1694

Charles Gildon(?), 'Vindication of *Paradise Lost*' (1694). Charles Gildon, ed., *Miscellaneous Letters and Essays on several Subjects* . . . (1694), 41–4. An *erratum* adds 'I.I.' as signature.

An editor and writer on miscellaneous subjects, Charles Gildon (1665–1724) shows strong influence from Milton by his frequent citation of Milton as authority.

To Mr. T. S. in Vindication of Mr. Milton's Paradise lost.

Sir,

You will pardon me, I am confident, tho' in Opposition to your Thoughts I positively declare my self extreamly well pleas'd with that part of Mr. *Milton*'s most excellent Poem, to which you discover the least Inclination. Those *Antient* and consequently *less Intelligible* Words, Phrases, and Similies, by which he frequently and *purposedly* affects to express his Meaning, in my Opinion do well suit with the *Venerable Antiquity* and *Sublime Grandeur* of his Subject. And how much soever some *Unthinking* have Condemn'd this his Choice, *You*, who have Maturely weigh'd how much deeper an Impression *less us'd* (so they be what you will grant his always are) *Significant words* make on a *Readers* fancy than such as are *more common*,—you, I say, must pay a vast deference to Mr. *Milton*'s great *Judiciousness* in this particular no less than to his *entire Manage* of every part of the *Charming Poem*, in which upon every Occasion he discovers himself a perfect, unimitable *Master of Language*. Here are you forc'd to give a profound Attention to the *Universal Creator*, speaking like *that Almighty* who by the *Fiat* of his Mouth made all things, and yet so *Gracious* are All his *Expressions*, as if he valued himself more on his *Good Will to Man* than on his *Prerogative* over him. There shall you read *Man*, addressing himself *Submissively* like a *Creature* who owes his Being to a better, wiser, and higher power, and yet not so *Abjectly* but you will easily perceive him to be *Lord* of the whole Creation. *Elsewhere* you may see an *Angel* discovering himself not a Little *Man's Superior* by Creation, in *Place* and *Power* more, but in *Knowledge* most of all. In *another place*, behold *Woman* appearing *Inferiour* to both these, and yet more *Ambitious* than either, but then *softer* much in her *Make* and *Manners* than her *rougher Spouse*, whom *down right Sincerity* and unaffected plainnes seem mostly to Delight. Nor can I now forget with what *vast complacency* we have oft together read the most *Natural, Lively*, yet (as their Sexes) different Descriptions our first *Parents* separately make of their own Apprehensions of themselves at their *first finding* themselves *Living Creatures*. Nay, the very *fallen Angels* are much Honour'd above the best of their deserts by the *Amazing Relation* we there meet with of their *Ambition, Malice, Inveteracy,* and *Cunning*; and never was *Scene* so livelily shown as that of his *Pandaemonium* in the first Book. Once more, and you are no less astonisht at his *Description* than he makes the *Angels* to be at the Report of their Adversaries Thund'ring Fireworks. And yet, if his Matter requires a *Meaner Style*, how much soever he speaks *Loftily* at one time, at another he does even to a *Miracle* suit his *Speech* to his *Subject*. This, I well know, has been rashly or maliciously censur'd in him for *Servile creeping*; but if 'tis well *consider'd* upon what *proper Occasion* he thus *humbles* his Style, 'twill be *Accounted* (as really it is) his *Great Commendation*. But in praise of Mr. *Milton's* admirable Dexterity in this his *Matchless Performance*, since All I can say must come exceeding short of his *due Merit*, that I bring not my self under the Correction of that known saying, *Praestat de Carthagine tacere quam pauca dicere*, I shall venture to add no more but this: tho' the Composing such a *compleat Poem* on such a no less *Obscure* than *weighty* Subject was a *Task* to be perform'd by Mr. *Milton* only, yet 'tis not out of doubt whether *himself* had ever been able so to Sing of *Unrevealed Heavenly Mysteries*, had he not been altogether depriv'd of his *Outward Sight*, and thereby made capable of such *continued Strenuous Inward Speculations* as he who has the use of his *Bodily Eyes* cannot possibly become possest with. *This*, however, must be Granted as indubitably true: The *bountiful Powers* above did more than make him amends for their taking away his Sight, by so *Illumining* his Mind as to enable him *most compleatly* to sing of *Matchless Beings, Matchless Things*, before *unknown* to, and even *unthought* of, by the whole Race of Men, thus rewarding him for a *Temporary Loss* with an *Eternal Fame*, of which *Envy* it self shall not be able ever to deprive this *best of Poems* or its most *Judicious Author*.

45. Hume's annotations of *Paradise Lost*

1695

Patrick Hume, 'Annotations on Milton's *Paradise Lost*', *Paradise Lost*, pub. Jacob Tonson (1695). Representative extracts.

Little is known about Patrick Hume except for his very learned annotations on *Paradise Lost*. They constitute one of the first scholarly treatments of the text of a modern author.

The last item is concerned with one correction by Richard Bentley in 1732 that is universally accepted: *Fowl* changed to *Soul*.

Book I [p. 1] *Paradise* . . . is a word of *Persian* Extraction, whence the *Jews* borrowed it, and of them the *Grecians*: Though they who affect such Gingles, derive [it from the word] to water round about; because it was a Place, according to the Description of *Moses*, watered by some of the most famous Rivers of the World. . . .

That *Paradise* was not Allegorical or Figurative, (according to *Origen*, St. *Ambrose* and others) is not only confirmed by the general Consent of the *Greek* and *Latin* Fathers; nor Fantastical, according to the *Jewish* Cabbala: But a part of *Asia*, where *Babylon* was afterwards built, and known by the Name of *Mesopotamia*, as lying between the *Euphrates* and the *Tygris*; both the Description of *Moses*, the Nature of the Soil, and the Comparison of many places of Scriptures most evidently make out. . . .

In this Garden of God, as it is called *Gen.* 13.10. abounding with all things, the choicest and most excellent the Earth ever bore, God seated our great Progenitors, in a Condition so superlatively happy, that our blessed Saviour was pleased by it to Typifie the high and happy State of Everlasting Life, *Luk.* 23.43. *This day thou shalt be with me in Paradise.*

The Forfeiture of this Innocent and Blissful Seat, by the Disobedience of our first Parents, and their deserved Expulsion out of this *Paradise*, is the sad Subject of this unparallell'd Poem.

I, 2 [pp. 1–2]

It imports not much to know, nor can it be determined, what kind this Interdicted Tree was of, the Prohibition having no regard to, or influence on, its Fruit, more than that it was made the Trial of Man's entire Obedience to his Maker. *Moses Barcepha* endeavours to prove it a Fig-Tree, because the Offenders had its Leaves so ready at hand to cover their Nakedness, *Gen.* 3.7. But this implies no more, than that a Tree of that kind, stood in its dangerous Neighborhood. It seemeth on the contrary, not reasonable to imagine, *Adam* should presume to cloath his Nakedness, the Consequence of his Offence, with the Leaves of the same Tree, the Eating of whose Fruit had been the cause of his Offending; especially when according to *Gen.* 3.3. the Prohibition was so strict and severe, that it had been a Daring second to his shameful Sin, but to have touch'd that sacred Tree; sacred (as our Author tells us) to Abstinence, secluded and set apart from all Enjoyment.

The common Opinion, That this Tree so set apart, and secluded by God's Command, was an Apple-Tree, is weakly grounded on *Cantic.* 8.5. . . .

I, 6 [p. 2]

. . . As our Author has attempted a greater Undertaking than that of either of those two Master-Poets [Homer and Spenser], so he had need to Invoke this Heavenly Muse, whom a little after he explains by God's Holy Spirit, to inspire and assist him: And well he might, being to sing, not only of the Beauteous Universe, and all Created Beings, but of the Creator Himself, and all those Revelations and Dispensations He had been pleased to make to Faln Man through the Great Redeemer of the World, His Son. This Argument might need a Divine Instructress, preferable to any of their Invoked Assistants, though styled . . . the Daughters of *Jove*.

III, 609 [p. 127]

Who would wonder if in the Suns Glorious Region, and those bright Fields, the Air should be as pure and preservative as the Alchymists fabulous Elixir, or there should be Rivers of Liquid Gold? Who would admire at this, that considers how here the Sun, the best of Chymists, though so far removed from this dark Globe, does by the Virtue of his powerful Touch, mixt with Terrestrial Moisture, beget so many things of Price, for Colour Glorious, and for Use most Rare and Wonderful? *Chymia* and *Alchymia* is a Science concerned in explaining the Principles,

Causes, Properties and Qualities of all Metals, and the manifold Alterations they are capable of; and further pretends to teach, how to change
and transmute the gross and imperfect, as Lead, Iron, Quicksilver, &c.
into the most perfect, Gold: To heighten the Light and Luster of all
Precious Stones to Perfection, and of this Philosophers Stone, to make
the most Cordial Preservative of Life, beyond the attack of all Diseases,
and even of Time and Old-Age it self. . . .

Well therefore does our Author shew the conceited Chymists the
Sun, the Noblest Chymist, whose Influence with Earth and Water mixt,
brings forth such wonderful Productions, according to that Admirable
Alchimie, that with a word brought all Things out of Nothing, while
these Presumptious Imitators of Nature, quickly bring all theirs to
nothing.

VII, 451 [p. 224]

'Tis unaccountable how our Author, who has hitherto kept so close to
the sacred Text, should deviate from it here, and make mention of
Fowl, when there is no such in *Gen.* i. 24. where the Works of the Sixth
Day are enumerated, having treated of 'em but just before; unless he
would insinuate (according to *Gen.* 2.19. above cited,) that Fowl, or at
least some kinds of 'em, were nearer of kin, in their Original to Earth,
than Water, which their Agility seems to contrary, thô the Elements
are no where so pure, at least these two inferior, but each has more or
less some mixture of the other.

46. Dennis on Milton's Devils

1696

Extract from John Dennis, 'Remarks on a Book Entituled, Prince Arthur, An Heroick Poem' (1696). E. N. Hooker, ed., *The Critical Works of John Dennis* (1939), i, 106–8.

'Tis true indeed, I am not ignorant that the most delightfull and most admirable Part of the sublimest of all our Poets, is that which relates the Rebellion and Fall of these Evil Angels, and their dismal Condition upon their Fall, and their Consult for the recovery of their native Mansions, and their Original Glory. But then we are to consider, that these Angels, according to the System of *Milton;* which an English Poet, who treats of those Matters after him, is certainly oblig'd to follow, were very different just upon their Fall, from what they are believ'd to be at present, or to have been in *Prince Arthur's* time. That this was *Milton's* Hypothesis, is apparent from several Passages. For God the Father, in the Sixth Book of *Paradise Lost,* speaking of the good and bad Angels, says to his Son: [VI, 690–92].

And *Milton,* in the First Book, describes *Lucifer,* as one whose Glory was not quite extinguish'd. The Verses deserve to be read every-where. [I, 589–621]

Here we may behold in *Lucifer* some Remains of Glory, and some Resemblance of Goodness; and consequently the Devils, according to *Milton,* were different then, from what they are believ'd to be now. Nor had they yet a while ruin'd Mankind, nor conceiv'd that unrelenting Hate against the whole Species, which now they are believ'd to have.

They had not resolv'd upon their design against Man till about the middle of the Second Book. And even afterwards, when *Lucifer* took his flight to the new-made World, in order to the executing what they had contriv'd; he shows Remorse upon the top of *Niphates,* in the Speech which is found in the Third [Fourth] Book, and which begins with that wonderfull Apostrophe to the Sun. [IV, 32–45]

And in the Eighth [Ninth] Book the Devil is made to relent, nay to be pleas'd upon the sight of *Eve.* [IX, 455–66]

By all which we may see, that *Milton*, to introduce his Devils with success, saw that it was necessary to give them something that was allied to Goodness. Upon which he very dextrously feign'd, that the Change which was caus'd by their Fall, was not wrought in them all at once; and that there was not an entire Alteration work'd in them, till they had a second time provok'd their Creatour by succeeding in their attempt upon Man. From whence it seems very apparent to me, that a Poet, who introduces Devils into a Poem writ on any more Modern Subject, cannot use them with the same success that *Milton* did, and ought certainly never to describe them, as Mr. *Blackmore* has done. For which reason I laid the Scene of the *Court of Death* between the Surface of the Earth and Hell, which is commonly believ'd to be at the Center, and endeavour'd to make what difference I could between those who compos'd it, and meer infernal Spirits.

47. Wesley on heroic poetry

1697

Extract from Samuel Wesley, The Preface, Being an Essay on Heroic Poetry, *The Life of Our Blessed Lord and Savior Jesus Christ* (1697), 23–4.

A divine and poet, Samuel Wesley (1662–1735) was father of the famous Methodist minister, John Wesley, who rewrote *Paradise Lost* in rhyme. He was an editor of *The Athenian Gazette,* which often praised Milton or quoted him in its pages.

As for Milton's *Paradise Lost* its an Original, and indeed he seems rather above the common Rules of Epic than ignorant of them. Its I'm sure a very lovely Poem, by what ever Name it's call'd, and in it he has many Thoughts and Images, greater than perhaps any either in Virgil or Homer. The Foundation is true History, but the turn is Fable: The Action is very Important, but not uniform; for one can't tell which is the Principal in the Poem, the Wars of the Angels or the Fall of Man, nor which is the Chief Person Michael or Adam. Its true, the former comes in as in Episode to the latter, but it takes up too great a part thereof, because its link'd to it. His Discourse of Light is incomparable; and I think 'twas worth the while to be blind to be its Author. His Description of Adam and Eve, their Persons and Love, is almost too lively to bear reading: Not but that he has his inequalities and repetitions, the latter pretty often, as have, more or less, all other Poets but Virgil. For this antique Words I'm not like to blame him whoever does: And for his blank Verse, I'm of a different mind from most others, and think they rather excuse his uncorrectness than the contraries; for I find its easier to run into it, in that sort of Verse, than in Rhyming Works where the Thought is oftner turned; whereas here the Fancy flows on, without check or controul. As for his Paradise Regain'd, I nothing wonder that it has not near the Life of his former Poem, any more than the Odysses fell short of the Iliads. Milton, when he write this, was grown older, probably poorer: He had not that scope for

Fable, was confin'd to a lower Walk, and draws out that in four Books which might have been well compriz'd in one: Notwithstanding all this, there are many strokes which appear truly his; as the Mustring of the Parthian Troops, the Description of Rome by the Devil to our Saviour, and several other places.

48. Bayle's notice

1697

Ectract from Peter Bayle, 'Milton', *The Dictionary Historical and Critical* (1697), ed. 2 (1737), iv, 219, note.

The French philosopher and critic Pierre Bayle (1647-1706) is best known for his *Dictionary*, which drew together encyclopedic materials on various topics and people. He adds nothing of importance on Milton that is not found elsewhere, but his entry is significant because so many gleaned knowledge of Milton from it. Bayle is unsympathetic toward the public life but laudatory of the poetry.

For the rest, Milton has written two Poems in blank verse; one upon the temptation of Eve; the other upon the temptation of Jesus Christ. The first is intituled, *Paradise Lost;* the second *Paradise Regained.* The former passes for one of the best pieces of Poetry that ever was seen in English. The famous Poet Dryden made a play out of it, which was extreamly applauded. The other is not near so good, which made some wags say, that Milton is easily found in Paradise lost, but not in Paradise regained.

49. Leslie on Milton's theology

1698

Extract from Charles Leslie, 'Preface to *The History of Sin and Heresy*' (1698). Charles Leslie, *The Theological Works* (1721), i, 777–8.

Amidst the controversy accompanying the rise of Deism, Charles Leslie (1650–1722) stood out as a learned defender of the sacraments and scriptural interpretation. Here Leslie shows his unhappiness with the imaginative treatment of angels in *Paradise Lost*, a treatment he perhaps justifiedly thought people read as truth.

The gravity and seriousness with which this subject ought to be treated, has not been regarded in the adventrous flight of Poets, who have dress'd Angels in Armour, and put Swords and Guns into their Hands, to form romantick Battels in the Plains of Heaven, a scene of licentious fancy; but the Truth has been greatly hurt thereby, and degraded at last even into a Play, which was design'd to have been acted upon the Stage: And tho' once happily prevented, yet it has pass'd the Press, and become the entertainment of prophane raillery.

This was one reason why I have endeavoured to give a more serious representation of that War in Heaven, and I hope I may say much better founded than *Milton*'s groundless supposition, who, in the fifth Book of his *Paradise Lost* makes the cause of the revolt of *Lucifer* and his Angels to have been, that God upon a certain day in Heaven, before the creation of this lower World, did summon all the Angels to attend, and then declar'd his Son to be their Lord and King; and applies to that day the seventh Verse of the second *Psalm, Thou art my Son, this day have I begotten thee*. The folly of this contrivance appears many ways: To make the Angels ignorant of the blessed Trinity; and to take it ill to acknowledge him for their King whom they had always ador'd as their God; or as if the Son had not been their King, or had not been begotten till that day. This scheme of the Angels revolt cannot answer either to the eternal Generation of the Son, which was before the Angels had a Being, or to his temporal Generation of the blessed Virgin, that being long after the fall of the Angels.

But if Mr. *Milton* had made the cause of their discontent to have been the Incarnation of *Christ,* then, at that time, reveal'd to the Angels; and their contesting in such manner as hereafter told for the dignity of the angelical above that of the human Nature, his contexture had been nearer to the truth, and might have been much more poetical, in the severe and just measure of Poetry, which ought not to exceed the bounds of probability, not to expatiate into effeminate romance, but to express Truth in an exalted and manly improvement of thought.

Milton, in the first Book of his *Paradise Lost,* makes *Lucifer* suppose himself to be self-existing, and so without beginning; which seems incongruous to the knowledge of an Angel, tho' he has deluded some foolish Men into that blasphemous and vain opinion, as hereafter shewn. And Philosophers of great name have held the Eternity of the World, because they were ignorant of its beginning; so that there are sore footsteps to warrant this conjecture of *Milton*'s than the former which I have mentioned.

In the repetition of the several Heresies which *Satan* has broach'd in the World against the truth of the Incarnation of *Christ,* I have but lightly nam'd those of former and early ages, but insisted a little more particularly upon those of our own times, because we are more nearly concern'd in them.

50. Toland on various poems

1698

Extract from John Toland, 'The Life of John Milton', *A Complete Collection of the Historical, Political, and Miscellaneous Works of John Milton* . . . (1698), 16, 30, 39–40, 43.

John Toland (1670–1722) was frequently in arguments over his deistic views and his comments on Socinianism and Arianism. The injection of such ideas into his biography of Milton, prefaced to a three-volume edition of the prose, created the controversy mentioned in the Introduction to this volume.

Thus far our Author, who afterwards made this Character good in his inimitable Poem of *Paradise Lost;* and before this time in his *Comus* or Mask presented at *Ludlow* Castle, like which Piece in the peculiar disposition of the Story, the sweetness of the Numbers, the justness of the Expression, and the Moral it teaches, there is nothing extant in any Language. . . .

And now we com to his Master-piece, his chief and favorit Work in Prose, for Argument the noblest, as being the Defence of a whole free Nation, the People of *England*; for stile and disposition the most eloquent and elaborat, equalling the old *Romans* in the purity of their own Language, and their highest Notions of Liberty; as universally spread over the learned World as any of their Compositions; and certain to endure while Oratory, Politics, or History, bear any esteem among Men. . . .

What imploy'd a good part of his Thoughts for many years before, and was at first only design'd to be a Tragedy, I mean his incomparable Epic Poem, intitul'd *Paradise Lost*, he now had sufficient leisure to prosecute and finish. It is a great wonder that this piece should ever be brought to perfection, considering the many Interruptions that obstructed it. His Youth was spent in Study, Travelling, and religious

Controversy; his Manhood was imploy'd in Affairs of State, or those of his Family; and in his latter years, to speak nothing of a decaying Fancy, nor of his personal Troubles, he was by reason of his Blindness oblig'd to write by whatsoever hand came next, ten, or twenty, or thirty Verses at a time; and consequently must trust the judgment of others at least for the Pointing and Orthography. But another difficulty that stopt its passage to the World was very singular: for his Vein never happily flow'd but from the Autumnal to the Vernal Equinox, as his Nephew *Edward Philips* affirms, who says he was told this particular by *Milton* himself; and yet I fancy he might be mistaken as to the time, because our Author in his *Latin* Elegy on the approach of Spring seems to say just the contrary, as if he could not make any Verses to his satisfaction till the Spring begun, according to these lines: [*Elegia quinta,* ll. 5–8]. A more judicious Friend of his informs me, that he could never compose well but in the Spring and Autumn: And let it be which way you will, it follows that this Piece was compos'd in half the time he was thought to be about it. As to the choice of his Subject, or the Particulars of his Story, I shall say nothing in defence of them against those People who brand 'em with Heresy and Impiety: for to incur the Displeasure of certain ignorant and supercilious Critics, argues free thinking, accurat Writing, and a generous Profession of Truth. I'm sure if *Hesiod,* or such other fabulous Authors in the rude ages of the World, had given so intelligible, coherent, and delightful an account of the Creation of the Universe, and the Origin of Mankind their System had past for Divine Inspiration; and the Unbelievers of it would appear to be so few, that any of 'em might well be shewn for a Monster rather than be thought worthy of Punishment or Confutation. As to the regularity of the Poem, I never knew it question'd by any but such as would build themselves a Reputation on the flaws and mistakes they discover in other Mens Labors. But the unparallel'd Sublimity and Force of the Expression, with the delicacy of his Thoughts, and the copiousness of his Invention, are unanimously own'd by all ranks of Writers. He has incontestably exceeded the fecundity of *Homer,* whose two Poems he could almost repeat without book: nor did he com much short of the correctness of Virgil. . . .

In the year 1670 he publish'd his *Paradise Regain'd,* consisting of four Books; but generally esteem'd much inferior to *Paradise Lost,* which he could not endure to hear, being quite of another mind: yet this occasion'd som body to say wittily enough that *Milton* might be seen in *Paradise Lost*, but not in *Paradise Regain'd*. With this last Book he publisht his *Samson Agonistes*, an admirable Tragedy, not a ridiculous mixture of Gravity and Farce according to most of the Modern, but after the Example of the yet unequal'd Antients, as they are justly cal'd, *Æschylus, Sophocles,* and *Euripides.*

51. Yalden on Milton's prose

1698

Thomas Yalden, 'On the Reprinting of Milton's Prose Works' [Toland's edition of 1698], from Robert Anderson, ed., *The Works of the British Poets* (1795), vii, 762–3.

Yalden (1670–1736), a minor poet of the period, obviously disliked Milton's ideas and resented the republication of the prose in 1698. Such attitudes coloured the appreciation of *Paradise Lost* for many readers. The poem reappeared a few times during the century.

These sacred lines with wonder we peruse,
And praise the flights of a seraphic muse,
Till thy seditious prose provokes our rage,
And soils the beauties of thy brightest page.
Thus here we see transporting scenes arise,
Heaven's radiant host, and opening paradise;
Then trembling view the dread abyss beneath,
Hell's horrid mansions, and the realms of death.
Whilst here thy bold majestic numbers rise,
And range th' embattled legions of the skies,
With armies fill the azure plains of light,
And paint the lively terrors of the fight,
We own the poet worthy to rehearse
Heaven's lasting triumphs in immortal verse:
But when thy impious mercenary pen
Insults the best of princes, best of men,
Our admiration turns to just disdain,
And we revoke the fond applause again.
Like the fall'n angels in their happy state,
Thou shar'dst their nature, insolence, and fate:
To harps divine, immortal hymns they sung,
As sweet thy voice, as sweet thy lyre was strung.
As they did rebels to th' Almighty grow,

So thou profane'st his image here below.
Apostate bard! may not thy guilty ghost,
Discover to its own eternal cost,
That as they heaven, thou paradise hast lost!

EIGHTEENTH-CENTURY COMMENT TO BENTLEY'S EDITION OF 'PARADISE LOST'

1700–1731

---

52. Oldys on Milton

1700

Extract from Alexander Oldys, 'An Ode By Way of Elegy on
. . . Mr. Dryden' (June 1700), Stanza V. George Saintsbury, ed.,
The Works of John Dryden (1893), xviii, 249.

The bard, who next the new-born saint addrest,
Was Milton, for his wonderous poem blest;
Who strangely found, in his Lost Paradise, rest.
   'Great bard', said he, ' 'twas verse alone
   Did for my hideous crime atone,
   Defending once the worst rebellion.
A double share of bliss belongs to thee,
For thy rich verse and thy firm loyalty;
Some of my harsh and uncouth points do owe
To thee a tuneful cadence still below.
Thine was indeed the state of innocence,
   Mine of offence,
With studied treason and self-interest stained,
Till Paradise Lost wrought Paradise Regained.'

53. Dennis on Milton's sublimity

1701

Extract from John Dennis, *The Advancement and Reformation of Modern Poetry* (1701). E. N. Hooker, ed., *The Critical Works of John Dennis* (1939), i, 219–20, 271–2, 276–8.

The following is one of the most significant statements of Milton's sublimity, illustrating both the importance of the translation of Longinus into English a few years before and the most constant factor in the high appraisal of Milton. Dennis's discussion of *Paradise Lost* in No. 54 elaborates the ideas presented here.

Let us now set before the Reader an Image, that only by its Greatness will move him, and exalt him. The Passage is in the First Book of *Milton's Paradise Lost*, where he thus describes *Lucifer*. [I, 589–601]

I desire the Reader, would give himself the Trouble of comparing these Ten Lines, with the Ten that preceded them, and then to tell me, Why the Spirit should be so much greater in these, than it is in the others, unless it proceeded from the Greatness of the Ideas? or, How the Greatness of the Ideas could cause it, but by infusing into the Poet, Admiration, and a noble Pride, which express'd, make the Spirit; which is stately and majestick till the last, and then it grows vehement, because the Idea which causes it, is not only great, but very terrible. For all the afflicting Passions that are violent, are express'd with Vehemence. The Reader cannot but observe of himself, that the greatest of these noble Ideas, is taken from Religion;

> But his face
> Deep Scars of Thunder had intrench'd. [I, 600–1] . . .

The next Instance is from *Milton*, who in the Seventh Book of the *Paradise Lost*, has handled the Subject of the Creation better than either *Ovid*, or *Virgil* himself has done; tho' he is certainly above *Ovid* by the Force of his own Genius, as much as by the Advantage of his Religion: But 'tis by the latter only, that he excels *Virgil*, than whom I do not believe that any Man can have a greater Genius. When I say that *Milton* excels *Virgil*, I mean, that he does so sometimes, both in his Thought, and in his Spirit, purely by the Advantage of his Religion. But at the same Time, I am very far from thinking, that he so much as equals him either in the continual Harmony of his Versification, or the constant Beauty of his Expression, or his perpetual Exaltation. He writ in a Language that was not capable of so much Beauty, or so much Harmony; and his Inequality proceeded from his want of Art to manage his Subject, and make it constantly great. For it would be an easy matter to prove that none of the Moderns understood the Art of Heroick Poetry, who writ before *Bossu* took Pains to unravel the Mystery. But nothing can make more for my Subject, than to shew that *Milton*, who lay under these vast Disadvantages, very often excell'd, even the Prince of the *Roman* Poets, both in the Greatness of his Thought, and his Spirit. . . .

And now any one may see how much *Virgil*'s God is inferior to *Milton*'s Angel. ' 'Tis true, I know very well, that it may be urg'd in *Virgil*'s Behalf, That he does not pretend to set down *Silenus*'s Song, but only the principal Heads of it; whereas *Milton* makes the Angel *Raphael* give an Account at large of the Creation. I know this very well, I say; but I am satisfied at the same Time, that *Virgil* making *Silenus* proceed upon the *Epicurean* Hypothesis, if he had given never so full and artful an Account of the Creation, could never possibly have equall'd *Milton*; for that Hypothesis runs directly counter to those lofty Thoughts, and those noble Images, which *Milton* has shewn in such wondrous Motion. For these Verses,

> *Tum durare solum, & discludere Nerea Ponto*
> *Cœperit, & rerum paulatim sumere formas;*

And this,

> *Rara per ignotos errent animalia montes,*

Are directly contradictory of those noble Images, which we find in the following Account of *Milton*. [VII, 449-453] Here are Four flat un-musical Verses again; but those which follow, will more than make Amends for them. [VII, 453-472]

What a Number of admirable Images are here crouding upon one another? So natural and peculiar to the Subject, that they would have been as absurd and extravagant in any other, as they are wonderfully just in this. And yet, even in this Subject, nothing could have supplied a Poet with them, but so Divine a Religion. So that at the same Time that the Eye is ravishingly entertain'd, Admiration is rais'd to a Height, and the Reason is supremely satisfied. For are not these Effects that are worthy of an infinite Cause? Can any thing be more surprizingly strong, than this energetick Image? [ll. 463–466] Is not the following one great and wonderful? [ll. 466–469] And how admirable is the next! [ll. 469–470] He began to rise even before he was finish'd, and his Horns were finish'd in rising.

I thought to have proceeded, and to have compar'd the Councils and Fights of *Virgil* and *Milton*; and above all, their Description of Hell and its Torments; in which both those great Poets seem to have exerted all their Strength. But I am afraid I have already run into Length, and there is Matter remaining for an intire Volume.

And thus I have endeavoured to shew in the former Part of this Book, that the principal Reason why the ancient Poets excell'd the Moderns in the Greatness of Poetry, was, Because they incorporated Poetry with Religion; and in the Second Part, That the Moderns, by joining the Christian Religion with Poetry, will have the Advantage of the Ancients; that is, That they will have the Assistance of a Religion that is more agreeable to the Design of Poetry, than the *Grecian* Religion.

54. Dennis on *Paradise Lost*

1704

Extract from John Dennis, 'The Grounds of Criticism in Poetry' (1704). E. N. Hooker, ed., *The Critical Works of John Dennis* (1939), i, 333–4, 342, 345, 347, 350–3, 368–70, 372.

SPECIMEN.

Being the Substance of what will be said in the Beginning of the Criticism *upon* Milton.

The next Poet of whom we shall treat is *Milton*, one of the greatest and most daring Genius's that has appear'd in the World, and who has made his Country a glorious present of the most lofty, but most irregular Poem, that has been produc'd by the Mind of Man. That great Man had a desire to give the World something like an Epick Poem; but he resolv'd at the same time to break thro' the Rules of *Aristotle*. Not that he was ignorant of them, or contemn'd them. On the contrary, no Man knew them better, or esteemed them more, because no Man had an Understanding that was more able to comprehend the necessity of them; and therefore when he mention'd them in the little Treatise which he wrote to Mr. *Hartlib*, he calls the Art which treats of them, a sublime Art. But at the same time he had discernment enough to see, that if he wrote a Poem which was within the compass of them, he should be subjected to the same Fate which has attended all who have wrote Epick Poems ever since the time of *Homer*; and that is to be a Copyist instead of an Original. Tis true, the Epick Poets who have liv'd since *Homer*, have most of them been Originals in their Fables, which are the very Souls of their Poems; but in their manner of treating those Fables, they have too frequently been Copyists. They have Copyed the Spirit and the Images of *Homer*; even the great *Virgil* himself is not to be excepted. *Milton* was the first, who in the space of almost 4000 Years, resolved, for his Country's Honour and his own, to present the World with an Original Poem; that is to say, a Poem that should have his own Thoughts, his own Images, and his own Spirit. In order to this he was resolved to write a Poem, that, by vertue of its extraordinary Subject, cannot so properly be said to be against the Rules, as it may be affirmed to be above them all. He had observ'd, that *Aristotle* had drawn his Rules which he has given us for Epick Poetry from the Reflections which he had made upon *Homer*. Now he knew very well, that in *Homer* the Action lay chiefly between Man and Man: For *Achilles* and *Hector* are properly the Principals, and the Gods are but Seconds. He was resolved therefore, that his Principals should be the Devil on one side and Man on the other: and the Devil is properly his Hero, because he bests the better. All the persons in his Poem, excepting two, are either Divine or Infernal. So that most of the Persons and particularly one of the Principals, being so very different from what *Homer* or *Aristotle* ever thought of, could not possibly be subjected to their Rules, either for the Characters or the Incidents. We shall now shew for what Reasons the choice of *Milton*'s Subject, as it set him free from the Obligation which he lay under to the Poetical Laws, so it necessarily threw him upon new Thoughts, new Images, and an Original Spirit. In the next place we shall shew, that his Thoughts, his Images, and by consequence too his Spirit, are actually new, and different from those of *Homer* and *Virgil*. Thirdly, We shall shew, that besides their Newness, they have vastly the Advantage of those of *Homer* and *Virgil*. And we shall make this appear from several things, but principally from the Description of Hell, which has been describ'd by those three great Poets with all their Force and with all their Art. After that, we shall proceed to say something of *Milton*'s Expression and his Harmony; and then we shall come to mark his Defects with so much the more exactness, because some of them ought to be avoided with the utmost Caution, as being so great, that they would be Insupportable in any one who had not his extraordinary Distinguishing Qualities. . . .

We have shown the *Hermogenes*, in the first Rank of these, reckons those Thoughts and Ideas of God, that are worthy of the Creator: Such is the Invocation of *Milton*, in the beginning of *Paradise Lost*. [I, 17–26)

And that it was these Divine Ideas, that rais'd his Soul, and fill'd it with Admiration, and with a noble Greatness, (which Passion express'd, makes the Greatness of the Spirit) the Reader who goes back to the beginning of the Poem, will find no manner of room to doubt. For *Milton*, like a Master, begins with a gentle Spirit, which he continues for the twelve first Lines: In the thirteenth, where he speaks of the

Boldness of his Attempt, he begins to rise; and in the nineteenth, where he talks of the Power of the Holy Ghost, he is quite upon the Wings.

Instruct me, for Thou know'st, Thou from the first. [I, 19]

And such are the Thoughts concerning God, which are spread thro that Divine Dialogue between God and *Adam*, in the eighth Book of the same Poem; I believe the Reader will pardon the length if I repeat it, which I am very much inclin'd to do, not only because I challenge the most zealous Admirers of Antiquity to produce any thing like it, from among all the Dialogues in *Homer* and *Virgil*, that are between either a God or a Man, or between one God and another; but because the Reader who sees the Inequalities in it, will easily see that it derives its Greatness and its Sublimity from the becoming Thoughts which it has of the Deity. That the Reader may thorowly understand it, without turning to the Book, the occasion of it is this: *Adam*, relating the History of the Creation to the Angel *Raphael*, tells him, how after he had given Names to the Birds and the Beasts, which God had brought before him for that purpose; he who understood their Natures, and saw none of them was fit for his Conversation, desir'd of God in the following Words a Partner fit for Human Society. . . .

I have the rather mention'd these Verses, to show that *Milton* was a little tainted with Socinianism, for by the first Verse 'tis evident, that he look'd upon the Son of God as a created Being. The last thing that I shall mention, is, what God says of Himself, in the Seventh Book; for speaking of Chaos, he says, that is boundless because He is infinite [VII, 168–173]. . . .

Where the Reader may take notice [in *Jerusalem Deliver'd*], that the Comparison of the Sun to *Michael* the Prince of the Arch-Angels, is extremely Just and Noble, because the top of the visible is admirably liken'd to the top of the invisible Creation: But in the two last Verses, *Tasso* has injudiciously been guilty of an Anticlimax. But now let us see how *Milton* describes the Descent of *Raphael* to Paradise, in the fifth Book of *Paradise Lost*. [V, 266–287]

Thus the Reader may see, by what has been said, that the Ideas of Angels are exceeding proper to raise Enthusiastick Admiration, as being the most glorious and admirable Beings of the Creation, and which lead the Soul immediately to its Creator. Next to these come the other Creatures of the immaterial World, as Demons, Apparitions of all sorts, and more particularly the Spirits of Men departed: then follow Prophecies, Visions, Miracles, Enchantments, Prodigies, and all things which have an immediate Relation to the Wonders of another World; of most of which we shall give Examples, when we come to speak of Terror, because they are rather wonderful, than they are admirable. We name those things wonderful, which we admire with fear. . . .

The following Verses of *Milton*, in the eighth Book of *Paradise Lost*, concerning the Magnitude and the Motions of the Heavens and Earth, derive a lofty Spirit from their Subject; for there says *Adam*. [VIII, 15–22]

I could here bring Examples of the same kind of Spirit, deriv'd in due Proportion from Ideas of Sublunary Things; as of the four Elements, Water, Earth, Air, Fire; Winds and Meteors of all sorts, Seas, Rivers, Mountains: but I am afraid of running into length, and heaping too many Citations one upon another. Besides, it will be very convenient to make two or three Remarks here.

First, That the Wonders of the Universe afford the more admirable Ideas, and a more admirable Spirit, the more they shew the Attributes of the Creator, or relate to his Worship. *Secondly*, That Natural Philosophy is absolutely necessary to a Poet, not only that he may adorn his Poem with the useful Knowledge it affords, but because the more he knows the immense Phaenomena of the Universe, the more he will be sure to admire them. For the more we know of Things that are never to be comprehended by us, the more that Knowledge must make them appear wonderful. The third Remark that I shall make is this, That they to whom Nature has given that happy Elevation of Thought, which alone can make a great Poet, will often be directed by that Tendency to Greatness, which they have within them to Ideas, from which they may derive a lofty Spirit; yet I shall shew, by the Example of *Milton*, that they may often very grossly fail, for want of a certain Knowledge of the Objects from which they are to draw their Ideas: for 'tis for want of that Knowledge that *Milton* has done the most unartful thing that perhaps ever was done, in the two or three last Books of the greatest Poem that ever was written by Man. For whereas in the first eight Books, he had by the Mouth of God or Angels, or of Man the Companion of Angels, divinely entertain'd us with the wondrous Works of God; in the latter end of his Poem, and more particularly, in the last Book, he makes an Angel entertain us with the Works of corrupted Man. From which it is very plain, by what has been deliver'd above, concerning the nature of Enthusiastick Passion, that the Angel could draw no sort of Enthusiasm, and least of all that of Admiration and Terror, which give the principal Greatness and Elevation to Poetry. For how flat, how low, and unmusical is the Relation of the Actions of fallen Man, in the tenth Book, tho deliver'd by the Voice of Divinity? [X, 197–208]

The late Mr. *Dryden*, with a great deal of Injustice, us'd to attribute the flatness of *Milton*, in this and some other Passages, to his getting into a Track of Scripture, as he was pleas'd to express himself: Whereas the thing that made him sink, was plainly the Poorness and Lowness of the Ideas. For how could the Works of corrupted Man afford any other to God or Angels? But what lofty, what glorious Ideas does a religious Mention of the Works of God afford to Man in his Primitive State, in that incomparable Hymn in the fifth Book of the same *Paradise Lost*? A Hymn, which tho it is intirely taken from Scripture, for it is apparently the 148th Psalm, yet will always stand alone, the Phoenix of lofty Hymns; and nothing equal to it, no nor second to it, can ever be produc'd from the *Grecian* Writers of Hymns. It is impossible I can do a greater pleasure to the Reader, who either has not read or does not remember *Milton*, than to insert it here. [V, 153–208]

.. 'Tis easy to discern here, with how much more Divinity *Milton* makes a Man speak concerning the Works of God, than he makes even the Creator himself speak concerning the Works of Man. But here if the Reader will pardon a Digression, I shall make an Observation which may not be disagreeable to him. The Observation is this, That all the Passages in *Paradise Lost,* where God is introduced speaking, are flat to the reserve of those in which he speaks of himself. Upon inquiring into the Reason of it, I found, that according to the Account which I have given of Poetical Enthusiasm, or of the Spirit of Poetry, it is nothing but that Admiration and Terror, and the rest of those Enthusiastical Passions which are produced by their proper Ideas, and which are to hold proportion with their Ideas, as their Ideas must with their Objects. Now nothing is more impossible than that God should either fear or admire his own Creatures. But where *Milton* makes him speak concerning himself, or his infinite Power, there he makes him speak with a great Spirit, as in that Passage of the sixth Book where he speaks to his Son.

> Go then thou mightiest in thy Father's Might,
> Ascend my Chariot, guide the rapid Wheels,
> That shake Heaven's Basis, bring forth all my War,
> My Bow and Thunder, my Almighty Arms. [VI, 710–3]

'Tis plain that here the Poet is guilty of a Mistake, but indeed a Mistake that is almost unavoidable; for 'tis the Admiration and Terror that make the Spirit in the preceding Verses; and it is impossible to conceive the Ideas without feeling the Passions: so that *Milton*, while he was rapt with Admiration, and moved with Terror by the Ideas which he had conceiv'd, shifts Persons insensibly, and forgetting who speaks, expresses himself with those Passions which indeed are proper enough in the Poet, but never can be so in the Deity. For neither his Bow, nor his Almighty Arms, his Thunder, nor the rapid Wheels that shake Heaven's Basis, can be in the least admirable or terrible to the Divinity; so that Mr. *Cowley* is certainly in the right in his Notes upon his *Davideis*, where he tells us, that God is to be introduced speaking simply. And this puts me in mind of an extraordinary Argument of Monsieur *Paschal*, proving the Divinity of our Saviour by the Simplicity of his Stile; for, says he, our Saviour speaks of the sublimest Subjects, even the Glories of the Kingdom of Heaven, without being moved at all, which shews that he was really God: for suppose a Peasant, says he, or an ordinary Man should be carry'd to the Court of some Prince, as for example the Great Mogul, and there be shewn all his Riches, his Pomp, and his Power; this Peasant at his return would certainly speak of these things in extravagant terms, in terms that would sufficiently declare his Transport. But if the Mogul himself was to speak of them, he who had been always used to them, would speak without any Emotion. So, says Monsieur *Paschal*, if any one else had deliver'd any thing concerning the Glories of the Kingdom of Heaven, he would certainly have done it with Transport, nay tho he had been a Fanatick or an Imposter: for let those Divine Ideas come how they will, 'tis impossible for Man to think of them without being ravish'd by them. But our Saviour, who was God, and who consequently had been used to them from all Eternity, spoke of them unconcern'd. . . .

But here it will be necessary to answer an Objection: for it may be urg'd perhaps that common Experience will destroy these new Speculations. For several of the Moderns have attempted Divine Poetry, and yet some of them have been contemptible to the last degree, and not one of them has excell'd the Antients.

To which we answer, That *Milton* has clearly the advantage of the Antients in several points, as shall be shewn in its proper place: and if the rest of the Moderns, who have attempted Sacred Poetry, have faln so very much short of them, it has been either for want of Genius, or for want of Art to know how to make use of Religion. For Sacred Poetry apparently requires a greater Capacity than the Profane does; because the greater the Ideas are, the greater must the Capacity be that receives them. But Sacred Ideas are greater than the Profane, as hath been shewn above. And therefore if the Rule of *Horace* be true, that a Poet ought to proportion his Subject to his Strength, it follows, that a Man may succeed pretty well in Human Poetry, and yet be despicable in the Divine. Besides, as Religion supplies us with greater Ideas than any thing Human can do; so it requires greater Enthusiasm, and a greater Spirit to attend them, as has been shewn above too. So that Sacred Poetry requires not only a very great Capacity, but a very warm and strong Imagination; which is a happy Mixture that is to be met with in a very few, and even of those few not one in a thousand perhaps applies himself to Sacred Poetry. And even of those rare ones who have apply'd themselves, hardly one of the Moderns has known the true use that ought to be made of Religion in Poetry. *Milton* indeed happen'd upon it, in his *Paradise Lost*; I say, happen'd upon it, because he has err'd very widely from it in his *Paradise Regain'd*, as shall be shewn in its proper place. The Rules for employing Religion in Poetry, are principally these which follow.

1. The first is, That the Religion ought to be one, that the Poet may be mov'd by it, and that he may appear to be in earnest. And the not observing of this Rule, was one Reason why *Spencer* miscarry'd, as we shall shew anon.

2. The second Rule, That the Religion which the Poet employs, ought to be the reigning one, that both the Poet and the Readers may be mov'd the more by a Religion in which they were bred. And this Rule may acquaint us with one of the Reasons why all who have translated *Homer* and *Virgil*, have succeeded so very indifferently.

3. The third is, That it may run through and be incorporated with the Action of the Poem, and consequently that it may always be a part of Action, and productive of Action; for from the Neglect of this third Rule, strange Inequalities would follow in a Poem, as shall be shewn more at large, when we treat of *Spencer* and *Cowley*.

4. The fourth Rule is, That the Religion may be managed so as to promote the Violence of the Enthusiastick Passions, and their Change and Variety; and the constituting his Subject contrary to this Rule, was one great Reason why *Milton* did not succeed in his *Paradise Regain'd*.

5. That it may not hinder the Violence of the ordinary Passions, nor the Change and Variety of them; and the not constituting his Subject according to this Rule, is the chief Reason why *Homer* in his *Odysses*

fell so far short of his *Iliads*; and *Milton* of his *Paradise Lost*, in his *Paradise Regain'd*.

6. That the Religion be managed so as not to obstruct the Violence of Action, which is always attended by the Violence of ordinary Passion; and the not observing of this, was one great Reason of the Miscarriage of *Homer* and *Milton*, in the fore-mention'd Poems.

7. That the divine and human Persons, if there by any, may have Inclinations and Affections; which *Tasso*'s celestial Persons have not, nor as I remember, *Cowley*'s.

8. That they be fairly distinguish'd from one another by those Inclinations and Affections. And this is the great advantage that the *Grecian* Machines have, for the most part, over those in our Religion. Yet *Milton* has pretty well distinguish'd his celestial Persons from one another, and his infernal ones admirably.

9. That they be fairly distinguish'd from the human Persons by the same Inclinations and Affections. And here *Milton*, in his infernal Persons, has undeniably the advantage both of Antients and Moderns. The Passions and Inclinations of the *Grecian* Gods are downright human Inclinations and Affections. The Passions of *Milton*'s Devils have enough of Humanity in them to make them delightful, but then they have a great deal more to make them admirable, and may be said to be the true Passions of Devils: but the time to speak more largely of this, will be when we come to the Epick Poets. . . .

For they of extraordinary Parts for the most part being extremely delighted with Poetry, and finding the greatest and most exalted Poetry upon Religious Subjects, would by degrees become more us'd to be mov'd by Sacred Ideas, than they would by Profane; that is, would by degrees become reform'd. That this is by no means a Chimera, Experience may serve to convince us: For I know several Gentlemen of very good Sense, who are extremely mov'd by *Milton*'s Hymn, in the fifth Book of *Paradise Lost,* and hardly at all stir'd with the Translation of the 148th Psalm, from whence that Hymn is taken. But if Men of very good Parts are more mov'd by the Hymn, it follows that they ought to be more mov'd by it; because Men of very good Sense are only mov'd to that degree by things by which they ought to be mov'd. So that we may conclude, that the Passion or Enthusiasm in that Hymn is exactly in Nature; that is, that the Enthusiasm, or Passion, or Spirit, call it what you will, flows from the Ideas, and bears a just Proportion to them.

But from hence at the same time it follows, that since those Persons, who are so much mov'd by the Hymn, are not equally stir'd by the translated Psalm, the Passion or Spirit is less in the latter, and does not come up to the Ideas; and therefore we may conclude, that *Milton*, by his Genius and Harmony, has restor'd that Spirit in composing the Hymn, which had been lost by the Weakness of the Translation, and the Want of Poetical Numbers: which last, as we have said before, contribute very much to the raising of Passion.

What *Milton* has done in relation to the 148th Psalm, others may do in a less proportion to other parts of the Old Testament, till the Favour of the Prince and publick Encouragement causes another *Milton* to arise, and apply himself to so necessary and so noble a Work. For this is certain, that there are not wanting great Genius's to every Age: But they do not equally appear in every Age, sometimes for want of knowing themselves, and sometimes for want of Encouragement and Leisure to exert themselves. The Business of the Treatise intended is to shew them how they may try, and know, and form themselves, which is all that I am capable of attempting towards the restoring so useful and so noble an Art. If I were in a Condition to give them Encouragement too, they should not be long without it. If they who so much exceed me in Power, did but equal me in Will, we should soon see Poetry raise up its dejected Head, and our own might come to emulate the happiest of *Grecian* and *Roman* Ages.

55. Trumbull on minor poems

1705

Sir William Trumbull, Letter to Pope (19 October 1705). George
Sherburn, ed., *The Correspondence of Alexander Pope* (1956), i,
10–11.

Pope's friend, Sir William Trumbull (1639–1716), who suggested
that he translate Homer, was Secretary of State. His comment
suggests the high regard in which Milton's works were held by
the non-literary figures of Augustan England.

Sir,—I return you the Book [an edition of *L'Allegro, Il Penseroso* and
Comus] you were pleas'd to send me, and with it your obliging letter,
which deserves my particular acknowledgment; for next to the pleasure of enjoying the company of so good a friend, the welcomest thing
to me is to hear from him. I expected to find, what I have met with, an
admirable genius in those Poems, not only because they were Milton's,
or were approved by Sir Hen. Wootton, but because you had commended them; and give me leave to tell you, that I know no body so
like to equal him, even at the age he wrote most of them, as your self.
Only do not afford more cause of complaints against you, that you
suffer nothing of yours to come abroad; which in this age, wherein wit
and true sense is more scarce than money, is a piece of such cruelty as
your best friends can hardly pardon. I hope you will repent and amend;
I could offer many reasons to this purpose, and such as you cannot
answer with any sincerity; but that I dare not enlarge, for fear of
engaging in a stile of Compliment, which has been so abused by
fools and knaves, that it is become almost scandalous. I conclude therefore with an assurance which shall never vary, of my being ever, &c.

56. Defoe on *Paradise Lost*

1706

Extract from Daniel Defoe, *Jure Divino: A Satyr* (1706), Book VII, 137, n.; 147 n.

Defoe (1661?–1731) noticed Milton in print only seldom, but his remarks point to esteem and attentive reading.

This would be a difficult Question to resolve ['Tell us from whence the Seeds of Crime began']. Mr. *Milton* brings *Satan*, whose Fall and Defection he makes to be prior to Man's Creation, tempting *Eve* to Evil, and so the Seeds of Sin are of the Devil; and his Description of it is very admirable [.]

[Referring to Milton's discussion of Satan's perverting of Mankind]: *Milton's Pandemonium*, is allow'd to be the deepest laid Thought, most capacious and extensive that ever appear'd in Print; and, I think, I cannot do too much Honour to the Memory of so Masterly a Genius, in confessing, the Manner of Mr. *Milton's* Poem, in that particular, forms to me the best Ideas of the Matter of Original Crime, of any Thing put into Words in our Language.

57. Watts's tribute to Milton

1706

Extract from Isaac Watts, 'The Adventurous Muse' (1706). Isaac Watts, *Horae Lyricae* (1789), 188–9.

This tribute to Milton by the hymn-writer Isaac Watts (1674–1748) was well known in the eighteenth century through the various editions of *Horae Lyricae*.

There Milton dwells: The mortal sung
Themes not presum'd by mortal tongue;
New terrors, or new glories, shine
In ev'ry page, and flying scenes divine
Surprize the wond'ring sense, and draw our souls along.
Behold his muse, sent out t' explore
The unapparent deep where waves of chaos roar,
And realms of night unknown before.
She trac'd a glorious path unknown,
Thro' fields of heav'nly war, and seraphs overthrown,
Where his advent'rous genius led:
Sovereign, she fram'd a model of her own,
Nor thank'd the living nor the dead.
The noble hater of degenerate rhime
Shook off the chains, and built his verse sublime;
A monument too high for coupled souls to climb.
He mourn'd the garden lost below;
(Earth is the scene for tuneful woe!)
Now bliss beats high in all his veins;
Now the lost Eden he regains,
Keeps his own air, and triumphs in unrivall'd strains.

Immortal bard! Thus thy own Raphael sings,
And knows no rule but native fire:
All heav'n sits silent while to his sov'reign strings
He talks unutterable things:

With graces infinite his untaught fingers rove
  Across the golden lyre:
  From ev'ry note devotion springs;
Rapture, and harmony, and love,
    O'erspread the list'ning choir.

58. Swift on Milton's divorce tracts

1708

Extract from Jonathan Swift, 'Remarks upon a Book Intituled "The Rights of the Christian Church, &c."' (1708). Temple Scott, ed., *The Prose Works of Jonathan Swift* (n.d.), Vol. 3: 'Writing on Religion and the Church, Part I', 81–2.

There are not many references to Milton by Jonathan Swift (1667–1745); the present one shows that Milton's notoriety as a writer favouring divorce had not died down.

[W]hen Milton writ his book of divorces, it was presently rejected as an occasional treatise; because every body knew, he had a shrew for his wife. Neither can there be any reason imagined, why he might not, after he was blind, have writ another upon the danger and inconvenience of eyes. But it is a piece of logic which will hardly pass on the world; that because one man hath a sore nose, therefore all the town should put plasters upon theirs.

59. Addison and Steele on
Paradise Lost
1709

Extract from Joseph Addison and Richard Steele, *Tatler*, No. 114, 31 December 1709.

A main influence in developing a taste for Milton was the *Tatler*, whose various papers quoted or alluded to Milton often. Sir Richard Steele (1672–1729) and Addison continued their cultural assault in the *Spectator* through similar papers as well as complete essays.

This additional satisfaction, from the taste of pleasures in the society of one we love, is admirably described in Milton, who represents Eve, though in Paradise itself, no further pleased with the beautiful objects around her than she sees them in company with Adam, in that passage so inexpressibly charming. [*PL*, IV, 639–56]

The variety of images in this passage is infinitely pleasing, and the recapitulation of each particular image, with a little varying of the expression, makes one of the finest turns of words that I have ever seen; which I rather mention, because Mr. Dryden has said in his preface to Juvenal, that he could meet with no turn of words in Milton.

It may further be observed, that though the sweetness of these verses has something in it of a pastoral, yet it excels the ordinary kind, as much as the scene of it is above an ordinary field or meadow. I might here, since I am accidentally led into this subject, show several passages in Milton that have as excellent turns of this nature as any of our English poets whatsoever; but shall only mention that which follows, in which he describes the fallen angels engaged in the intricate disputes of predestination, free-will, and foreknowledge; and to humour the perplexity, makes a kind of labyrinth in the very words that describe it [*PL*, II, 557–61].

60. Anonymous statement of Milton's sublimity

1709

Extract from *Milton's Sublimity Asserted: In A Poem. Occasion'd by a late Celebrated Piece, Entituled, Cyder, a Poem; In Blank Verse, By Philo-Milton* (1709), 20–1, 26–8.

  Milton's [Muse] was warm'd with a Celestial heat,
Whilst thine is grip'd, and chill'd with Acid Tiff;
His matchless *Genius* in transcendent Layes,
Sung the great *Anthem* of his Makers Works
Immense of *Eden*, and the *Innocents*,
Blest Pair! who fell by the forbidden Fruit;
That Cursed Fatal Fruit, whose damning Juice,
Is made the Favo'rite Subject of thy Song;
When subtile *Thou*, by Charm of *Milton*'s Name
Delightful, play a second *Fiends* Deceit,
To Guile the World with Interdicted Verse;
And whilst in moving Numbers, he excites
The Vig'rous Soul to the sublimest Thoughts;
Thou like a *Bankrupt* Wit, with Cheerful Ale,
And Voice; dull as a Bag-pipes Drone, dost Buzz
Incessant, Thy self pleasing *Madrigal*;
Of *Shilling*, *Breeches*, and *Chimera*'s Dire.
. . . He Art and Judgment, in Alliance binds;
Nature from Force he rescues, and sets free,
Then places *Method* in an easy Seat;
Reflection with a solemn Pomp is grac'd,
Whilst each Transition like some pleasing Scene,
Commands our Wonder, and compels Delight:
If Vagrant in Digression, *Milton* roves,
Beyond the Confines of his *Eden*'s ground,
'Tis like the *Bee*, hard Traveller on Flowers,

For Honey Foraging to store her Hive;
When laden with the Amber Drops she comes
To hoard her Riches, in their waxen Cells;
Each sparkling Epithet, with Vigour glows,
And oft within a bright *Parenthesis*;
Instructive *Morals* gracefully appear,
To Guard from vain *Ideas* Reasons Throne:
His vast *Invention* unexhausted flows,
A Thousand Beautys Reign in ev'ry Page,
With all the Majesty of Eloquence,
Of *Nervous Eloquence*; so when a Silver Stream
Transparent, glides along a pleasing Shoar;
It's Waters add more Blessings to the Soil,
And Party-colour'd Flowr's adorn the place.

61. Shaftesbury on heroic poetry

1710

Extract from Anthony Ashley Cooper, Earl of Shaftesbury, 'Soliloquy: or, Advice to an Author' (1710), *Characteristicks of Men, Manners, Opinions, Times* (1727), i, 276, 358-9.

The first Baron Ashley and first Earl of Shaftesbury (1621-83) was an aesthetician and poet, whose praise of Milton is representative of the early eighteenth-century attitude.

Upon the whole: since in the two great poetick Stations, the *Epick* and *Dramatick*, we may observe the moral Genius so naturally prevalent: since our most approv'd *heroick Poem* [Milton's *Paradise Lost*] has neither the Softeness of Language, nor the fashionable Turn of Wit; but merely solid Thought, strong Reasoning, noble Passion, and a continu'd Thred of moral Doctrine, Piety, and Virtue to recommend it; we may justly infer, that it is not so much the *publick Ear*, as the *ill Hand* and *vitious Manner* of our Poets, which needs redress. . . .

I shou'd be unwilling to examine rigorously the Performance of our great Poet [Milton], who sung so piously the *Fall of Man*. The *War in Heaven*, and the *Catastrophe* of that original *Pair* from whom the Generations of Mankind were propagated, are Matters so abstrusely reveal'd, and with such a resemblance of *Mythology*, that they can more easily bear what figurative Construction or fantastick Turn the Poet may think fit to give 'em. But shou'd he venture farther, into the Lives and Characters of the Patriarchs, the holy Matrons, Heroes and Heroines of the chosen Seed; shou'd he employ the sacred *Machine*, the Exhibitions and Interventions of Divinity, according to Holy Writ, to support the *Action* of his Piece; he wou'd soon find the Weakness of his pretended *Orthodox* MUSE, and prove how little those Divine Patterns were capable of human Imitation, or of being rais'd to any other Majesty, or Sublime, than that in which they originally appear.

62. Defoe on the two epics

1711

Extract from Daniel Defoe, *A Review of the State of the British Nation*, Vol. VIII, No. 63 (18 August 1711), 254–5.

The Famous Mr. *Milton* wrote two Poems, *Paradise lost*, and *Paradise regain'd*, which tho' form'd in the same Mould, the Work of the same bright Genius, yet have met with a most differing Reception in the World; the first passes with a general Reputation for the greatest, best, and most sublime Work now in the *English* Tongue, and it would be to lessen a Man's own Reputation to say any Thing less of it—The other is call'd a Dull Thing, infinitely short of the former, nothing to compare with it, and not like the same Author, and this is the Universal Opinion of the Age about these two Books: Mr. *Milton* was told this by several, for it was the Opinion then as well as now, and his Answer was this—Well, I see the Reason plainly, why this Book is not liked so well as the other, for I am sure it is the better Poem of the two, but People have not the same Gust of Pleasure at the regaining Paradise, as they have concern at the loss of it, and therefore they do not relish this so well as they did the other, tho' it be without Comparison the best Performance.

63. Addison's papers on *Paradise Lost*

1712

Joseph Addison, *Notes Upon the Twelve Books of* Paradise Lost, London, 1719.

Without question Addison's six general papers on *Paradise Lost* and the twelve papers on each book have been reprinted more often than any other work on Milton, and they have been a major influence in forming opinion since their original publication.

Originally published in the *Spectator*: No. 267, 5 January 1712; No. 273, 12 January 1712; No. 279, 19 January 1712; No. 285, 26 January 1712; No. 291, 2 February 1712; No. 297, 9 February 1712; No. 303, 16 February 1712; No. 309, 23 February 1712; No. 315, 1 March 1712; No. 321, 8 March 1712; No. 327, 15 March 1712; No. 333, 22 March 1712; No. 339, 29 March 1712; No. 345, 5 April 1712; No. 351, 12 April 1712; No. 357, 19 April 1712; No. 363, 26 April 1712; No. 369, 3 May 1712. Latin epigraphs are omitted as well as one insertion in No. 303 in the 1719 edition.

Spectator, No. 267

There is Nothing in Nature more irksome than general Discourses, especially when they turn chiefly upon Words. For this Reason I shall wave the Discussion of that Point which was started some Years since, Whether *Milton's Paradise Lost* may be called an *Heroic Poem*? Those who will not give it that Title, may call it (if they please) a *Divine Poem*. It will be sufficient to its Perfection, if it has in it all the Beauties of the highest Kind of Poetry; and as for those who alledge it is not an Heroick Poem, they advance no more to the Diminution of it, than if they should say *Adam* is not *Aeneas*, nor *Eve* Helen.

I shall therefore examine it by the Rules of Epic Poetry, and see whether it falls short of the *Iliad* or *Aeneid*, in the Beauties which are essential to that Kind of Writing. The first Thing to be consider'd in an Epic Poem, is the Fable, which is perfect or imperfect, according as the Action which it relates is more or less so. This Action should have three Qualifications in it. First, It should be but One Action. Secondly, It should be an Entire Action; and Thirdly, It should be a Great Action. To consider the Action of the *Iliad*, *Aeneid*, and *Paradise Lost*, in these three several Lights. *Homer* to preserve the Unity of his Action hastens into the Midst of Things, as *Horace* has observed: Had he gone up to *Leda*'s Egg, or begun much later, even at the Rape of *Helen*, or the Investing of *Troy*, it is manifest that the Story of the Poem would have been a Series of Several Actions. He therefore opens his Poem with the Discord of his Princes, and artfully interweaves, in the several succeeding Parts of it, an Account of every Thing material which relates to them, and had passed before this fatal Dissension. After the same Manner, *Aeneas* makes his first Appearance in the *Tyrrhene* Seas, and within Sight of *Italy*, because the Action proposed to be celebrated was that of his settling himself in *Latium*. But because it was necessary for the Reader to know what had happened to him in the taking of *Troy*, and in the preceding Parts of his Voyage, *Virgil* makes his Heroe relate it by Way of Episode in the second and third Books of the *Aeneid*: the Contents of both which Books come before those of the first Book in the Thread of the Story, tho' for preserving of this Unity of Action, they follow it in the Disposition of the Poem. *Milton* in Imitation of these two great Poets, opens his *Paradise Lost* with an infernal Council plotting the Fall of Man, which is the Action he proposed to celebrate; and as for those Great Actions, the Battle of the Angels, and the Creation of the World (which preceded in Point of Time, and which, in my Opinion, would have entirely destroyed the Unity of his Principal Action, had he related them in the same Order that they happened) he cast them into the fifth, sixth and seventh Books, by way of Episode to this noble Poem.

Aristotle himself allows, that *Homer* has nothing to boast of as to the Unity of his Fable, tho' at the same Time that great Critick and Philosopher endeavours to palliate this Imperfection in the *Greek* Poet by imputing it in some Measure to the very Nature of an Epic Poem. Some have been of Opinion, that the *Aeneid* also labours in this Particular, and has Episodes which may be looked upon as Excrescencies rather than as Parts of the Action. On the contrary, the Poem, which we have now under our Consideration, hath no other Episodes than such as naturally arise from the Subject, and yet is filled with such a Multitude of astonishing Incidents, that it gives us at the same Time a

Pleasure of the greatest Variety, and of the greatest Simplicity; uniform in its Nature, tho' diversified in the Execution.

I must observe also, that, as *Virgil* in the Poem which was designed to celebrate the Original of the *Roman* Empire, has described the Birth of its great Rival, the *Carthaginian* Common-wealth: *Milton*, with the like Art in his Poem on the Fall of Man, has related the Fall of those Angels who are his professed Enemies. Beside the many other Beauties in such an Episode, it's running parallel with the great Action of the Poem, hinders it from breaking the Unity so much as another Episode would have done, that had not so great an Affinity with the principal Subject. In short, this is the same Kind of Beauty which the Criticks admire in the *Spanish Fryar*, or the *Double Discovery*, where the two different Plots look like Counterparts and Copies of one another.

The second Qualification required in the Action of an Epic Poem is, that it should be an *entire* Action: An Action is entire when it is compleat in all its Parts; or as *Aristotle* describes it, when it consists of a Beginning, a Middle, and an End. Nothing should go before it, be intermix'd with it, or follow after it, that is not related to it. As on the contrary, no single Step should be omitted in that just and regular Progress which it must be supposed to take from its Original to its Consummation. Thus we see the Anger of *Achilles* in its Birth, its Continuance, and Effects; and *Aeneas*'s Settlement in *Italy*, carried on through all the Oppositions in his Way to it both by Sea and Land. The Action in *Milton* excells (I think) both the former in this Particular; we see it contrived in Hell, executed upon Earth, and punished by Heaven. The Parts of it are told in the most distinct Manner, and grow out of one another in the most natural Order.

The third Qualification of an Epic Poem is its *Greatness*. The Anger of *Achilles* was of such Consequence, that it embroiled the Kings of *Greece*, destroy'd the Heroes of *Asia*, and engaged all the Gods in Factions. *Aeneas*'s Settlement in *Italy* produc'd the *Caesars*, and gave Birth to the *Roman* Empire. *Milton*'s Subject was still greater than either of the former; it does not determine the Fate of single Persons or Nations, but of a whole Species. The United Powers of Hell are joined together for the Destruction of Mankind, which they effected in Part, and would have completed, had not Omnipotence it self interposed. The principal Actors are Man in his greatest Perfection, and Woman in her highest Beauty. Their Enemies are the fallen Angels: The Messiah their Friend, and the Almighty their Protector. In short, every Thing that is great in the whole Circle of Being, whether within the

Verge of Nature, or out of it, has a proper Part assigned it in this admirable Poem.

In Poetry, as in Architecture, not only the Whole, but the principal Members, and every Part of them, should be Great. I will not presume to say, that the Book of Games in the *Aeneid*, or that in the *Iliad*, are not of this Nature, nor to reprehend *Virgil*'s Simile of the Top, and many other of the same Kind in the *Iliad*, as liable to any Censure in this Particular; but I think We may say, without derogating from those wonderful Performances, that there is an Indisputable and Unquestioned Magnificence in every Part of *Paradise Lost*, and indeed a much greater than could have been formed upon any Pagan System.

But *Aristotle*, by the Greatness of the Action, does not only mean that it should be great in its Nature, but also in its Duration; or in other Words, That it should have a due Length in it, as well as what we properly call Greatness. The just Measure of this Kind of Magnitude, he explains by the following Similitude. An animal, no bigger than a Mite, cannot appear perfect to the Eye, because the Sight takes it in at once, and has only a confused Idea of the Whole, and not a distinct Idea of all its Parts; If on the contrary you should suppose an Animal of ten thousand Furlongs in Length, the Eye would be so filled with a single Part of it, that it could not give the Mind an Idea of the whole. What these Animals are to the Eye, a very short or a very long Action would be to the Memory. The first would be, as it were, lost and swallowed up by it, and the other difficult to be contained in it. *Homer* and *Virgil* have shewn their principal Art in this Particular; the Action of the *Iliad*, and that of the *Aeneid*, were in themselves exceeding short, but are so beautifully extended and diversified by the Invention of *Episodes*, and the Machinery of Gods, with the like poetical Ornaments, that they make up an agreeable Story sufficient to employ the Memory without overcharging it. *Milton*'s Action is enriched with such a Variety of Circumstances, that I have taken as much Pleasure in reading the Contents of his Books, as in the best invented Story I ever met with. It is possible, that the Traditions, on which the *Iliad* and *Aeneid* were built, had more Circumstances in them than the History of *the Fall of Man*, as it is related in Scripture. Besides it was easier for *Homer* and *Virgil* to dash the Truth with Fiction, as they were in no Danger of offending the Religion of their Country by it. But as for *Milton*, he had not only a very few Circumstances upon which to raise his Poem, but was also obliged to proceed with the greatest Caution in every Thing that he added out of his own Invention. And, indeed, notwithstanding all the Restraints he was under, he has filled his Story with so many surprising Incidents, which bear so close Analogy with what is delivered in Holy Writ, that it is capable of pleasing the most delicate Reader, without giving Offence to the most scrupulous.

The modern Criticks have collected from several Hints in the *Iliad* and *Aeneid* the Space of Time, which is taken up by the Action of each of those Poems; but as a great Part of *Milton*'s Story was transacted in Regions that lie out of the Reach of the Sun and the Sphere of Day, it is impossible to gratifie the Reader with such a Calculation, which indeed would be more curious than instructive; None of the Criticks, either Antient or Modern, having laid down Rules to circumscribe the Action of an Epic Poem with any Determined Number of Years, Days, or Hours.

But of this more particularly hereafter.

Spectator, No. 273

Having examined the Action of *Paradise Lost*, let us in the next Place consider the Actors. This is *Aristotle*'s Method of considering; first the Fable, and secondly the Manners, or as we generally call them in *English*, the Fable and the Characters.

Homer has excelled all the Heroic Poets that ever wrote, in the Multitude and Variety of his Characters. Every God that is admitted into his Poem, acts a Part which would have been suitable to no other Deity. His Princes are as much distinguished by their Manners as by their Dominions; and even those among them, whose Characters seem wholly made up of Courage, differs from one another as to the particular Kinds of Courage in which they excel. In short, there is scarce a Speech or Action in the *Iliad*, which the Reader may not ascribe to the Person that speaks or acts, without seeing his Name at the Head of it.

Homer does not only out-shine all other Poets in the Variety, but also in the Novelty of his Characters. He has introduced among his *Grecian* Princes a Person, who had lived in three Ages of Men, and conversed with *Theseus, Hercules, Polyphemus*, and the first Race of Heroes. His principal Actor is the Son of a Goddess, not to mention the Offspring of other Deities, who have likewise a Place in his Poem, and the venerable *Trojan* Prince who was the Father of so many Kings and Heroes. There is in these several Characters of *Homer*, a certain Dignity as well as Novelty, which adapts them in a more peculiar Manner to the Nature of an heroic Poem. Tho' at the same Time, to give them the greater Variety, he has described a *Vulcan*, that is, a Buffoon among his Gods, and a *Thersites* among his Mortals.

Virgil falls infinitely short of *Homer* in the Characters of his Poem, both as to their Variety and Novelty. *Aeneas* is indeed a perfect Character, but as for *Achates*, tho' he is stiled the Heroe's Friend, he does nothing in the whole Poem which may deserve that Title. *Gyas*, *Mnestheus*, *Sergestus*, and *Cloanthus*, are all of them Men of the same Stamp and Character,

. . . fortemque Gyan, fortemque Cloanthum: Virg.

There are indeed several very natural Incidents in the Part of *Ascanius*; as that of *Dido* cannot be sufficiently admired. I do not see any Thing new or particular in *Turnus*. *Pallas* and *Evander* are remote Copies of *Hector* and *Priam*, as *Lausus* and *Mezentius* are almost Parallels to *Pallas* and *Evander*. The Characters of *Nisus* and *Eurialus* are beautiful, but common. We must not forget the Parts of *Sinon*, *Camilla*, and some few others, which are fine Improvements on the Greek Poet. In short, there is neither that Variety nor Novelty in the Persons of the *Aeneid*, which we meet with in those of the *Iliad*.

If we look into the Characters of *Milton*, we shall find that he has introduced all the Variety his Fable was capable of receiving. The whole Species of Mankind was in two Persons at the Time to which the Subject of his Poem is confined. We have, however, four distinct Characters in these two Persons. We see Man and Woman in the highest Innocence and Perfection, and in the most abject State of Guilt and Infirmity. The two last Characters are, indeed, very common and obvious, but the two first are not only more magnificent, but more new than any Characters either in *Virgil* or *Homer*, or indeed in the whole Circle of Nature.

Milton was so sensible of this Defect in the Subject of his Poem, and of the few Characters it would afford him, that he has brought into it two Actors of a shadowy and fictitious Nature, in the Persons of Sin and Death, by which Means he has wrought into the Body of his Fable a very beautiful and well-invented Allegory. But notwithstanding the Fineness of this Allegory may atone for it in some Measure; I cannot think that Persons of such a chimerical Existence are proper Actors in an Epic Poem; because there is not that Measure of Probability annexed to them, which is requisite in Writings of this Kind, as I shall shew more at large hereafter.

Virgil has, indeed, admitted *Fame* as an Actress in the *Aeneid*, but the

Part she acts is very short, and none of the most admired Circumstances in that Divine Work. We find in Mock-Heroic Poems, particularly in the *Dispensary* and the *Lustrin*, several allegorical Persons of this Nature, which are very beautiful in those Compositions, and may, perhaps, be used as an Argument, that the Authors of them were of Opinion, such Characters might have a Place in an Epic Work. For my own Part, I should be glad the Reader would think so, for the Sake of the Poem I am now examining, and must further add, that if such empty unsubstantial Beings may be ever made Use of on this Occasion, never were any more nicely imagined, and employed in more proper Actions, than those of which I am now speaking.

Another principal Actor in this poem is the great Enemy of Mankind. The Part of *Ulysses* in *Homer*'s *Odyssey* is very much admired by *Aristotle*, as perplexing that Fable with very agreeable Plots and Intricacies, not only by the many Adventures in his Voyage, and the Subtility of his Behaviour, but by the various Concealments and Discoveries of his Person in several Parts of that Poem. But the crafty Being I have now mentioned, makes a much longer Voyage than *Ulysses*, puts in Practice many more Wiles and Stratagems, and hides himself under a greater Variety of Shapes, and Appearances, all of which are severally detected, to the great Delight and Surprise of the Reader.

We may likewise observe with how much Art the Poet has varied several Characters of the Persons that speak in his infernal Assembly. On the contrary, how has he represented the whole Godhead exerting it self towards Man in its full Benevolence under the Three-fold Distinction of a Creator, a Redeemer, and a Comforter!

Nor must we omit the Person of *Raphael*, who, amidst his Tenderness and Friendship for Man, shews such a Dignity and Condescention in all his Speech and Behaviour, as are suitable to a superior Nature. The Angels are indeed as much diversified in *Milton*, and distinguished by their proper Parts, as the Gods are in *Homer* or *Virgil*. The Reader will find nothing ascribed to *Uriel*, *Gabriel*, *Michael*, or *Raphael*, which is not in a particular manner suitable to their respective Characters.

There is another Circumstance in the principal Actors of the *Iliad* and *Aeneid*, which give a peculiar Beauty to those two Poems, and was therefore contrived with very great Judgment. I mean the Authors having chosen for their Heroes Persons who were so nearly related to the People for whom they wrote. *Achilles* was a *Greek*, and *Aeneas* the remote Founder of *Rome*. By this Means their Countrymen (whom they principally proposed to themselves for their Readers) were particularly attentive to all the Parts of their Story, and sympathized with their Heroes in all their Adventures. A *Roman* could not but rejoice in the Escapes, Successes, and Victories of *Aeneas*, and be grieved at any Defeats, Misfortunes, or Disappointments that befel him; as a *Greek* must have had the same Regard for *Achilles*. And it is plain, that each of those Poems have lost this great Advantage, among those Readers to whom their Heroes are as Strangers, or indifferent Persons.

Milton's Poem is admirable in this respect, since it is impossible for any of its Readers, whatever Nation, Country or People he may belong to, not to be related to the Persons who are the principal Actors in it; but what is still infinitely more to its Advantage, the principal Actors in this Poem are not only our Progenitors, but our Representatives. We have an Actual Interest in every Thing they do, and no less than our utmost Happiness is concerned, and lies at Stake in all their Behaviour.

I shall subjoin as a Corollary to the foregoing Remark, an admirable Observation out of *Aristotle*, which hath been very much misrepresented in the Quotations of some Modern Criticks. 'If a Man of perfect and consummate Virtue falls into a Misfortune, it raises our Pity, but not our Terror, because we do not fear that it may be our own Case, who do not resemble the suffering Person.' But as that great Philosopher adds, 'If we see a Man of Virtue, mixt with Infirmities, fall into any Misfortune, it does not only raise our Pity but our Terror; because we are afraid that the like Misfortunes may happen to our selves, who resemble the Character of the suffering Person.'

I shall only remark in this Place, that the foregoing Observation of *Aristotle*, tho' it may be true in other Occasions, does not hold in this; because in the present Case, though the Persons who fall into Misfortune are of the most perfect and consummate Virtue, it is not to be considered as what may possibly be, but what actually is our own Case; since we are embark'd with them on the same Bottom, and must be Partakers of their Happiness or Misery.

In this, and some other very few Instances, *Aristotle*'s Rules for Epic Poetry (which he had drawn from his Reflections upon *Homer*) cannot be supposed to square exactly with the heroic Poems which have been made since his Time; since it is evident to every impartial Judge his Rules would still have been more perfect, could he have perused the *Aeneid* which was made some hundred Years after his Death.

In my next, I shall go through other Parts of *Milton*'s Poem; and hope that what I shall there advance, as well as what I have already written, will not only serve as a Comment upon *Milton*, but upon *Aristotle*.

Spectator, No. 279

We have already taken a general Survey of the Fable and Characters in *Milton*'s *Paradise Lost*: The Parts which remain to be consider'd, according to *Aristotle*'s Method, are the *Sentiments* and the *Language*. Before I enter upon the first of these, I must advertise my Reader, that it is my Design as soon as I have finished my general Reflections on these four several Heads, to give particular Instances out of the Poem now before us of Beauties and Imperfections which may be observed under each of them, as also of such other Particulars as may not properly fall under any of them. This I thought fit to premise, that the Reader may not judge too hastily of this Piece of Criticism, or look upon it as imperfect before he has seen the whole Extent of it.

The Sentiments in an Epic Poem are the Thoughts and Behaviour which the Author ascribes to the Persons whom he introduces, and are *just* when they are conformable to the Characters of the several Persons. The Sentiments have likewise a Relation to *Things* as well as *Persons*, and are then perfect when they are such as are adapted to the Subject. If in either of these Cases the Poet endeavours to argue or explain, to magnifie or diminish, to raise Love or Hatred, Pity or Terror, or any other Passion, we ought to consider whether the Sentiments he makes Use of are proper for those Ends. *Homer* is censured by the Criticks for his Defect as to this Particular in several Parts of the *Iliad* and *Odyssey*, tho' at the same Time those who have treated this great Poet with Candour, have attributed this Defect to the Times in which he lived. It was the Fault of the Age, and not of *Homer*, if there wants that Delicacy in some of his Sentiments, which now appears in the Works of Men of a much inferior Genius. Besides, if there are Blemishes in any particular Thoughts, there is an infinite Beauty in the greatest Part of them. In short, if there are many Poets who would not have fallen into the Meanness of some of his Sentiments, there are none who could have risen up to the Greatness of others. *Virgil* has excelled all others in the Propriety of his Sentiments. *Milton* shines likewise very much in this Particular: Nor must we omit one Consideration which adds to his Honour and Reputation. *Homer* and *Virgil* introduced Persons whose Characters are commonly known among Men, and such as are to be met with either in History, or in ordinary Conversation. *Milton*'s Characters, most of them, lie out of Nature, and were to be formed purely by his own Invention. It shews a greater Genius in *Shakespear* to have drawn his *Calyban*, than this *Hotspur* or *Julius Caesar*: The one was to be supplied out of his own Imagination, whereas the other might have been formed upon Tradition, History and Observation. It was much easier therefore for *Homer* to find proper Sentiments for an Assembly of *Grecian* Generals, than for *Milton* to diversifie his infernal Council with proper Characters, and inspire them with a Variety of Sentiments. The Loves of *Dido* and *Aeneas* are only Copies of what has passed between other Persons. *Adam* and *Eve* before the Fall, are a different Species from that of Mankind, who are descended from them; and none but a Poet of the most unbounded Invention, and the most exquisite Judgment, cou'd have filled their Conversation and Behaviour with so many apt Circumstances during their State of Innocence.

Nor is it sufficient for an Epic Poem to be filled with such Thoughts as are *natural*, unless it abound also with such as are *sublime*. *Virgil* in this Particular falls short of *Homer*. He has not indeed so many Thoughts that are sublime and noble. The Truth of it is, *Virgil* seldom rises into very astonishing Sentiments, where he is not fired by the *Iliad*. He every where charms and pleases us by the Force of his own Genius; but seldom elevates and transports us where he does not fetch his Hints from *Homer*.

Milton's chief Talent, and indeed his distinguishing Excellence lies in the Sublimity of this Thoughts. There are others of the Moderns who rival him in every other Part of Poetry; but in the Greatness of his Sentiments he triumphs over all the Poets both Modern and Ancient, *Homer* only excepted. It is impossible for the Imagination of Man to distend it self with greater Ideas, than those which he has laid together in his first, second and sixth Books. The seventh, which describes the Creation of the World, is likewise wonderfully sublime, tho' not so apt to stir up Emotion in the Mind of the Reader, nor consequently so perfect in the Epic Way of Writing, because it is filled with less Action. Let the judicious Reader compare what *Longinus* has observed on several Passages in *Homer*, and he will find Parallels for most of them in the *Paradise Lost*.

From what has been said we may infer, that as there are two Kinds of Sentiments, the Natural and the Sublime, which are always to be pursued in an heroic Poem, there are also two Kinds of Thoughts which are carefully to be avoided. The first are such as are affected and un-natural; the second such as are mean and vulgar. As for the first Kind of Thoughts we meet with little or Nothing that is like them in *Virgil*: He has none of those trifling Points and Puerilities that are so often to be met with in *Ovid*, none of the Ephigrammatick Turns of *Lucan*, none of those swelling Sentiments which are so frequently in *Statius* and *Claudian*, none of those mixed Embellishments of *Tasso*. Every Thing is just and natural. His Sentiments shew that he had a perfect Insight into humane Nature, and that he knew every Thing which was the most proper to affect it.

Mr. *Dryden* has in some Places, which I may hereafter take Notice of, misrepresented *Virgil*'s Way of Thinking as to this Particular, in the Translation he has given us of the *Aeneid*. I do not remember that *Homer* any where falls into the Faults abovementioned, which were indeed the false Refinements of later Ages. *Milton*, it must be confest, has sometimes erred in this Respect, as I shall shew more at large in another Paper; tho' considering all the Poets of the Age in which he writ, were infected with this wrong Way of Thinking, he is rather to be admired that he did not give more into it, than that he did sometimes comply with the vicious Taste which still prevails so much among modern Writers.

But since several Thoughts may be natural which are low and groveling, an Epic Poet should not only avoid such Sentiments as are unnatural or affected, but also such as are mean and vulgar. *Homer* has opened a great Field of Raillery to Men of more Delicacy than Greatness of Genius, by the Homeliness of some of his Sentiments. But, as I have before said, these are rather to be imputed to the Simplicity of the Age in which he lived, to which I may also add, of that which he described, than to any Imperfection in that Divine Poet. *Zoilus*, among the Ancients, and Monsieur *Perrault*, among the Moderns, pushed their Ridicule very far upon him, on Account of some such Sentiments. There is no Blemish to be observed in *Virgil*, under this Head, and but a very few in *Milton*.

I shall give but one Instance of this Impropriety of Thought in *Homer*, and at the same Time compare it with an Instance of the same Nature, both in *Virgil* and *Milton*. Sentiments which raise Laughter, can very seldom be admitted with any Decency into an heroic Poem, whose Business is to excite Passions of a much nobler Nature. *Homer*, however, in his Characters of *Vulcan* and *Thersites*, in his Story of *Mars* and *Venus*, in his Behaviour of *Irus*, and in other Passages, has been observed to have lapsed into the Burlesque Character, and to have departed from that serious Air which seems essential to the Magnificence of an Epic Poem. I remember but one Laugh in the whole *Aeneid*, which rises in the fifth book upon *Monoetes*, where he is represented as thrown overboard, and drying himself upon a Rock. But this Piece of Mirth is so well timed, that the severest Critick can have Nothing to say against it, for it is in the Book of Games and Diversions, where the Reader's Mind may be supposed to be sufficiently relaxed for such an Entertainment. The only Piece of Pleasantry in *Paradise Lost*, is where the evil Spirits are described as rallying the Angels upon the Success of their new invented Artillery. This Passage I look upon to be the most exceptionable in the whole Poem, as being nothing else but a String of Puns, and those too very indifferent. [VI, 470 ff.]

Spectator, No. 285

Having already treated of the Fable, the Characters and Sentiments in the *Paradise lost*, we are in the last Place to consider the *Language*; and as the learned World is very much divided upon *Milton* as to this Point, I hope they will excuse me if I appear particular in any of my Opinions, and encline to those who judge the most advantagiously of the Author.

It is requisite that the Language of an Heroic Poem should be both Perspicuous and Sublime. In Proportion as either of these two Qualities are wanting, the Language is imperfect. Perspicuity is the first and most necessary Qualification; insomuch that a good-natur'd Reader sometimes overlooks a little Slip even in the Grammar or Syntax, where it is impossible for him to mistake the Poet's Sense. Of this kind is that Passage in *Milton*, wherein he speaks of *Satan*.

> God and his Son except,
> Created thing nought valu'd he nor shunn'd. [II, 678–9]

And that in which he describes *Adam* and *Eve*.

> *Adam* the goodliest Man of Men since born
> His Sons, the fairest of her Daughters *Eve*. [IV, 323–4]

It is plain, that in the former of these Passages, according to the natural Syntax, the Divine Persons mentioned in the first Line are represented as created Beings; and that in the other, *Adam* and *Eve* are confounded with their Sons and Daughters. Such little Blemishes as these, when the Thought is great and natural, we should, with *Horace*, impute to a pardonable Inadvertency, or to the Weakness of Human Nature, which cannot attend to each minute Particular, and give the last finishing to every Circumstance in so long a Work. The Ancient Criticks therefore, who were acted by a Spirit of Candour, rather than that of Cavilling, invented certain Figures of Speech, on purpose to palliate little Errors of this Nature in the Writings of those Authors who had so many greater Beauties to attone for them.

If Clearness and Perspicuity were only to be consulted, the Poet would have nothing else to do but to cloath his Thoughts in the most plain and natural Expressions. But since it often happens that the most obvious Phrases, and those which are used in ordinary Conversation, become too familiar to the Ear, and contract a kind of Meanness by passing through the Mouths of the Vulgar, a Poet should take particular Care to guard himself against Idiomatick Ways of speaking. *Ovid* and *Lucan* have many Poornesses of Expression upon this account, as taking up with the first Phrases that offered, without putting themselves to the Trouble of looking after such as would not only be natural, but also elevated and sublime. *Milton* has but a few Failings in this kind, of which, however, you may meet with some Instances, as in the following Passages. [III, 474–6; V, 395–7; X, 733–6] The great Masters in Composition know very well that many an elegant Phrase becomes improper for a Poet or an Orator, when it has been debased by common Use. For this Reason the Works of Antient Authors, which are written in dead Languages, have a great Advantage over those which are written in Languages that are now spoken. Were there any Mean Phrases or Idioms in *Virgil* and *Homer*, they would not shock the Ear of the most delicate Modern Reader, so much as they would have done that of an old *Greek* or *Roman*, because we never hear them pronounced in our Streets, or in ordinary Conversation.

It is not therefore sufficient, that the Language of an Epic Poem be Perspicuous, unless it be also Sublime. To this End it ought to deviate from the common Forms and ordinary Phrases of Speech. The Judgment of a Poet very much discovers it self in shunning the common Roads of Expression, without falling into such ways of Speech as may seem stiff and unnatural; he must not swell into a false Sublime, by endeavouring to avoid the other Extream. Among the *Greeks*, *Aeschylus*, and some times *Sophocles* were guilty of this Fault; among the *Latins*, *Claudian* and *Statius*; and among our own Countrymen, *Shakespear* and *Lee*. In these Authors the Affectation of Greatness often hurts the Perspicuity of the Stile, as in many others the Endeavour after Perspicuity prejudices its Greatness.

Aristotle has observed, that the Idiomatick Stile may be avoided, and the Sublime formed, by the following Methods. First, by the Use of Metaphors: such are those in *Milton*,

Imparadised in anothers Arms, [IV, 506]

And in his Hand a Reed
Stood waving *tipt* with Fire; [VI, 579–80]

The grassie Clods now *calv'd*. [VII, 463]

Spangled with eyes . . . [IX, 130]

In these and innumerable other Instances, the Metaphors are very bold but just; I must however observe, that the Metaphors are not thick sown in *Milton*, which always savours too much of Wit; that they never clash with one another, which, as *Aristotle* observes, turns a Sentence into a Kind of an Enigma or Riddle; and that he seldom has Recourse to them where the proper and natural Words will do as well.

Another way of raising the Language, and giving it a Poetical Turn, is to make Use of the Idioms of other Tongues. *Virgil* is full of the *Greek* Forms of Speech, which the Criticks call *Hellenisms*, as *Horace* in his Odes abounds with them much more than *Virgil*. I need not mention the several Dialects which *Homer* has made use of for this End. *Milton* in Conformity with the Practice of the Ancient Poets, and with *Aristotle*'s Rule, has infused a great many *Latinisms* as well as *Graecisms*, and sometimes *Hebraisms*, into the Language of his Poem; as towards the Beginning of it, [I, 335–7; II, 523–8; XI, 376–7].

Under this Head may be reckoned the placing the Adjective after the Substantive, the Transposition of Words, the turning the Adjective into a Substantive, with several other Foreign Modes of Speech, which this Poet has naturalized to give his Verse the greater Sound, and throw it out of Prose.

The third Method mentioned by *Aristotle*, is what agrees with the Genius of the *Greek* Language more than with that of any other Tongue, and is therefore more used by *Homer* than by any other Poet. I mean the lengthening of a Phrase by the Addition of Words, which may either be inserted or omitted, as also by the extending or contracting of particular Words by the Insertion or Omission of certain Syllables. *Milton* has put in practice this Method of raising his Language, as far as the Nature of our Tongue will permit, as in the Passage above-mentioned, *Eremite*, for what is Hermite, in common Discourse. If you observe the Measure of his Verse, he has with great Judgment suppressed a Syllable in several Words, and shortened those of two Syllables into one, by which Method, besides the above-mentioned Advantage, he has given a greater Variety to his Numbers. But this Practice is more particularly remarkable in the Names of Persons and of Countries, as *Beëlzebub*, *Hessebon*, and in many other Particulars, wherein he has either changed the Name, or made use of that which is not the most commonly known, that he might the better depart from the Language of the Vulgar.

The same Reason recommended to him several old Words, which also makes his Poem appear the more venerable, and gives it a greater Air of Antiquity.

I must likewise take notice, that there are in *Milton* several Words of his own Coining, as *Cerberean*, *miscreated*, *hell-doom'd*, *Embryon* Atoms, and many others. If the Reader is offended at this Liberty in our *English* Poet, I would recommend him to a Discourse in *Plutarch*, which shews us how frequently *Homer* has made use of the same Liberty.

Milton by the above-mentioned Helps, and by the Choice of the noblest Words and Phrases which our Tongue would afford him, has carried our Language to a greater height than any of the *English* Poets have ever done before or after him, and made the Sublimity of his Stile equal to that of his Sentiments,

I have been the more particular in these Observations on *Milton's* Stile, because it is that part of him in which he appears the most singular. The Remarks I have here made upon the Practice of other Poets, with my Observations out of *Aristotle*, will perhaps alleviate the Prejudice which some have taken to his Poem upon this Account; tho' after all, I must confess, that I think his Stile, tho' admirable in general, is in some places too much stiffened and obscured by the frequent Use of those Methods, which *Aristotle* has prescribed for the raising of it.

This Redundancy of those several Ways of Speech which *Aristotle* calls *foreign Language*, and with which *Milton* has so very much enriched, and in some places darkned the Language of his Poem, was the more proper for his use, because his Poem is written in Blank Verse. Rhyme, without any other Assistance, throws the Language off from Prose, and very often makes an indifferent Phrase pass unregarded; but where the Verse is not built upon Rhymes, there Pomp of Sound, and Energy of Expression, are indispensably necessary to support the Stile, and keep it from falling into the Flatness of Prose.

Those who have not a Taste for this Elevation of Stile, and are apt to ridicule a Poet when he goes out of the common Forms of Expression, would do well to see how *Aristotle* has treated an Ancient Author, called *Euclid*, for his insipid Mirth upon this Occasion. Mr. *Dryden* used to call this sort of Men his Prose-Criticks.

I should, under this Head of the Language, consider *Milton*'s Numbers, in which he has made use of several Elisions, that are not customary among other *English* Poets, as may be particularly observed in his cutting off the Letter *Y*, when it precedes a Vowel. This, and some other Innovations in the Measure of his Verse, has varied his Numbers, in such a manner, as makes them incapable of satiating the Ear and cloying the Reader, which the same uniform Measure would certainly have done, and which the perpetual Returns of Rhyme never fail to do in long Narrative Poems. I shall close these Reflections upon the Language of *Paradise Lost*, with observing that *Milton* has copied after *Homer*, rather than *Virgil*, in the length of his Periods, the Copiousness of his Phrases, and the running of his Verses into one another.

Spectator, No. 291

I have now consider'd *Milton*'s *Paradise Lost* under those four great Heads of the Fable, the Characters, the Sentiments, and the Language; and have shewn that he excels, in general, under each of these Heads. I hope that I have made several Discoveries which may appear new, even to those who are versed in Critical Learning. Were I indeed to chuse my Readers, by whose Judgment I would stand or fall, they should not be such as are acquainted only with the *French* and *Italian* Criticks, but also with the Antient and Modern who have written in either of the learned Languages. Above all, I would have them well versed in the *Greek* and *Latin* Poets, without which a Man very often fancies that he understands a Critick, when in reality he does not comprehend his Meaning.

It is in Criticism, as in all other Sciences and Speculations; one who brings with him any implicit Notions and Observations which he has made in his reading of the Poets, will find his own Reflections methodized and explained, and perhaps several little Hints that had passed in his Mind, perfected and improved in the Works of a good Critick; whereas one who has not these previous Lights, is very often an utter Stranger to what he reads, and apt to put a wrong Interpretation upon it.

Nor is it sufficient, that a Man who sets up for a Judge in Criticism, should have perused the Authors above-mentioned, unless he has also a clear and logical Head. Without this Talent he is perpetually puzzled and perplexed amidst his own Blunders, mistakes the Sense of those he would confute, or if he chances to think right, does not know how to convey his Thoughts to another with Clearness and Perspicuity. *Aristotle*, who was the best Critick, was also one of the best Logicians that ever appeared in the World.

Mr. *Lock*'s Essay on Human Understanding would be thought a very odd Book for a Man to make himself Master of, who would get a Reputation by Critical Writings; though at the same Time it is very certain, that an Author who has not learned the Art of distinguishing between Words and Things, and of ranging his Thoughts, and setting them in proper Lights, whatever Notions he may have, will lose himself in Confusion and Obscurity. I might further observe, that there is not a *Greek* or *Latin* Critick who has not shewn, even in the Stile of his Criticisms, that he was a Master of all the Elegance and Delicacy of his Native Tongue.

The Truth of it is, there is nothing more absurd than for a Man to set up for a Critick, without a good Insight into all the Parts of Learning; whereas many of those who have endeavoured to signalize themselves by Works of this Nature among our *English* Writers, are not only defective in the above-mentioned Particulars, but plainly discover by the Phrases which they make use of, and by their confused way of thinking, that they are not acquainted with the most common and ordinary Systems of Arts and Sciences. A few general Rules extracted out of the *French* Authors, with a certain Cant of Words, has sometimes set up an illiterate heavy Writer for a most judicious and formidable Critick.

One great Mark, by which you may discover a Critick who has neither Taste nor Learning, is this, that he seldom ventures to praise any Passage in an Author which has not been before received and applauded by the Publick, and that his Criticism turns wholly upon little Faults and Errors. This Part of a Critick is so very easy to succeed in, that we find every ordinary Reader, upon the publishing of a new Poem, has Wit and Ill-nature enough to turn several Passages of it into Ridicule, and very often in the right Place. This Mr. *Dryden* has very agreeably remarked in those two celebrated Lines,

> Errors, like Straws, upon the Surface flow;
> He who would search for Pearls must dive below.

A true Critick ought to dwell rather upon Excellencies than Imperfections, to discover the concealed Beauties of a Writer, and communicate to the World such Things as are worth their Observation. The most exquisite Words and finest Strokes of an Author are those which very often appear the most doubtful and exceptionable, to a Man who wants a Relish for polite Learning; and they are these, which a soure undistinguishing Critick generally attacks with the greatest Violence. *Tully* observes, that it is very easy to brand or fix a Mark upon what he calls *Verbum ardens*, or, as it may be rendered into *English*, *a glowing bold Expression*, and to turn it into Ridicule by a cold ill-natured Criticism. A little Wit is equally capable of exposing a Beauty, and of aggravating a Fault; and though such a Treatment of an Author naturally produces Indignation in the Mind of an understanding Reader, it has however its Effect among the Generality of those whose Hands it falls into, the Rabble of Mankind being very apt to think that everything which is laughed at with any Mixture of Wit, is ridiculous in itself.

Such a Mirth as this, is always unseasonable in a Critick, as it rather prejudices the Reader than convinces him, and is capable of making a Beauty, as well as Blemish, the Subject of Derision. A Man, who cannot write with Wit on a proper Subject, is dull and stupid, but one who shews it in an improper Place, is as impertinent and absurd. Besides, a Man who has the Gift of Ridicule, is apt to find Fault with any Thing that gives him an Opportunity of exerting his beloved Talent, and very often censures a Passage, not because there is any Fault in it, but because he can be merry upon it. Such kinds of Pleasantry are very unfair and disingenous in Works of Criticism, in which the greatest Masters, both antient and modern, have always appeared with a serious and instructive Air.

As I intend in my next Paper to shew the Defects of *Milton's Paradise Lost,* I thought fit to premise these few Particulars, to the End that the Reader may know I enter upon it, as on a very ungrateful Work, and that I shall just point at the Imperfections, without endeavouring to enflame them with Ridicule. I must also observe with *Longinus*, that the Productions of a great Genius, with many Lapses and Inadvertencies, are infinitely preferable to the Works of an inferior Kind of Author, which are scrupulously exact and conformable to all the Rules of correct Writing.

I shall conclude my Paper with a Story out of *Bastalini*, which sufficiently shews us the Opinion that judicious Author entertained of the Sort of Criticks I have been here mentioning. A famous Critick, says he, having gathered together all the Faults of an eminent Poet, made a Present of them to *Apollo*, who received them very graciously, and resolved to make the Author a suitable Return for the Trouble he had been at in collecting them. In Order to this, he set before him a Sack of Wheat, as it had been just threshed out of the Sheaf. He then bid him pick out the Chaff from among the Corn, and lay it aside by itself. The Critick applied himself to the Task with great Industry and Pleasure, and after having made the due Separation, was presented by *Apollo* with the Chaff for his Pains.

Specatator, No. 297

After what I have said in my last *Saturday*'s Paper, I shall enter on the Subject of this without further Preface, and remark the several Defects which appear in the Fable, the Characters, the Sentiments, and the Language of *Milton*'s *Paradise Lost*; not doubting but the Reader will pardon me, if I alledge at the same Time whatever may be said for the Extenuation of such Defects. The first Imperfection which I shall observe in the Fable is, that the Event of it is unhappy.

The Fable of every Poem is according to *Aristotle*'s Division either *Simple* or *Implex*. It is called Simple when there is no Change of Fortune in it, Implex when the Fortune of the chief Actor changes from Bad to Good, or from Good to Bad. The Implex Fable is thought the most perfect; I suppose, because it is more proper to stir up the Passions of the Reader, and to surprize him with a greater Variety of Accidents.

The Implex Fable is therefore of two Kinds: In the first the chief Actor makes his Way through a long Series of Dangers and Difficulties, 'till he arrives at Honour and Prosperity, as we see in the Story of *Ulysses*. In the second, the chief Actor in the Poem falls from some eminent Pitch of Honour and Prosperity, into Misery and Disgrace. Thus we see *Adam* and *Eve* sinking from a State of Innocence and Happiness, into the most abject Condition of Sin and Sorrow.

The most taking Tragedies among the Antients were built on this last Sort of Implex Fable, particularly the Tragedy of *Oedipus*, which proceeds upon a Story, if we may believe *Aristotle*, the most proper for Tragedy that could be invented by the Wit of Man. I have taken some Pains in a former Paper to shew, that this Kind of Implex Fable, wherein the Event is unhappy, is more apt to affect an Audience than that of the first Kind; notwithstanding many excellent Pieces among the Antients, as well as most of those which have been written of late Years in our own Country, are raised upon contrary Plans. I must however own, that I think this Kind of Fable, which is the most perfect in Tragedy, is not so proper for an Heroick Poem.

Milton seems to have been sensible of this Imperfection in his Fable, and has therefore endeavoured to cure it by several Expedients; particularly by the Mortification which the great Adversary of Mankind meets with upon his Return to the Assembly of Infernal Spirits, as it is described in a beautiful Passage of the tenth Book; and likewise by the Vision, wherein *Adam* at the Close of the Poem sees his Off-spring triumphing over his Great enemy, and himself restored to a happier *Paradise* than that from which he fell.

There is another Objection against *Milton*'s Fable, which is indeed almost the same with the former, tho' placed in a different Light, namely, That the Hero in the *Paradise Lost* is unsuccessful, and by no Means a Match for his Enemies. This gave Occasion to Mr. *Dryden's* Reflection, that the Devil was in reality *Milton*'s Hero. I think I have obviated this Objection in my first Paper. The *Paradise Lost* is an Epic, or a Narrative Poem, and he that looks for an Hero in it, searches for that which *Milton* never intended; but if he will needs fix the Name of an Hero upon any Person in it, 'tis certainly the *Messiah* who is the Hero, both in the Principal Action, and in the chief Episodes. Paganism could not furnish out a real Action for a Fable greater than that of the *Iliad* or *Aeneid*, and therefore an Heathen could not form a higher Notion of a Poem than one of the Kind which they call an Heroic. Whether *Milton*'s is not of a sublimer Nature I will not presume to determine: It is sufficient, that I shew there is in the *Paradise Lost* all the Greatness of Plan, Regularity of Design, and masterly Beauties which we discover in *Homer* and *Virgil*.

I must in the next Place observe, that *Milton* has interwoven in the Texture of his Fable some Particulars which do not seem to have Probability enough for an Epic Poem, particularly in the Actions which he draws of the *Limbo of Vanity*, with other Passages in the second Book. Such Allegories rather savour of the Spirit of *Spenser* and *Ariosto*, than of *Homer* and *Virgil*.

In the Structure of his Poem he has likewise admitted of too many Digressions. It is finely observed by *Aristotle*, that the Author of an Heroic Poem should seldom speak himself, but throw as much of his Work as he can into the Mouths of those who are his principal Actors. *Aristotle* has given no Reason for his Precept; but I presume it is because the Mind of the Reader is more awed and elevated when he hears *Aeneas* or *Achilles* speak, than when *Virgil* or *Homer* talk in their own Persons. Besides that assuming the Character of an eminent Man is apt to fire the Imagination, and raise the Ideas of the Author. *Tully* tells us, mentioning his Dialogue of old Age, in which *Cato* is the chief Speaker, that upon a Review of it he was agreeably imposed upon, and fancied that it was *Cato*, and not he himself, who uttered his Thoughts on that Subject.

If the Reader would be at the Pains to see how the Story of the *Iliad* and *Aeneid* is delivered by those Persons who act in it, he will be surprised to find how little in either of these Poems proceeds from the Authors. *Milton* has, in the general Disposition of his Fable, very finely observed this great Rule; insomuch, that there is scarce a third Part of it which comes from the Poet; the rest is spoken either by *Adam* and *Eve*, or by some Good or Evil Spirit who is engaged either in their Destruction or Defence.

From what has been here observed, it appears that Digressions are by no Means to be allowed of in an Epic Poem. If the Poet, even in the ordinary Course of his Narration, should speak as little as possible, he should certainly never let his Narrative sleep for the sake of any Reflections of his own. I have often observed, with a secret Admiration, that the longest Reflection in the *Aeneid* is in that Passage of the Tenth Book, where *Turnus* is represented as dressing himself in the Spoils of *Pallas*, whom he had slain. *Virgil* here lets his Fable standstill for the Sake of the following Remark. *How is the Mind of Man ignorant of Futurity, and unable to bear prosperous Fortune with Moderation? The Time will come when* Turnus *shall wish that he had left the Body of* Pallas *untouched, and curse the Day in which he dressed himself in these Spoils.* As the great Event of the *Aeneid*, and the Death of *Turnus,* whom *Aeneas* slew, because he saw him adorned with the Spoils of *Pallas,* turns upon this Incident, *Virgil* went out of his Way to make this Reflection upon it, without which so small a Circumstance might possibly have slipped out of his Reader's Memory. *Lucan,* who was an Injudicious Poet, lets drop his Story very frequently for the Sake of his unnecessary Digressions, or his *Diverticula,* as *Scaliger* calls them. If he gives us an Account of the Prodigies which preceded the Civil War, he declaims upon the Occasion, and shews how much happier it would be for Man, if he did not feel his evil Fortune before it comes to pass, and suffer not only by its real Weight, but by the Apprehension of it. *Milton*'s Complaint for his Blindness, his Panegyrick on Marriage, his Reflections on *Adam* and *Eve*'s going naked, of the Angels eating, and several other Passages in his Poem, are liable to the same Exception, tho' I must confess there is so great a Beauty in these very Digressions that I would not wish them out of his Poem.

I have, in a former Paper, spoken of the *Characters* of *Milton*'s *Paradise Lost*, and declared my Opinion, as to the Allegorical Persons who are introduced in it.

If we look into the *Sentiments*, I think they are sometimes defective under the following Heads; First, as there are several of them too much pointed, and some that degenerate even into Punns. Of this last Kind, I am afraid is that in the First Book, where, speaking of the Pigmies, he calls them

> The small *Infantry*
> Warr'd on by Cranes . . . [I, 575–6]

Another Blemish that appears in some of his Thoughts, is his frequent Allusion to Heathen Fables, which are not certainly of a Piece with the Divine Subject, of which he treats. I do not find Fault with these Allusions, where the Poet himself represents them as fabulous, as he does in some Places, but where he mentions them as Truths and Matters of Fact. The Limits of my Paper will not give me Leave to be particular in Instances of this Kind: The Reader will easily remark them in his Perusal of the Poem.

A Third Fault in his Sentiments, is an unnecessary Ostentation of Learning, which likewise occurs very frequently. It is certain, that both *Homer* and *Virgil* were Masters of all the Learning of their Times, but it shews itself in their Works, after an indirect and concealed Manner. *Milton* seems ambitious of letting us know, by his Excursions on Free-Will and Predestination, and his many Glances upon History, Astronomy, Geography and the like, as well as by the Terms and Phrases he sometimes makes Use of, that he was acquainted with the whole Circle of Arts and Sciences.

If, in the last Place, we consider the *Language* of this great Poet, we must allow what I have hinted in a former Paper, that it is often too much laboured, and sometimes obscured by old Words, Transpositions, and Foreign Idioms. *Seneca*'s Objection to the Stile of a great Author, *Riget ejus oratio, nihil is placidum nihil lene*, is what many Criticks make to *Milton*: As I cannot wholly refute it, so I have already apologized for it in another Paper; to which I may further add, that *Milton*'s Sentiments and Ideas were so wonderfully sublime, that it would have been impossible for him to have represented them in their full Strength and Beauty, without having Recourse to these Foreign Assistances. Our Language sunk under him, and was unequal to that Greatness of Soul, which furnished him with such glorious Conceptions.

A second Fault in his Language is, that he often affects a Kind of Jingle in his Words, as in the following Passages, and many others:

> And brought into the *World* a *World of* Woe. [I, 3]
>
> Begirt th' Almighty Throne
> *Beseeching* or *besieging* . . .   [V, 868-9]
>
> This *tempted* our *Attempt* . . .   [I, 642]
>
> At one slight *Bound* high over-leapt all *Bound.* [IV, 181]

I know there are Figures for this Kind of Speech, that some of the greatest Antients have been guilty of it, and that *Aristotle* himself has given it a Place in his Rhetorick among the Beauties of that Art. But as it is in itself poor and trifling, it is I think at present universally exploded by all the Masters of polite Writing.

The last Fault which I shall take Notice of in *Milton's* Stile, is the frequent Use of what the Learned call *Technical Words*, or Terms of Art. It is one of the great Beauties of Poetry, to make hard Things intelligible, and to deliver what is abstruse of it self in such easy Language as may be understood by ordinary Readers: Besides, that the Knowledge of a Poet should rather seem born with him, or inspired, than drawn from Books and Systems. I have often wondered, how Mr. *Dryden* could translate a Passage out of *Virgil*, after the following Manner,

> Tack to the Larboard, and stand off to Sea,
> Veer Star-board Sea and Land.

Milton makes Use of *Larboard* in the same Manner. When he is upon Building, he mentions *Doric Pillars, Pilasters, Cornice, Freeze, Architrave.* When he talks of Heavenly Bodies, you meet with *Ecliptic,* and *Eccentric,* the *Trepidation, Stars dropping from the Zenith, Rays culminating from the Equator.* To which might be added many Instances of the like Kind in several other Arts and Sciences.

I shall in my next Papers give an Account of the many particular Beauties in *Milton*, which would have been too long to insert under those general Heads I have already treated of, and with which I intend to conclude this Piece of Criticism.

Spectator, No. 303

I have seen in the Works of a Modern Philosopher, a Map of the Spots in the Sun. My last Paper of the Spots in the Sun, My last Paper of the

Faults and Blemishes in *Milton's Paradise Lost*, may be considered as a Piece of the same Nature. To pursue the Allusion: As it is observed, that among the bright Parts of the luminous Body above-mentioned, there are some which glow more intensely, and dart a stronger Light than others; so, notwithstanding I have already shewn *Milton's* Poem to be very beautiful in general. I shall now proceed to take notice of such Beauties as appear to me more exquisite than the rest. *Milton* has proposed the Subject of his Poem in the following Verses. [I, 1–6]

These Lines are perhaps as plain, simple and unadorned as any of the whole Poem, in which Particular the Author has conform'd himself to the Example of *Homer*, and the Precept of *Horace*.

His Invocation to a Work which turns in a great Measure upon the Creation of the World, is very properly made to the Muse who inspired *Moses* in those Books from whence our Author drew his Subject, and to the Holy Spirit who is therein represented as operating after a particular Manner in the first Production of Nature. This whole Exordium rises very happily into noble Language and Sentiment, as I think the Transition to the Fable is exquisitely beautiful and natural.

The Nine-days Astonishment, in which the Angels lay entranced after their dreadful Overthrow and Fall from Heaven, before they could recover either the Use of Thought or Speech, is a noble *Circumstance*, and very finely imagined. The Division of Hell into Seas of Fire and into firm Ground impregnate with the same furious Element, with that particular Circumstance of the Exclusion of *Hope* from those Infernal Regions, are Instances of the same great and fruitful Invention.

The Thoughts in the first Speech and Description of *Satan*, who is one of the principal Actors, in this Poem, are wonderfully proper to give us a full Idea of him. His Pride, Envy and Revenge, Obstinacy, Despair and Impenitence, are all of them very artfully interwoven. In short, his first Speech is a Complication of all those Passions which discover themselves separately in several other of his Speeches in the Poem. The whole Part of this great Enemy of Mankind is filled with such Incidents as are very apt to raise and terrify the Reader's Imagination. Of this Nature, in the Book now before us, is his being the first that awakens out of the general Trance, with his Posture on the burning Lake, his rising from it, and the Description of his Shield and Spear. [192–6, 221–7, 284–6]

To which we may add his Call to the fallen Angels that lay plunged and stupified in the Sea of Fire. [314–5]

But there is no single Passage in the whole Poem worked up to a greater Sublimity, than that wherein his Person is described in those celebrated Lines:

> He, above the rest
> In shape and gesture proudly eminent
> Stood like a Tower, &c. [589–91]

His Sentiments are every way answerable to his Character, and suitable to a created Being of the most exalted and most depraved Nature. Such is that in which he takes possession of his Place of Torments. [250–3]

And afterwards, [258–63]

Amidst those Impieties which this Enraged Spirit utters in other Places of the Poem, the Author has taken care to introduce none that is not big with Absurdity, and incapable of shocking a Religious Reader; his Words, as the Poet himself describes them, bearing only a *Semblance of Worth, not Substance*. He is likewise with great Art described as owning his Adversary to be Almighty. Whatever perverse Interpretation he puts on the Justice, Mercy, and other Attributes of the Supreme Being, he frequently confesses his Omnipotence, that being the Perfection he was forced to allow him, and the only Consideration which could support his Pride under the Shame of his Defeat.

Nor must I here omit that beautiful Circumstance of his bursting out in Tears, upon his Survey of those innumerable Spirits whom he had involved in the same Guilt and Ruin with himself. [615–20]

The Catalogue of Evil Spirits has Abundance of Learning in it, and a very agreeable Turn of Poetry, which rises in a great measure from its describing the Places where they were worshipped, by those beautiful Marks of Rivers so frequent among the Antient Poets. The Author has doubtless in this place *Homer*'s Catalogue of Ships, and *Virgil*'s List of Warriors in his View. The Characters of *Moloch* and *Belial* prepare the Reader's Mind for their respective Speeches and Behaviour in the second and sixth Book. The Account of *Thammuz* is finely Romantick, and suitable to what we read among the Antients of the Worship which was paid to that Idol.

The Passage in the Catalogue, explaining the manner how Spirits transform themselves by Contraction, or Enlargement of their Dimensions, is introduced with great Judgment, to make way for several surprising Accidents in the Sequel of the Poem. There follows one, at the very End of the First Book, which is what the *French* Criticks call

Marvellous, but at the same Time *probable* by reason of the Passage last mentioned. As soon as the Infernal Palace is finished, we are told the Multitude and Rabble of Spirits immediately shrunk themselves into a small Compass, that there might be Room for such a numberless Assembly in this capacious Hall. But it is the Poet's Refinement upon this Thought, which I most admire, and which is indeed very noble in its self. For he tells us, that notwithstanding the vulgar, among the fallen Spirits, contracted their Forms, those of the first Rank and Dignity still preserved their natural Dimensions. [789-97]

The Character of *Mammon*, and the Description of the *Pandaemonium*, are full of Beauties.

There are several other Strokes in the First Book wonderfully poetical, and Instances of that Sublime Genius so peculiar to the Author. Such is the Description of *Azazel's* Stature, and the Infernal Standard, which he unfurls; as also of that ghastly Light, by which the Fiends appear to one another in their Place of Torments.

> The Seat of Desolation, void of Light,
> Save what the glimm'ring of those livid Flames
> Casts pale and dreadful . . . [181-3]

The Shout of the whole Host of fallen Angels when drawn up in Battel Aray;

> . . . The Universal Host up sent
> A Shout that tore Hell's Concave, and beyond
> Frighted the Reign of *Chaos* and old *Night*. [541-3]

The Review, which the Leader makes of his Infernal Army; [567-73]

The Flash of Light, which appeared upon the drawing of their Swords; [663-6] The sudden Production of the *Pandaemonium*; [710-2] The artificial Illuminations made in it; [726-730].

There are also several noble Similes and Allusions in the first Book of *Paradise Lost*. And here I must observe, that when *Milton* alludes either to Things or Persons, he never quits his Simile till it rises to some very great Idea, which is often foreign to the Occasion that gave Birth to it. The Resemblance does not, perhaps, last above a Line or two, but the Poet runs on with the Hint, till he has raised out of it some glorious Image or Sentiment, proper to inflame the Mind of the Reader, and to give it that sublime Kind of Entertainment, which is suitable to the Nature of an Heroick Poem. Those, who are acquainted with *Homer's* and *Virgil*'s Way of Writing, cannot but be pleased with this kind of Structure in *Milton*'s Similitudes. I am the more particular on his Head, because ignorant Readers, who have formed their Taste upon the quaint Similes and little Turns of Wit, which are so much in Vogue among modern Poets, cannot relish these Beauties which are of a much higher Nature, and are therefore apt to censure *Milton*'s Comparisons, in which they do not see any surprising Points of Likeness. Monsieur *Perrault* was a Man of this vitiated Relish, and for that very Reason has endeavoured to turn into Ridicule several of *Homer*'s Similitudes, which he calls *Comparaisons à longue queue, Long-tail'd Comparisons*. I shall conclude this Paper on the First Book of *Milton* with the Answer which Monsieur *Boileau* makes to *Perrault* on this Occasion; 'Comparisons,' says he, 'in Odes and Epic Poems are not introduced only to illustrate and embellish the Discourse, but to amuse and relax the Mind of the Reader, by frequently disengaging him from too painful an Attention to the principal Subject, and by leading him into other agreeable Images. '*Homer*,' says he, 'excelled in this Particular, whose Comparisons abound with such Images of Nature as are proper to relieve and diversifie his Subjects. He continually instructs the Reader, and makes him take notice, even in Objects which are every Day before our Eyes, of such Circumstances as we should not otherwise have observed.' *To this he adds, as a Maxim universally acknowledged,* 'That it is not necessary in Poetry for the Points of the Comparison to correspond with one another exactly, but that a general Resemblance is sufficient, and that too much Nicety in this Particular savours of the Rhetorician and Epigrammatist.'

In short, if we look into the Conduct of *Homer*, *Virgil* and *Milton*, as the great Fable is the Soul of each Poem, so to give their Works an agreeable Variety, their Episodes are so many short Fables, and their Similes so many short Episodes; to which you may add, if you please, that their Metaphors are so many short Similes. If the Reader considers the Comparisons in the first Book of *Milton*, of the Sun in an Eclipse, of the sleeping *Leviathan*, of the Bees swarming about their Hive, of the fairy Dance, in the View wherein I have here placed them, he will easily discover the great Beauties that are in each of those Passages.

Spectator, No. 309

I have before observed in general, that the Persons whom *Milton* introduces into his Poem always discover such Sentiments and Behaviour, as are in a peculiar Manner conformable to their respective Characters.

Every Circumstance in their Speeches and Actions, is with great Justness and Delicacy adapted to the Persons who speak and act. As the Poet very much excels in this Consistency of his Characters, I shall beg Leave to consider several Passages of the Second Book in this Light. That superior Greatness, and Mock-Majesty, which is ascribed to the Prince of the fallen Angels, is admirably preserved in the Beginning of this Book. His opening and closing the Debate; his taking on himself that great Enterprize at the Thought of which the whole internal Assembly trembled; his encountring the hideous Phantom who guarded the Gates of Hell, and appeared to him in all his Terrors, are Instances of that proud and daring Mind which could not brook Submission even to Omnipotence. [674-8]

The same Boldness and Intrepidity of Behaviour discovers it self in the several Adventures which he meets with during his Passage through the Regions of unformed Matter, and particularly in his Address to those tremendous Powers who are described as presiding over it.

The Part of *Moloch* is likewise in all its Circumstances full of that Fire and Fury which distinguish this Spirit from the rest of the fallen Angels. He is described in the first Book as besmeared with the Blood of humane Sacrifices, and delighted with the Tears of Parents and the Cries of Children. In the second Book he is marked out as the fiercest Spirit that fought in Heaven; and if we consider the Figure which he makes in the sixth Book, where the Battel of the Angels is described, we find it every Way answerable to the same furious enraged Character. [355-63]

It may be worth while to observe, that *Milton* has represented this violent impetuous Spirit, who is hurried on by such precipitate Passions, as the *first* that rises in the Assembly, to give his Opinion upon their present Posture of Affairs. Accordingly he declares himself abruptly for War, and appears incensed at his Companions, for losing so much Time as even to deliberate upon it. All his Sentiments are rash, audacious, and desperate. Such is that of arming themselves with their Tortures, and turning their Punishments upon him who inflicted them. [60-70]

His preferring Annihilation to Shame or Misery, is also highly suitable to his Character; as the Comfort he draws from their disturbing the Peace of Heaven, that if it be not Victory [it] is Revenge, is a Sentiment truly diabolical, and becoming the Bitterness of this implacable Spirit.

Belial is described, in the first Book, as the Idol of the lewd and luxurious. He is in the second Book, pursuant to that Description, characterised as timorous and slothful; and if we look in the sixth Book we find him celebrated in the Battel of Angels for Nothing but that Scoffing Speech which he makes to *Satan*, on their supposed Advantage over the Enemy. As his Appearance is uniform, and of a Piece, in these three several Views, we find his Sentiments in the infernal Assembly every Way conformable to his Character. Such are his Apprehensions of a second Battel, his Horrors of Annihilation, his preferring to be miserable rather than *not to be*. I need not observe, that the Contrast of Thought in this Speech, and that which precedes it, gives an agreeable Variety to the Debate.

Mammon's Character is so fully drawn in the first Book, that the Poet adds Nothing to it in the Second. We were before told, that he was the first who taught Mankind to ransack the Earth for Gold and Silver, and that he was the Architect of *Pandaemonium*, or the infernal Palace, where the evil Spirits were to meet in Council. His Speech in this Book is every where suitable to so depraved a Character. How proper is that Reflection, of their being unable to taste the Happiness of Heaven were they actually there, in the Mouth of one, who while he was in Heaven, is said to have had his Mind dazzled with the outward Pomps and Glories of the Place, and to have been more intent on the Riches of the Pavement, than on the beatifick Vision. I shall also leave the Reader to judge how agreeable the following Sentiments are to the same Character. [262-73]

Beelzebub, who is reckon'd the second in Dignity that fell, and is, in the first Book, the second that awakens out of the Trance, and confers with *Satan* upon the Situation of their Affairs, maintains his Rank in the Book now before us. There is a wonderful Majesty described in his rising up to speak. He acts as a Kind of Moderator between the two opposite Parties, and proposes a third Undertaking, which the whole Assembly gives into. The Motion he makes of detaching one of their Body in Search of a new World is grounded upon a Project devised by *Satan*, and cursorily proposed by him in the following Lines of the first book. [650-60]

It is on this Project that *Beelzebub* grounds his Proposal. [344-53]

The Reader may observe how just it was, not to omit in the first Book the Project upon which the whole Poem turns: As also that the Prince of the fall'n Angels was the only proper Person to give it Birth, and that the next to him in Dignity was the fittest to second and support it.

There is besides, I think, something wonderfully beautiful, and very apt to affect the Reader's Imagination, in this antient Prophecy or Report in Heaven, concerning the Creation of Man. Nothing could shew more the Dignity of the Species, than this Tradition which ran of them before their Existence. They are represented to have been the Talk of Heaven, before they were created. *Virgil* in compliment to the *Roman* Common-wealth, makes the Heroes of it appear in their State of Pre-existence; but *Milton* does a far greater Honour to Mankind in general, as he gives us a Glimpse of them even before they are in Being.

The rising of this great Assembly is described in a very sublime and poetical Manner.

> Their rising all at once was as the sound
> Of Thunder heard remote . . . [476-7]

The Diversions of the fallen Angels, with the particular Account of their Place of Habitation, are described with great Pregnancy of Thought, and Copiousness of Invention. The Diversions are every way suitable to Beings who had Nothing left them but Strength and Knowledge misapplied. Such are their Contentions at the Race, and in Feats of Arms, with their Entertainment in the following Lines.

> Others with vast *Typhaean* Rage more fell
> Rend up both Rocks and Hills and ride the Air
> In Whirlwind; Hell scarce holds the wild uproar. [539-41]

Their Musick is employed in celebrating their own criminal Exploits, and their Discourse in sounding the unfathomable Depths of Fate, Free-will, and Fore-Knowledge.

The several Circumstances in the Description of Hell are very finely imagined; as the four Rivers which disgorge themselves into the Sea of Fire, the Extreams of Cold and Heat, and the River of Oblivion. The monstrous Animals produced in that infernal World are represented by a single Line, which gives us a more horrid Idea of them, than a much longer Description would have done. [624-8]

This Episode of the fallen Spirits, and their Place of Habitation, comes in very happily to unbend the Mind of the Reader from its Attention to the Debate. An ordinary Poet would indeed have spun out so many Circumstances to a great Length, and by that Means have weakned, instead of illustrated, the principal Fable.

The Flight of *Satan* to the Gates of Hell is finely imaged.

I have already declared my Opinion of the Allegory concerning *Sin* and *Death*, which is however a very finished Piece in its Kind, when it is not considered as Part of an Epic Poem. The Genealogy of the several Persons is contrived with great Delicacy. *Sin* is the Daughter of *Satan*, and *Death* the Offspring of *Sin*. The incestuous Mixture between *Sin* and *Death* produces these Monsters and Hell-hounds which from Time to Time enter into their Mother, and tear the Bowels of her who gave them Birth. These are the Terrors of an evil Conscience, and the proper Fruits of *Sin*, which naturally rise from the Apprehensions of *Death*. This last beautiful Moral is, I think, clearly intimated in the Speech of *Sin*, where complaining of this her dreadful Issue, she adds,

> *Before mine Eyes in Opposition sits*
> *Grim Death thy Son and Foe, who sets them on.*
> And me his Parent would full soon devour
> For want of other Prey, but that he knows
> His End with mine involv'd . . . [803–7]

I need not mention to the Reader the beautiful Circumstance in the last Part of this Quotation. He will likewise observe how naturally the three Persons concerned in this Allegory are tempted by one common Interest to enter into a Confederacy together, and how properly Sin is made the Portress of Hell, and the only Being that can open the Gates to that World of Tortures.

The descriptive Part of this Allegory is likewise very strong, and full of sublime Ideas. The Figure of Death, the Regal Crown upon his Head, his Menace to Satan, his advancing to the Combat, the Outcry at his Birth, are Circumstances too noble to be past over in Silence, and extreamly suitable to this *King of Terrors*. I need not Mention the Justness of Thought which is observed in the Generation of these several Symbolical Persons, that Sin was produced upon the first Revolt of Satan, that Death appeared soon after he was cast into Hell, and that the Terrors of Conscience were conceived at the Gate of this Place of Torments. The Description of the Gates is very poetical, as the opening of them is full of *Milton*'s Spirit. [879–89]

In Satan's Voyage through the Chaos there are several imaginary Persons described, as residing in that immense Waste of Matter. This may perhaps be conformable to the Taste of those Criticks who are pleased with Nothing in a Poet which has not Life and Manners ascribed to it; but for my own Part, I am pleased most with those Passages in this Description which carry in them a greater Measure of

Probability, and are such as might possibly have happened. Of this Kind is his first Mounting in the Smoak, that rises from the infernal Pit, his falling into a Cloud of Nitre, and the like combustible Materials, that by their Explosion still hurried him forward in his Voyage; his springing upward like a Pyramid of Fire, with his laborious Passage through that Confusion of Elements, which the Poet calls

The Womb of Nature, and perhaps her Grave. [911]

The Glimmering Light which shot into the *Chaos* from the utmost Verge of the Creation, with the distant Discovery of the Earth that hung close by the Moon, are wonderfully Beautiful and Poetical.

Spectator, No. 315

Horace advises a Poet to consider thoroughly the Nature and Force of his Genius. *Milton* seems to have known, perfectly well, wherein his Strength lay, and has therefore chosen a Subject entirely conformable to those Talents, of which he was Master. As his Genius was wonderfully turned to the Sublime, his Subject is the noblest that could have entered into the Thoughts of Man. Every Thing that is truly great and astonishing, has a Place in it. The whole Systeme of the intellectual World; the *Chaos*, and the Creation; Heaven, Earth and Hell; enter into the Constitution of his Poem.

Having in the First and Second Book represented the Infernal World with all its Horrours, the Thread of his Fable naturally leads him into the opposite Regions of Bliss and Glory.

If *Milton*'s Majesty forsakes him any where, it is in those Parts of his Poem, where the Divine Persons are introduced as Speakers. One may, I think, observe that the Author proceeds with a Kind of Fear and Trembling, whilst he describes the Sentiments of the Almighty. He dares not give his Imagination its full Play, but chuses to confine himself to such Thoughts as are drawn from the Books of the most Orthodox Divines, and to such Expressions as may be met with in Scripture. The Beauties, therefore, which we are to look for in these Speeches, are not of a poetical Nature, or so proper to fill the Mind with Sentiments of Grandeur, as with Thoughts of Devotion. The Passions, which they are designed to raise, are a Divine Love and Religious Fear. The particular Beauty of the Speeches in the Third Book, consists in that Shortness and Perspicuity of Stile, in which the Poet has couched the greatest Mysteries of Christianity, and drawn together, in a regular

Scheme, the whole Dispensation of Providence, with respect to Man. He has represented all the abstruse Doctrines of Predestination, Free-Will and Grace, as also the great Points of Incarnation and Redemption (which naturally grow up in a Poem that treats of the Fall of Man), with great Energy of Expression, and in a clearer and stronger Light than I ever met with in any other Writer. As these Points are dry in themselves to the Generality of Readers, the concise and clear Manner in which he has treated them, is very much to be admired, as is likewise that particular Art which he has made Use of, in the interspersing of all those Graces of Poetry, which the Subject was capable of receiving.

The Survey of the whole Creation, and of every Thing that is transacted in it, is a Prospect worthy of Omniscience; and as much above that, in which *Virgil* had drawn his *Jupiter*, as the Christian Idea of the Supream Being is more Rational and Sublime than that of the Heathens. The particular Objects on which he is described to have cast his Eye, are represented in the most beautiful and lively Manner: [56–79].

Satan's Approach to the Confines of the Creation, is finely imaged in the Beginning of the Speech, which immediately follows. The Effects of this Speech in the blessed Spirits, and in the divine Person to whom it was addressed, cannot but fill the Mind of the Reader with a secret Complacency. [135–42]

I need not Point out the Beauty of that Circumstance, wherein the whole Host of Angels are represented as standing mute; nor shew how proper the Occasion was to produce such a Silence in Heaven. The Close of this Divine Colloquy, with the Hymn of Angels that follows upon it, are so wonderfully beautiful and poetical, that I should not forbear inserting the whole Passage, if the Bounds of my Paper would give me leave. [344–9]

Satan's Walk upon the Outside of the Universe, which, at a Distance, appeared to him of a globular Form, but, upon his nearer Approach, looked like an unbounded Plain, is natural and noble. As his Roaming upon the Frontiers of the Creation, between that Mass of Matter, which was wrought into a World, and that shapeless unformed Heap of Materials, which still lay in *Chaos* and Confusion, strikes the Imagination with something astonishingly great and wild. I have before spoken of the Limbo of Vanity, which the Poet places upon this outermost Surface of the Universe, and shall here explain my self more at large on that, and other Parts of the Poem, which are of the same shadowy Nature.

Aristotle observes, that the Fable of an Epic Poem should abound in Circumstances that are both credible and astonishing; or, as the *French* Criticks chuse to phrase it, the Fable should be filled with the Probable and the Marvellous. This Rule is as fine and just as any in *Aristotle*'s whole Art of Poetry.

If the Fable is only probable, it differs Nothing from a true History; if it is only marvellous, it is no better than a Romance. The great Secret therefore of Heroick Poetry, is to relate such Circumstances, as may produce in the Reader at the same Time both Belief and Astonishment. This is brought to pass in a *well chosen* Fable, by the Account of such Things as have really happened, or at least of such Things as have happened according to the received Opinions of Mankind. *Milton*'s Fable is a Master-piece of this Nature; as the War in Heaven, the Condition of the fallen Angels, the State of Innocence, the Temptation of the Serpent, and the Fall of Man, though they are very astonishing in themselves, are not only credible, but Actual Points of Faith.

The next Method of reconciling Miracles with Credibility, is by a happy Invention of the Poet; as in particular, when he introduces Agents of a superior Nature, who are capable of effecting what is wonderful, and what is not to be met with in the ordinary Course of Things. *Ulysses*'s Ship being turned into a Rock, and *Aeneas*'s Fleet into a Shoal of Water Nymphs, though they are very surprising Accidents, are nevertheless probable, when we are told that they were the Gods who thus transformed them. It is this Kind of Machinery which fills the Poems both of *Homer* and *Virgil* with such Circumstances as are wonderful, but not impossible, and so frequently produce in the Reader the most pleasing Passion that can rise in the Mind of Man, which is Admiration. If there be any Instance in the *Aeneid* liable to Exception upon this Account, it is in the Beginning of the Third Book, where *Aeneas* is represented as tearing up the Myrtle that dropped Blood. To qualifie this wonderful Circumstance, *Polydorus* tells a Story from the Root of the Myrtle, that the barbarous Inhabitants of the Country having pierced him with Spears and Arrows, the Wood which was left in his Body took Root in his Wounds, and gave Birth to that bleeding Tree. This Circumstance seems to have the Marvellous without the Probable, because it is represented as proceeding from natural Causes, without the Interposition of any God, or other supernatural Power capable of producing it. The Spears and Arrows grow of themselves, without so much as the modern Help of an Enchantment. If we look into the Fiction of *Milton*'s Fable, though we find it full of surprising

Incidents, they are generally suited to our Notions of the Things of Persons described, and tempered with a due Measure of Probability. I must only make an Exception to the Limbo of Vanity, with his Episode of Sin and Death, and some of the imaginary Persons in his *Chaos*. These Passages are astonishing, but not credible; the Reader cannot so far impose upon himself as to see a Possibility in them; they are the Description of Dreams and Shadows, not of Things or Persons. I know that many Criticks look upon the Stories of *Circe, Polypheme*, the *Sirens*, nay the whole *Odissey* and *Illiad* to be Allegories; but allowing this to be true, they are Fables, which considering the Opinions of Mankind that prevailed in the Age of the Poet, might possibly have been according to the Letter. The Persons are such as might have acted what is ascribed to them, as the Circumstances, in which they are represented, might possibly have been Truths and Realities. This Appearance of Probability is so absolutely requisite in the greater Kinds of Poetry, that *Aristotle* observes the ancient tragick Writers made Use of the Names of such great Men as had actually lived in the World, tho' the Tragedy proceeded upon Adventures they were never engaged in, on Purpose to make the Subject more credible. In a Word, besides the hidden Meaning of an Epic Allegory, the plain literal Sense ought to appear probable. The Story should be such as an ordinary Reader may acquiesce in, whatever natural, moral, or political Truth may be discovered in it by Men of greater Penetration.

Satan after having long wandred upon the Surface, or outmost Wall of the Universe, discovers at last a wide Gap in it, which led into the Creation, and is described as the Opening through which the Angels pass to and fro into the lower World, upon their Errands to Mankind. His Sitting upon the Brink of this Passage, and taking a Survey of the whole Face of Nature, that appeared to him new and fresh in all its Beauties, with the Simile illustrating this Circumstance, fills the Mind of the Reader with as surprising and glorious an Idea as any that arises in the whole Poem. He looks down into that vast Hollow of the Universe with the Eye, or (as *Milton* calls it in his first Book) with the Kenn of an Angel. He surveys all the Wonders in this immense Amphitheatre that lye between both the Poles of Heaven, and takes in at one View the whole Round of the Creation.

His Flight between the several Worlds that shined on every Side of him, with the particular Description of the Sun, are set forth in all the Wantonness of a luxuriant Imagination. His Shape, Speech and Behaviour upon his transforming himself into an Angel of Light, are touched with exquisite Beauty. The Poet's Thought of directing *Satan* to the Sun, which in the Vulgar Opinion of Mankind is the most conspicuous Part of the Creation, and the placing in it an Angel, is a Circumstance very finely contrived, and the more adjusted to a poetical Probability, as it was a received Doctrine among the most famous Philosophers, that every Orb had its *Intelligence*; and as an Apostle in sacred Writ is said to have seen such an Angel in the Sun. In the Answer which this Angel returns to the disguised Evil Spirit, there is such a becoming Majesty as is altogether suitable to a superior Being. The Part of it in which he represents himself as present at the Creation, is very noble in it self, and not only proper where it is introduced, but requisite to prepare the Reader for what follows in the Seventh Book. [708–13]

In the following Part of the Speech he points out the Earth with such Circumstances, that the Reader can scarce forbear fancying himself employed on the same distant View of it. [722–5]

I must not conclude my Reflections upon this third Book of *Paradise Lost*, without taking Notice of that celebrated Complaint of *Milton* with which it opens, and which certainly deserves all the Praises that have been given it; tho' as I have before hinted, it may rather be looked upon as an Excrescence, than as an essential Part of the Poem. The same Observation might be applied to that beautiful Digression upon Hypocrisie, in the same Book.

Spectator, No. 321

Those, who know how many Volumes have been written on the Poems of *Homer* and *Virgil*, will easily pardon the Length of my Discourse upon *Milton*. The *Paradise Lost* is looked upon, by the best Judges, as the greatest Production, or at least the noblest Work of Genius, in our Language, and therefore deserves to be set before an *English* Reader in its full Beauty. For this Reason, tho' I have endeavoured to give a general Idea of its Graces and Imperfections in my six first Papers, I thought my self obliged to bestow one upon every Book in particular. The Three first Books I have already dispatched, and am now entring upon the Fourth. I need not acquaint my Reader, that there are Multitudes of Beauties in this great Author, especially in the descriptive Parts of this Poem, which I have not touched upon; it being my Intention to point out those only, which appear to me the most exquisite, or those which are not so obvious to ordinary Readers. Every one that has read the Criticks, who have written upon the *Odissy*, the *Illiad* and the *Aeneid*, knows very well, that though they agree in their Opinions of the great Beauties in those Poems, they have nevertheless each of them discovered several Master-Strokes, which have escaped the Observation of the rest. In the same Manner, I question not, but any Writer, who shall treat of this Subject after me, may find several Beauties in *Milton*, which I have not taken notice of. I must likewise observe, that as the greatest Masters of critical Learning differ among one another, as to some particular Points in an Epic Poem, I have not bound my self scrupulously to the Rules which any one of them has laid down upon that Art, but have taken the Liberty sometimes to join with one, and sometimes with another, and sometimes to differ from all of them, when I have thought that the Reason of the Thing was on my side.

We may consider the Beauties of the Fourth Book under three Heads. In the first are those Pictures of Still-Life, which we meet with in the Description of *Eden, Paradise, Adam*'s Bower, &c. In the next are the Machines, which comprehend the Speeches and Behaviour of the good and bad Angels. In the last is the Conduct of *Adam* and *Eve*, who are the principal Actors in the Poem.

In the Description of *Paradise*, the Poet has observed *Aristotle*'s Rule of lavishing all the Ornaments of Diction on the weak unactive Parts of the Fable, which are not supported by the Beauty of Sentiments and Characters. Accordingly the Reader may observe, that the Expressions are more florid and elaborate in these Descriptions, than in most other Parts of the Poem. I must further add, that tho' the *Drawings* of Gardens, Rivers, Rainbows, and the like dead Pieces of Nature, are justly censured in an heroic Poem, when they run out into an unnecessary Length; the Description of *Paradise* would have been faulty, had not the Poet been very particular in it, not only as it is the Scene of the principal Action, but as it is requisite to give us an Idea of that Happiness from which our first Parents fell. The Plan of it is wonderfully beautiful, and formed upon the short Sketch which we have of it, in Holy Writ. *Milton*'s Exuberance of Imagination, has poured forth such a Redundancy of Ornaments on this Seat of Happiness and Innocence, that it would be endless to point out each Particular.

I must not quit this Head, without further observing, that there is scarce a Speech of *Adam* or *Eve* in the whole Poem, wherein the Sentiments and Allusions are not taken from this their delightful Habitation. The Reader, during their whole Course of Action, always finds himself in the Walks of *Paradise*. In short, as the Criticks have remarked, that in those Poems, wherein Shepherds are Actors, the Thoughts ought always to take a Tincture from the Woods, Fields and Rivers; so we may observe, that our first Parents seldom lose Sight of their happy Station in any Thing they speak or do; and, if the Reader will give me Leave to use the Expression, that their Thoughts are always *paradisiacal*.

We are in the next Place to consider the Machines of the Fourth Book. *Satan* being now within Prospect of *Eden*, and looking round upon the Glories of the Creation, is filled with Sentiments different from those which he discovered whilst he was in Hell. The Place inspires him with Thoughts more adapted to it: He reflects upon the happy Condition from whence he fell, and breaks forth into a Speech that is softned with several transient Touches of Remorse and Self-Accusation: But at length, he confirms himself in Impenitence, and in his Design of drawing Man into his own State of Guilt and Misery. This Conflict of Passions is raised with a great deal of Art, as the Opening of his Speech to the Sun is very bold and noble. [32–9]

This Speech is, I think, the finest that is ascribed to *Satan* in the whole Poem. The Evil Spirit afterwards proceeds to make his Discoveries concerning our first Parents, and to learn after what Manner they may be best attacked. His bounding over the Walls of *Paradise*; his sitting in the Shape of a Cormorant upon the Tree of Life, which stood in the Center of it, and over-topped all the other Trees of the Garden; his alighting among the Herd of Animals, which are so beautifully represented as playing about *Adam* and *Eve*, together with his transforming himself into different Shapes, in order to hear their Conversation, are Circumstances that give an agreeable Surprise to the Reader, and are devised with great Art, to connect that Series of Adventures in which the Poet has engaged this Artificer of Fraud.

The Thought of *Satan*'s Transformation into a Cormorant, and placing himself on the Tree of Life, seems raised upon that Passage in the *Iliad*, where two Deities are described, as perching on the Top of an Oak in the Shape of Vulturs.

His planting himself at the Ear of *Eve* under the Form of a Toad, in order to produce vain Dreams and Imaginations, is a Circumstance of the same Nature; as his starting up in his own Form is wonderfully fine, both in the Literal Description, and in the Moral which is concealed under it. His Answer upon his being discovered, and demanded to give an Account of himself, is conformable to the Pride and intrepidity of his Character. [827–31]

Zephon's Rebuke, with the Influence it had on *Satan*, is exquisitely graceful and moral. *Satan* is afterwards led away to *Gabriel*, the chief of the guardian Angels, who kept Watch in *Paradise*. His disdainful Behaviour on this Occasion is so remarkable a Beauty, that the most ordinary Reader cannot but take Notice of it. *Gabriel*'s discovering his Approach at a Distance, is drawn with great Strength and Liveliness of Imagination. [866–73]

The Conference between *Gabriel* and *Satan* abounds with Sentiments proper for the Occasion, and suitable to the Persons of the two Speakers. *Satan*'s cloathing himself with Terror, when he prepares for the Combat, is truly sublime, and at least equal to *Homer*'s Description of Discord celebrated by *Longinus*, or to that Fame in *Virgil*, who are both represented with their Feet standing upon the Earth, and their Heads reaching above the Clouds. [977–80, 985–9]

I must here take notice, that *Milton* is every where full of Hints, and sometimes literal Translations, taken from the greatest of the *Greek* and *Latin* Poets. But this I may reserve for a Discourse by it self, because I would not break the Thread of these Speculations, that are designed for *English* Readers, with such Reflections as would be of no Use but to the Learned.

I must however observe in this Place, that the breaking off the Combat between *Gabriel* and *Satan*, by the hanging out of the golden Scales in Heaven, is a Refinement upon *Homer*'s Thought, who tells us, that before the Battle between *Hector* and *Achilles*, *Jupiter* weighed the Event of it in a Pair of Scales. The Reader may see the whole Passage in the 22d *Iliad*.

Virgil, before the last decisive Combat, describes *Jupiter* in the same Manner, as weighing the Fates of *Turnus* and *Aeneas*. *Milton*, though he fetched this beautiful Circumstance from the *Iliad* and *Aeneid*, does not only insert it as a poetical Embellishment, like the Authors abovementioned; but makes an artful Use of it for the proper carrying on of his Fable, and for the breaking off the Combat between the two Warriors, who were upon the point of engaging. To this we may further add, that *Milton* is the more justified in this Passage, as we find the same noble Allegory in Holy Writ, where a wicked Prince is said to have been *weigh'd in the Scales, and to have been found wanting*.

I must here take Notice under the Head of the Machines, that *Uriel*'s gliding down to the Earth upon a Sunbeam, with the Poet's Device to make him *descend*, as well in his Return to the Sun, as in his coming from it, is a Prettiness that might have been admired in a little fanciful Poet, but seems below the Genius of *Milton*. The Description of the Host of armed Angels walking their nightly Round in *Paradise*, is of another Spirit;

> So saying, on he led his radiant files,
> Dazling the Moon; [797-8]

as that Account of the Hymns which our first Parents used to hear them sing in these their Midnight-Walks, is altogether Divine, and inexpressibly amusing to the Imagination.

We are, in the last place, to consider the Parts which *Adam* and *Eve* act in the fourth Book. The Description of them as they first appeared to *Satan*, is exquisitely drawn, and sufficient to make the fallen Angel gaze upon them with all that Astonishment, and those Emotions of Envy, in which he is represented. [288-322]

There is a fine Spirit of Poetry in the Lines which follow, wherein they are described as sitting on a Bed of Flowers by the Side of a Fountain, amidst a mixed Assembly of Animals.

The Speeches of these two first Lovers flow equally from Passion and Sincerity. The Professions they make to one another are full of Warmth; but at the same Time founded on Truth. In a Word, they are the Gallantries of *Paradise*. [408, 411-2, 436-48]

The remaining Part of *Eve*'s Speech, in which she gives an Account of her self upon her first Creation, and the Manner in which she was brought to *Adam*, is I think as beautiful a Passage as any in *Milton*, or perhaps in any other Poet whatsoever. These Passages are all worked off with so much Art, that they are capable of pleasing the most delicate Reader, without offending the most severe.

> That Day I oft remember, when from Sleep, &c. [449]

A Poet of less Judgment and Invention than this great Author, would have found it very difficult to have filled these tender Parts of the Poem with Sentiments proper for a State of Innocence; to have described the Warmth of Love, and the Professions of it, without Artifice or Hyperbole; to have made the Man speak the most endearing Things, without descending from his natural Dignity, and the Woman receiving them without Departing from the Modesty of her Character; in a Word, to adjust the Prerogatives of Wisdom and Beauty, and make each appear to the other in its proper Force and Loveliness. This mutual Subordination of the two Sexes is wonderfully kept up in the whole Poem, as particularly in the Speech of *Eve* I have beforementioned, and upon the Conclusion of it in the following Lines; [492-9]

The Poet adds, that the Devil turned away with Envy at the Sight of so much Happiness.

We have another View of our first Parents in their evening Discourses, which is full of pleasing Images, and Sentiments suitable to their Condition and Characters. The Speech of *Eve*, in particular, is dressed up in such a soft and natural Turn of Words and Sentiments, as cannot be sufficiently admired.

I shall close my Reflections upon this Book, with observing the Masterly Transition which the Poet makes to their Evening Worship, in the following Lines. [720-5]

Most of the modern heroick Poets have imitated the Ancients, in beginning a Speech without premising, that the Person said thus or thus; but as it is easie to imitate the Ancients in the Omission of two or three Words, it requires Judgment to do it in such a Manner as they shall not be missed, and that the Speech may begin naturally without them. There is a fine Instance of this Kind out of *Homer*, in the Twenty Third Chapter of *Longinus*.

Spectator, No. 327

We were told in the foregoing Book how the Evil Spirit practised upon *Eve* as she lay asleep, in order to inspire her with Thoughts of Vanity, Pride and Ambition. The Author, who shews a wonderful Art throughout his whole Poem, in preparing the Reader for the several Occurrences that arise in it, founds, upon the above-mention'd Circumstance, the First Part of the Fifth Book. *Adam* upon his Awaking finds *Eve* still asleep, with an unusual Discomposure in her Looks. The Posture in which he regards her, is described with a Tenderness not to be express'd, as the Whisper with which he awakens her is the softest that ever was conveyed to a Lover's Ear. [9-30]

I cannot but take Notice that *Milton*, in the Conferences between *Adam* and *Eve*, had his Eye very frequently upon the Book of *Canticles*, in which there is a noble Spirit of Eastern Poetry, and very often not unlike what we meet with in *Homer*, who is generally placed near the Age of *Solomon*. I think there is no Question but the Poet in the preceding Speech remember'd those two Passages which are spoken on the like Occasion, and fill'd with the same pleasing Images of Nature. [Song of Songs ii. 10-3, vii, 11-2]

His preferring the Garden of *Eden* to that

> . . . Where the *Sapient* King
> Held Dalliance with his fair *Egyptian* Spouse, [IX, 442–3]

shews that the Poet had this delightful Scene in his Mind.

Eve's Dream is full of those *high Conceits engendring Pride*, which, we are told, the Devil endeavoured to instil into her. Of this Kind is that Part of it where she fancies herself awaken'd by *Adam* in the following beautiful Lines. [38–47]

An injudicious Poet would have made *Adam* talk thro' the whole Work, in such Sentiments as these. But Flattery and Falshood are not the Courtship of *Milton*'s *Adam*, and could not be heard by *Eve* in her State of Innocence, excepting only in a Dream produc'd on purpose to taint her Imagination. Other vain Sentiments of the same Kind in this Relation of her Dream, will be obvious to every Reader. Tho' the catastrophe of the Poem is finely presaged on this Occasion, the Particulars of it are so artfully shadow'd, that they do not anticipate the Story which follows in the Ninth Book. I shall only add, that tho' the Vision it self is founded upon Truth, the Circumstances of it are full of that Wildness and Inconsistency which are natural to a Dream. *Adam*, conformable to his superior Character for Wisdom, instructs and comforts *Eve* upon this Occasion. [129–35]

The Morning Hymn is written in Imitation of one of those Psalms, where, in the Overflowings of Gratitude and Praise, the Psalmist calls not only upon the Angels, but upon the most conspicuous Parts of the inanimate Creation, to joyn with him in extolling their Common Maker. Invocations of this Nature fill the Mind with glorious Ideas of God's Works, and awaken that divine Enthusiasm, which is so natural to Devotion. But if this Calling upon the dead Parts of Nature, is at all Times a proper Kind of Worship, it was in a particular Manner suitable to our first Parents, who had the Creation fresh upon their Minds, and had not seen the various Dispensations of Providence, nor consequently could be acquainted with those many Topicks of Praise which might afford Matter to the Devotions of their Posterity. I need not remark the beautiful Spirit of Poetry, which runs through this whole Hymn, nor the Holiness of that Resolution with which it concludes.

Having already mentioned those Speeches which are assigned to the Persons in this Poem, I proceed to the Description which the Poet gives of *Raphael*. His Departure from before the Throne, and his Flight thro' the Choirs of Angels, is finely imaged. As *Milton* every where fills his Poem with Circumstances that are marvellous and astonishing, he des-

cribes the Gate of Heaven as framed after such a Manner, that it open'd
of it self upon the Approach of the Angel who was to pass through it.
[253–6]

The Poet here seems to have regarded two or three Passages in the
18th *Iliad*, as that in particular, where, speaking of *Vulcan*, *Homer* says,
that he had made twenty *Tripodes* running on Golden Wheels, which,
upon Occasion, might go of themselves to the Assembly of the Gods,
and, when there was no more Use for them, return again after the
same Manner. *Scaliger* has rallied *Homer* very severely upon this Point,
as M. *Dacier* has endeavoured to defend it. I will not pretend to determine, whether in this Particular of *Homer*, the Marvellous does not lose
Sight of the Probable. As the miraculous Workmanship of *Milton*'s
Gates is not so extraordinary as this of the *Tripodes*, so I am Perswaded
he would not have mentioned it, had not he been supported in it by
a Passage in the Scripture, which speaks of Wheels in Heaven that had
Life in them, and moved of themselves, or stood still, in Conformity
with the Cherubims, whom they accompanied.

There is no Question but *Milton* had this Circumstance in his
Thoughts, because in the following Book he describes the Chariot of
the *Messiah* with *living* Wheels, according to the Plan in *Ezekiel*'s
Vision. [VI, 749–52]

I question not but *Bossu*, and the two *Daciers*, who are for vindicating
every Thing that is censured in *Homer*, by something parallel in Holy
Writ, would have been very well pleased had they thought of con-
fronting *Vulcan*'s *Tripodes* with *Ezekiel*'s Wheels.

Raphael's Descent to the Earth, with the Figure of his Person, is
represented in very lively Colours. Several of the *French*, *Italian*, and
English Poets have given a Loose to their Imaginations in the Description of Angels: But I do not remember to have met with any so finely
drawn, and so conformable to the Notions which are given of them in
Scripture, as this in *Milton*. After having set him forth in all his heavenly
Plumage, and represented him as alighting upon the Earth, the Poet
concludes his Description with a Circumstance, which is altogether
new, and imagined with the greatest Strength of Fancy. [285–7]

Raphael's Reception by the Guardian Angels; his passing through the
Wilderness of Sweets; his distant Appearance to *Adam*, have all the
Graces that Poetry is capable of bestowing. The Author afterwards
gives us a particular Description of *Eve* in her Domestick Employ-
ments. [331–7]

Though in this, and other Parts of the same Book, the Subject is only the Housewifry of our First Parent, it is set off with so many pleasing Images and strong Expressions, as make it none of the least agreeable Parts in this Divine Work.

The natural Majesty of *Adam*, and at the same Time his submissive Behaviour to the superior Being, who had vouchsafed to be his Guest; the solemn Hail which the Angel bestows upon the Mother of Mankind, with the Figure of *Eve* ministring at the Table, are Circumstances which deserve to be admired.

Raphael's Behaviour is every Way suitable to the Dignity of his Nature, and to that Character of a sociable Spirit, with which the Author has so judiciously introduced him. He had received Instructions to converse with *Adam*, as one Friend converses with another, and to warn him of the Enemy, who was contriving his Destruction: Accordingly he is represented as sitting down at Table with *Adam*, and eating of the Fruits of *Paradise*. The Occasion naturally leads him to his Discourse on the Food of Angels. After having thus entered into Conversation with Man upon more indifferent Subjects, he warns him of his Obedience, and makes a natural Transition to the History of that fallen Angel, who was employed in the Circumvention of our first Parents.

Had I followed Monsieur *Bossu*'s Method, in my first Paper on *Milton*, I should have dated the Action of *Paradise List* from the Beginning of *Raphael*'s Speech in this Book, as he supposes the Action of the *Aeneid* rather from its immediate Beginning in the first Book, than from its remote Beginning in the second, and shew why I have considered the sacking of *Troy* as an *Episode*, according to the common Acceptation of that Word. But as this would be a dry unentertaining Piece of Criticism, and perhaps unnecessary to those who have read my first Paper, I shall not enlarge upon it. Whichever of the Notions be true, the Unity of *Milton*'s Action is preserved according to either of them; whether we consider the Fall of Man in its immediate Beginning, or proceeding from the Resolutions taken in the infernal Council, or in its more remote Beginning, or proceeding from the first Revolt of the Angels in Heaven. The Occasion which *Milton* assigns for this Revolt, as it is founded on Hints in Holy Writ, and on the Opinion of some great Writers, so it was the most proper that the Poet could have made use of.

The Revolt in Heaven is described with great Force of Imagination and a fine Variety of Circumstances. The learned Reader cannot but be pleased with the Poet's Imitation of *Homer* in the last of the following Lines. [755–62]

Homer mentions Persons and Things, which he tells us in the Language of the Gods are call'd by different Names from those they go by in the Language of Men. *Milton* has imitated him with his usual Judgment in this particular Place, wherein he has likewise the Authority of Scripture to justify him. The Part of *Abdiel*, who was the only Spirit that in this infinite Host of Angels preserved his Allegiance to his Maker, exhibits to us a noble Moral of religious Singularity. The Zeal of the Seraphim breaks forth in a becoming Warmth of Sentiments and Expressions, as the Character which is given us of him denotes that generous Scorn and Intrepidity which attends heroick Virtue. The Author doubtless designed it as a Pattern to those who live among Mankind in their present State of Degeneracy and Corruption. [896–907]

Spectator, No. 333

We are now entering upon the Sixth Book of *Paradise Lost*, in which the Poet describes the Battel of Angels; having raised his Reader's Expectation, and prepar'd him for it by several Passages in the preceding Books. I omitted quoting these Passages in my Observations on the former Books, having purposely reserved them for the Opening of this, the Subject of which gave Occasion to them. The Author's Imagination was so inflamed with this great Scene of Action, that wherever he speaks of it, he rises, if possible, above himself. Thus where he mentions Satan in the Beginning of his Poem. [I, 44–9]

We have likewise several noble Hints of it in the Infernal Conference. [I, 128–37, 169–77]

There are several other very sublime Images on the same Subject in the First Book, as also in the Second. [II, 165–8]

In short, the Poet never mentions any thing of this Battel but in such Images of Greatness and Terrour as are suitable to the Subject. Among several others, I cannot forbear quoting that Passage where the Power, who is describ'd as presiding over the Chaos, speaks in the Third Book. [II, 988–98]

It required great Pregnancy of Invention, and Strength of Imagination, to fill this Battel with such Circumstances as should raise and astonish the Mind of the Reader; and, at the same time, an Exactness of Judgment to avoid every thing that might appear light or trivial. Those who look into *Homer*, are surpriz'd to find his Battels still rising one above another, and improving in Horrour, to the Conclusion of the *Iliad*. *Milton's* Fight of Angels is wrought up with the same Beauty. It is usher'd in with such Signs of Wrath as are suitable to Omnipotence incensed. The first Engagement is carried on under a Cope of Fire, occasion'd by the Flights of innumerable burning Darts and Arrows which are discharged from either Host. The second Onset is still more terrible, as it is filled with those artificial Thunders, which seem to make the Victory doubtful, and produce a kind of Consternation even in the good Angels. This is follow'd by the tearing up of Mountains and Promontories; till, in the last Place, the Messiah comes forth in the Fulness of Majesty and Terrour. The Pomp of his Appearance, amidst the Roarings of his Thunders, the Flashes of his Lightnings, and the Noise of his Chariot-Wheels, is described with the utmost Flights of Humane Imagination.

There is nothing in the first and last Day's Engagement which does not appear natural, and agreeable enough to the ideas most Readers would conceive of a Fight between two Armies of Angels.

The second Day's Engagement is apt to startle an Imagination, which has not been raised and qualified for such a Description, by the Reading of the ancient Poets, and of *Homer* in particular. It was certainly a very bold Thought in our Author, to ascribe the first Use of Artillery to the Rebel Angels. But as such a pernicious Invention may be well supposed to have proceeded from such Authors, so it entered very properly into the Thoughts of that Being, who is all along described as aspiring to the Majesty of his Maker. Such Engines were the only Instruments he could have made use of to imitate those Thunders, that in all Poetry, both Sacred and Prophane, are represented as the Arms of the Almighty. The Tearing up the Hills was not altogether so daring a Thought as the former. We are, in some measure, prepared for such an Incident by the Description of the Gyants' War which we meet with among the ancient Poets. What still made this Circumstance the more proper for the Poet's Use, is the Opinion of many Learned Men, that the Fable of the Gyants' War, which makes so great a Noise in Antiquity, and gave Birth to the sublimest Description in *Hesiod*'s Works, was an Allegory founded upon this very Tradition of a Fight between the good and bad Angels.

It may, perhaps, be worth while to consider with what Judgment *Milton*, in this Narration, has avoided every Thing that is mean and trivial in the Descriptions of the *Latin* and *Greek* Poets; and, at the same time, improv'd every great Hint which he met with in their Works upon this Subject. *Homer* in that Passage, which *Longinus* has celebrated for its Sublimeness, and which *Virgil* and *Ovid* have copied after him, tells us, that the Gyants threw *Ossa* upon *Olympus*, and *Pelion* upon

Ossa. He adds an Epithet to *Pelion* . . . which very much swells the Idea, by bringing up to the Reader's Imagination all the Woods that grew upon it. There is further a great Beauty in his singling out by Name these three remarkable Mountains, so well known to the *Greeks*. This last is such a Beauty as the Scene of *Milton*'s War could not possibly furnish him with. *Claudian*, in his Fragment upon the Gyants' War, has given full Scope to that Wildness of Imagination which was natural to him. He tells us, that the Gyants tore up whole Islands by the Roots and threw them at the Gods. He describes one of them in particular, taking up *Lemnos* in his Arms, and whirling it to the Skies, with all *Vulcan*'s Shop in the midst of it. Another tears up Mount *Ida*, with the River *Vulcan*'s Shop in the midst of it. Another tears up Mount *Ida*, with the River *Enipeus*, which ran down the Sides of it; but the Poet, not content to describe him with this Mountain upon his Shoulders, tells us that the River flow'd down his Back, as he held it up in that Posture. It is visible to every judicious Reader, that such Ideas savour more of Burlesque than of the Sublime. They proceed from a Wantonness of Imagination, and rather divert the Mind than astonish it. *Milton* has taken every thing that is Sublime in these several Passages, and composes out of them the following great Image. [643–6]

We have the full Majesty of *Homer* in this short Description, improved by the Imagination of *Claudian*, without its Puerilities.

I need not point out the Description of the fallen Angels seeing the Promontories hanging over their Heads in such a dreadful Manner, with the other numberless Beauties in this Book, which are so conspicuous, that they cannot escape the Notice of the most ordinary Reader.

There are indeed so many wonderful Stroaks of Poetry in this Book, and such a Variety of sublimes Ideas, that it would have been impossible to have given them a Place within the Bounds of this Paper. Besides that, I find it in a great measure done to my Hand at the End of my Lord *Roscommon*'s Essay on translated Poetry. I shall refer my Reader thither for some of the Master-Stroaks in the Sixth Book of *Paradise Lost*, though at the same time there are many others which that noble Author has not taken notice of.

Milton, notwithstanding the sublime Genius he was Master of, has in this Book drawn to his Assistance all the Helps he could meet with among the ancient Poets. The Sword of *Michael*, which makes so great a Havock among the bad Angels, was given him, we are told, out of the Armory of God. [320–5]

This Passage is a Copy of that in *Virgil*, wherein the Poet tells us, that the Sword of *Aeneas*, which was given him by a Deity, broke into Pieces the Sword of *Turnus*, which came from a mortal Forge. As the Moral in this Place is Divine, so by the way we may observe, that the bestowing on a Man who is favour'd by Heaven such an Allegorical Weapon, is very conformable to the old Eastern Way of Thinking. Not only *Homer* has made use of it, but we find the *Jewish* Hero in the Book of *Maccabees*, who had fought the Battels of the chosen People with so much Glory and Success, receiving in his Dream a Sword from the Hand of the Prophet *Jeremiah*. The following Passage, wherein Satan is described as wounded by the Sword of *Michael*, is in Imitation of *Homer*. [329–34]

Homer tells us in the same manner, that upon *Diomedes* wounding the Gods, there flow'd from the Wound an *Ichor*, or pure kind of Blood, which was not bred from mortal Viands; and that tho' the Pain was exquisitely great, the Wound soon closed up and healed in those Beings who are vested with Immortality.

I question not but *Milton* in his Description of his furious *Moloch* flying from the Battel, and bellowing with the Wound he had received, had his Eye on *Mars* in the *Iliad*, who, upon his being wounded, is represented as retiring out of the Fight, and making an Outcry louder than that of a whole Army when it begins the Charge. *Homer* adds, that the *Greeks* and *Trojans* who were engaged in a general Battel, were terrified on each Side with the bellowing of this wounded Deity. The Reader will easily observe how *Milton* has kept all the Horrour of this Image without running into the Ridicule of it. [355–62]

Milton has likewise raised his Description in this Book with many Images taken out of the Poetical Parts of Scripture. The Messiah's Chariot, as I have before taken Notice, is form'd upon a Vision of *Ezekiel*, who, as *Grotius* observes, has very much in him of *Homer*'s Spirit in the Poetical Parts of his Prophecy.

The following Lines in that glorious Commission which is given the Messiah to extirpate the Host of Rebel Angels, is drawn from a sublime Passage in the Psalms. [710–4]

The Reader will easily discover many other Stroaks of the same Nature.

There is no question but *Milton* has heated his Imagination with the Fight of the Gods in *Homer*, before he entered upon this Engagement of the Angels. *Homer* there gives us a Scene of Men, Heroes, and Gods mixed together in Battel. *Mars* animates the contending Armies, and lifts up his Voice in such a manner, that it is heard distinctly amidst all the Shouts and Confusion of the Fight. *Jupiter* at the same time thunders over their Heads; while *Neptune* raises such a Tempest that the whole Field of Battel and all the Tops of the Mountains, shake about them. The Poet tells us, that *Pluto* himself, whose Habitation was in the very Center of the Earth, was so affrighted at the Shock, that he leapt from his Throne. *Homer* afterwards describes *Vulcan* as pouring down a Storm of Fire upon the River *Xanthus*, and *Minerva* as throwing a Rock at *Mars*; who, he tells us, covered seven Acres in his Fall.

As *Homer* has introduced into his Battel of the Gods every thing that is great and terrible in Nature, *Milton* has filled his Fight of Good and Bad Angels with all the like Circumstances of Horrour. The Shout of Armies, the Rattling of Brazen Chariots, the Hurling of Rocks and Mountains, the Earthquake, the Fire, the Thunder, are all of them employ'd to lift up the Reader's Imagination, and give him a suitable Idea of so great an Action. With what Art has the Poet represented the whole Body of the Earth trembling, even before it was created. [217-9]

In how sublime and just a Manner does he afterwards describe the whole Heaven shaking under the Wheels of the Messiah's Chariot, with that exception to the Throne of God? [832-4]

Notwithstanding the Messiah appears cloathed with so much Terrour and Majesty, the Poet has still found Means to make his Readers conceive an Idea of him beyond what he himself was able to describe. [835-55]

In a Word, *Milton*'s Genius, which was so great in it self, and so strengthened by all the Helps of Learning, appears in this Book every way equal to his subject, which was the most sublime that could enter into the Thoughts of a Poet. As he knew all the Arts of Affecting the Mind, he knew it was necessary to give it certain Resting-places and Opportunities of recovering it self from Time to Time: He has therefore with great Address interspersed several Speeches, Reflections, Similitudes, and the like Reliefs, to diversifie his Narration, and ease the Attention of the Reader, that he might come fresh to his great Action, and by such a Contrast of Ideas, have a more lively Taste of the noble Parts of his Description.

Spectator, No. 339

Longinus has observed, that there may be a Loftiness in Sentiments, where there is no Passion, and brings Instances out of ancient Authors to support this his Opinion. The Pathetick, as that great Critick observes, may animate and inflame the Sublime, but is not essential to it. Accordingly, as he further remarks, we very often find that those who excel most in stirring up the Passions very often want the Talent of writing in the great and sublime Manner; and so on the contrary. *Milton* has shewn himself a Master in both these Ways of Writing. The seventh Book, which we are now entering upon, is an Instance of that Sublime which is not mixt and work'd up with Passion. The Author appears in a kind of composed and sedate Majesty; and tho' the Sentiments do not give so great an Emotion as those in the former Book, like a troubled Ocean, represents Greatness in Confusion; the seventh affects the Imagination like the Ocean in a Calm, and fills the Mind of the Reader, without producing in it any thing like Tumult or Agitation.

The Critick above-mentioned, among the Rules which he lays down for succeeding in the sublime way of writing, proposes to his Reader, that he should imitate the most celebrated Authors who have gone before him, and have been engaged in Works of the same Nature; as in particular that if he writes on a poetical Subject, he should consider how *Homer* would have spoken on such an Occasion. By this Means one great Genius often catches the Flame from another, and writes in his Spirit without copying servilely after him. There are a thousand shining Passages in *Virgil*, which have been lighted up by *Homer*.

Milton, tho' his own natural Strength of Genius was capable of furnishing out a perfect Work, has doubtless very much raised and enabled his conceptions, by such an Imitation as that which *Longinus* has recommended.

In this Book, which gives us an Account of the Six Days Works, the Poet received but very few Assistances from Heathen Writers, who were Strangers to the Wonders of Creation. But as there are many glorious Stroaks of Poetry upon this Subject in Holy Writ, the Author has numberless Allusions to them through the whole Course of this Book. The great Critick I have before mentioned, though an Heathen, has taken Notice of the sublime Manner in which the Law-giver of the *Jews* has described the Creation in the First Chapter of *Genesis*; and there are many other Passages in Scripture, which rise up to the same Majesty, where this Subject is touched upon. *Milton* has shewn his Judgment very remarkably, in making use of such of these as were proper for his Poem, and in duly qualifying those high Strains of Eastern Poetry, which were suited to Readers whose Imaginations were set to an higher Pitch than those of colder Climates.

Adam's Speech to the Angel, wherein he desires an Account of what had passed within the Regions of Nature before the Creation, is very great and solemn. The following Lines, in which he tells him, that the Day is not too far spent for him to enter upon such a Subject, are exquisite in their Kind. [98–102]

The Angel's encouraging our First Parents in a modest Pursuit after Knowledge, with the Causes which he assigns for the Creation of the World, are very just and beautiful. The Messiah, by whom, as we are told in Scripture, the Heavens were made, comes forth in the Power of his Father, surrounded with an Host of Angels, and cloathed with such a Majesty as becomes his entering upon a Work, which, according to our Conceptions, appears the utmost Exertion of Omnipotence. What a beautiful Description has our Author raised upon that Hint in one of the Prophets. *And behold there came four Chariots out from between two Mountains, and the Mountains were Mountains of Brass.* [Zech. vi.1; *PL*, VII, 197–207]

I have before taken Notice of these Chariots of God, and of these Gates of Heaven, and shall here only add, that *Homer* gives us the same Idea of the latter as opening of themselves, tho' he afterwards takes off from it, by telling us, that the Hours first of all removed those prodigious Heaps of Clouds which lay as a Barrier before them.

I do not know any thing in the whole Poem more sublime than the Description which follows, where the Messiah is represented at the Head of his Angels, as looking down into the *Chaos*, calming its Confusion, riding into the midst of it, and drawing the first Out Line of the Creation. [210–31]

The Thought of the Golden Compasses is conceiv'd altogether in *Homer's* Spirit, and is a very noble Incident in this wonderful Description. *Homer*, when he speaks of the Gods, ascribes to them several Arms and Instruments with the same Greatness of Imagination. Let the Reader only peruse the Description of *Minerva's* Aegis, or Buckler, in the Fifth Book, with her Spear which would overturn whole Squadrons, and her Helmet, that was sufficient to cover an Army drawn out of an Hundred Cities: The Golden Compasses in the above-mentioned Passage appear a very natural Instrument in the Hand of him, whom *Plato* somewhere calls the Divine Geometrician. As Poetry delights in cloathing abstracted Ideas in Allegories and sensible Images, we find a magnificent Description of the Creation form'd after the same manner in one of the Prophets, wherein he describes the Almighty Architect as measuring the Waters in the Hollow of his Hand, meeting out the Heavens with his Span, comprehending the Dust of the Earth in a Measure, weighing the Mountains in Scales, and the Hills in a Ballance.

Another of them describing the Supreme Being in this great Work of Creation, represents him as laying the Foundations of the Earth, and stretching out the North over the empty Place, and hanging the Earth upon nothing. This last noble Thought *Milton* has express'd in the following Verse.

And Earth self-ballanc'd on her Center hung. [242]

The Beauties of Description in this Book lie so very thick, that it is impossible to enumerate them in this Paper. The Poet has employ'd on them the whole Energy of our Tongue. The several great Scenes of the Creation rise up to view one after another, in such a Manner that the Reader seems present at this wonderful Work, and to assist among the Choirs of Angels, who are the Spectators of it. How glorious is the Conclusion of the first Day. [252-6]

We have the same Elevation of Thought in the third Day, when the Mountains were brought forth, and the Deep was made. [285-90]

We have also the Rising of the whole vegetable World describ'd in this Day's Work, which is fill'd with all the Graces that other Poets have lavished on their Description of the Spring, and leads the Reader's Imagination into a Theatre equally surprizing and beautiful.

The several Glories of the Heav'ns make their Appearance on the fourth Day. [370-84]

One would wonder how the Poet could be so concise in his Description of the Six Days' Works, as to comprehend them within the Bounds of an Episode, and at the same Time so particular, as to give us a lively Idea of them. This is still more remarkable in his Account of the fifth and sixth Days, in which he has drawn out to our View the whole Animal Creation, from the Reptil to the Behemoth. As the Lion and the Leviathan are two of the noblest Productions in the World of living Creatures, the Reader will find a most exquisite Spirit of Poetry in the Account which our Author gives us of them. The Sixth Day concludes with the Formation of Man, upon which the Angel takes Occasion, as he did after the Battle in Heaven, to remind *Adam* of his Obedience, which was the principal Design of this his Visit.

The Poet afterwards represents the Messiah, returning into Heaven, and taking a Survey of his great Work. There is something inexpressibly sublime in this Part of the Poem, where the Author describes that great Period of Time, filled with so many glorious Circumstances; when the Heavens and Earth were finished; when the Messiah ascended up in Triumph through the Everlasting Gates; when he looked down with Pleasure upon his new Creation; when every Part of Nature seem'd to rejoice in its Existence; when the Morning Stars sang together, and all the Sons of God shouted for Joy. [550–68]

I cannot conclude this Book upon the Creation, without mentioning a Poem which has lately appear'd under that Title. The Work was undertaken with so good an Intention, and is executed with so great a Mastery, that it deserves to be looked upon as one of the most useful and noble Productions in our *English* Verse. The Reader cannot but be pleased to find the Depths of Philosophy enlivened with all the Charms of Poetry, and to see so great a Strength of Reason, amidst so beautiful a Redundancy of the Imagination. The Author has shewn us that Design in all the Works of Nature, which necessarily leads us to the Knowledge of its first Cause. In short, he has illustrated, by numberless and incontestible Instances, that Divine Wisdom, which the Son of *Sirach* has so nobly ascribed to the Supreme Being in his Formation of the World, when he tells us, that *He created her, and saw her, and numbered her, and poured her out upon all his Works.*

Spectator, No. 345

The Accounts which *Raphael* gives of the Battle of Angels, and the Creation of the World, have in them those Qualifications which the Criticks judge requisite to an Episode. They are nearly related to the principal Action, and have a just Connection with the Fable.

The Eighth Book opens with a beautiful Description of the Impression which this Discourse of the Archangel made on our first Parent. *Adam* afterwards, by a very natural Curiosity, enquires concerning the Motions of those Celestial Bodies which make the most glorious Appearance among the six Days Works. The Poet here, with a great deal of Art, represents *Eve* as withdrawing from this Part of their Conversation to Amusements more suitable to her Sex. He well knew, that the Episode in this Book, which is filled with *Adam*'s Account of his Passion and Esteem for *Eve*, would have been improper for her Hearing, and has therefore devised very just and beautiful Reasons for her retiring. [39–58]

The Angel's returning a doubtful Answer to *Adam*'s Enquiries, was not only proper for the moral Reason which the Poet assigns, but because it would have been highly absurd to have given the Sanction of an Archangel to any particular System of Philosophy. The chief Points in the *Ptolomaick* and *Copernican* Hypothesis are described with great

Conciseness and Perspicuity, and at the same Time dressed in very pleasing and poetical Images.

Adam, to detain the Angel, enters afterwards upon his own History, and relates to him the Circumstances in which he found himself upon his Creation; as also his Conversation with his Maker, and his first meeting with *Eve*. There is no Part of the Poem more apt to raise the Attention of the Reader, than this Discourse of our great Ancestor; as nothing can be more surprizing and delightful to us, than to hear the Sentiments that arose in the first Man while he was yet new and fresh from the Hands of his Creator. The Poet has interwoven every thing which is delivered upon this Subject in Holy Writ with so many beautiful Imaginations of his own, that nothing can be conceived more just and natural than this whole Episode. As our Author knew this Subject could not but be agreeable to his Reader, he would not throw it into the Relation of the six Days Works, but reserved it for a distinct Episode, that he might have an Opportunity of expatiating upon it more at large. Before I enter on this Part of the Poem, I cannot but take Notice of two shining Passages in the Dialogue between *Adam* and the Angel. The first is that wherein our Ancestor gives an Account of the Pleasure he took in conversing with him, which contains a very noble Moral. [210–6]

The other I shall mention is that in which the Angel gives a Reason why he should be glad to hear the story *Adam* was about to relate. [229–36]

There is no Question but our Poet drew the Image in what follows from that in *Virgil*'s Sixth Book, where *Aeneas* and the Sybil stand before the Adamantine Gates, which are there describ'd as shut upon the Place of Torments, and listen to the Groans, the Clank of Chains, and the Noise of Iron Whips, that were heard in those Regions of Pain and Sorrow. [240–4]

Adam then proceeds to give an Account of his Condition and Sentiments immediately after his Creation. How agreeably does he represent the Posture in which he found himself, the beautiful Landskip that surrounded him, and the Gladness of Heart which grew up in him on that Occasion? [253–66]

Adam is afterwards describ'd as surpriz'd at his own Existence, and taking a Survey of himself, and of all the Works of Nature. He likewise is represented as discovering by the Light of Reason, that he and every thing about him must have been the Effect of some Being infinitely good and powerful, and that this Being had a Right to his

Worship and Adoration. His first Address to the Sun, and to those Parts of the Creation which made the most distinguished Figure, is very natural and amusing to the Imagination. [273-7]

His next Sentiment, when upon his first going to sleep he fancies himself losing his Existence, and falling away into nothing, can never be sufficiently admired. His Dream, in which he still preserves the Consciousness of his Existence, together with his Removal into the Garden which was prepared for his Reception, are also Circumstances finely imagined, and grounded upon what is delivered in sacred Story.

These and the like wonderful Incidents in this Part of the Work, have in them all the Beauties of Novelty, at the same Time that they have all the Graces of Nature. They are such as none but a great Genius could have thought of, though, upon the Perusal of them, they seem to rise of themselves from the Subject of which he treats. In a Word, though they are natural they are now obvious, which is the true Character of all fine Writing.

The Impression which the Interdiction of the Tree of Life left in the Mind of our first Parent, is described with great Strength and Judgment; as the Image of the several Beasts and Birds passing in Review before him is very beautiful and lively. [349-52]

Adam, in the next Place, describes a Conference which he held with his Maker upon the Subject of Solitude. The Poet here represents the supreme Being, as making an Essay of his own Work, and putting to the Trial that reasoning Faculty with which he had endued his Creature. *Adam* urges, in this divine Colloquy the Impossibility of his being happy, tho' he was the Inhabitant of *Paradise*, and Lord of the whole Creation, without the Conversation and Society of some rational Creature, who should partake those Blessings with him. This Dialogue, which is supported chiefly by the Beauty of the Thoughts, without other poetical Ornaments, is as fine a Part as any in the whole Poem: The more the Reader examines the Justness and Delicacy of its Sentiments, the more he will find himself pleased with it. The Poet has wonderfully preserved the Character of Majesty and Condescension in the Creator, and at the same Time that of Humility and Adoration in the Creature, as particularly in those beautiful Lines. [367-8, 377-80]

Adam then proceeds to give an Account of his second Sleep, and of the Dream in which he beheld the Formation of *Eve*. The new Passion that was awakened in him at the Sight of her is touched very finely. [470-7]

Adam's Distress upon losing Sight of this beautiful Phantom, with his

Exclamations of Joy and Gratitude at the Discovery of a real Creature, who resembled the Apparition which had been presented to him in his Dream; the Approaches he makes to her, and his Manner of Courtship, are all laid together in a most most exquisite Propriety of Sentiments.

Tho' this Part of the Poem is work'd up with great Warmth and Spirit, the Love which is described in it is every way suitable to a State of Innocence. If the Reader compares the Description which *Adam* here gives of his leading *Eve* to the Nuptial Bower, with that which Mr. *Dryden* has made on the same Occasion in a Scene of his *Fall of Man*, he will be sensible of the great Care which *Milton* took to avoid all Thoughts on so delicate a Subject, that might be offensive to Religion or good Manners. The Sentiments are chaste, but not cold, and convey to the Mind Ideas of the most transporting Passion, and of the greatest Purity. What a Noble Mixture of Rapture and Innocence has the Author joined together, in the Reflection which *Adam* makes on the Pleasures of Love, compared to those of Sense. [521–39, 546–59]

These Sentiments of Love, in our first Parent, gave the Angel such an Insight into humane Nature, that he seems apprehensive of the Evils which might befal the Species in general, as well as *Adam* in particular, from the Excess of this Passion. He therefore fortifies him against it by timely Admonitions; which very artfully prepare the Mind of the Reader for the Occurrences of the next Book, where the Weakness of which *Adam* here gives such distant Discoveries brings about tht fatal Event which is the Subject of the Poem. His Discourse, which follows the gentle Rebuke he receiv'd from the Angel, shews that his Love, however violent it might appear, was still founded in Reason, and consequently not improper for *Paradise*. [596–605]

Adam's Speech, at parting with the Angel, has in it a Deference and Gratitude agreeable to an inferior Nature, and at the same Time a certain Dignity and Greatness suitable to the Father of Mankind in his State of Innocence.

Spectator, No. 351

If we look into the three great Heroic Poems which have appear'd in the World, we may observe that they are built upon very slight Foundations. *Homer* lived near 300 Years after the *Trojan* War, and, as the writing of History was not then in use among the *Greeks*, we may very well suppose, that the Tradition of *Achilles* and *Ulysses* had brought down but very few Particulars to his Knowledge, tho' there is no

Question but he has wrought into his two Poems such of their remark-able Adventures as were still talked of among his Contemporaries.

The story of *Aeneas*, on which *Virgil* founded his Poem, was like-wise very bare of Circumstances, and by that Means afforded him an Opportunity of embellishing it with Fiction, and giving a full Range to his own Invention. We find, however, that he has interwoven, in the Course of his Fable, the principal Particulars, which were generally believed among the *Romans*, of *Aeneas* his Voyage and Settlement in *Italy*.

The Reader may find an Abridgment of the whole Story as collected out of the ancient Historians, and as it was received among the *Romans*, in *Dionysius Halicarnasseus*.

Since none of the Criticks have considered *Virgil's* Fable, with relation to this History of *Aeneas*, it may not, perhaps, be amiss to examine it in this Light, so far as regards my present Purpose. Whoever looks into the Abridgment above-mentioned, will find that the Character of *Aeneas* is filled with Piety to the Gods, and a superstitious Observation of Prodigies, Oracles, and Predictions. *Virgil* has not only preserved this character in the Person of *Aeneas*, but has given a Place in his Poem to those particular Prophecies which he found recorded of him in History and Tradition. The Poet took the Matters of Fact as they came down to him, and circumstanced them after his own Manner, to make them appear the more natural, agreeable, or surprizing. I believe very many Readers have been shocked at that ludicrous Pro-phecy, which one of the *Harpyes* pronounces to the *Trojans* in the Third Book, namely, that, before they had built their intended City, they should be reduced by Hunger to eat their very Tables. But, when they hear that this was one of the Circumstances that had been trans-mitted to the *Romans* in the History of *Aeneas*, they will think the Poet did very well in taking Notice of it. The Historian above-mentioned acquaints us, a Prophetess had foretold *Aeneas*, that he should take his Voyage Westward, till his Companions should eat their Tables; and that accordingly, upon his landing in *Italy*, as they were eating their Flesh upon Cakes of Bread, for want of other Conveniencies, they afterwards fed on the Cakes themselves; upon which one of the Com-pany said merrily, *We are eating our Tables*. They immediately took the Hint, says the Historian, and concluded the Prophecy to be fulfilled. As *Virgil* did not think it proper to omit so material a Particular in the History of *Aeneas*, it may be worth while to consider with how much Judgment he has qualified it, and taken off every thing that might have appeared improper for a Passage in an Heroic Poem. The Prophetess who foretells it is an hungry *Harpy*, as the Person who discovers it is young *Ascanius*. . . .

Such an Observation, which is beautiful in the Mouth of a Boy, would have been ridiculous from any other of the Company. I am apt to think that the changing of the *Trojan* Fleet into Water-Nymphs, which is the most violent Machine in the whole *Aeneid*, and has given Offence to several Criticks, may be accounted for the same way. *Virgil* himself, before he begins that Relation, premises that what he was going to tell appeared incredible, but that it was justified by Tradition. What further confirms me that this Change of the Fleet was a celebrated Circumstance in the History of *Aeneas*, is, that *Ovid* has given a Place to the same *Metamorphosis* in his Account of the heathen Mythology.

None of the Criticks I have met with having considered the Fable of the *Aeneid* in this Light, and taken Notice how the Tradition, on which it was founded, authorizes those Parts in it which appear the most exceptionable; I hope the Length of this Reflection will not make it unacceptable to the curious Part of my Readers.

The History, which was the Basis of *Milton*'s Poem, is still shorter than either that of the *Iliad* or *Aeneid*. The Poet has likewise taken Care to insert every Circumstance of it in the Body of his Fable. The Ninth Book, which we are here to consider, is raised upon that brief Account in Scripture, wherein we are told that the Serpent was more subtle than any Beast of the Field, that he tempted the Woman to eat of the forbidden Fruit, that she was overcome by this Temptation, and that *Adam* followed her Example. From these Few Particulars *Milton* has formed one of the most entertaining Fables that Invention ever produced. He has disposed of these several Circumstances among so many beautiful and natural Fictions of his own, that his whole Story looks only like a comment upon sacred Writ, or rather seems to be a full and compleat Relation of what the other is only an Epitome. I have insisted the longer on this consideration, as I look upon the Disposition and Contrivance of the Fable to be the principal Beauty of the Ninth Book, which has more *Story* in it, and is fuller of Incidents, than any other in the whole Poem. *Satan*'s traversing the Globe, and still keeping within the Shadow of the Night, as fearing to be discovered by the Angel of the Sun, who had before detected him, is one of those beautiful Imaginations with which he introduces this his second Series of Adventures. Having examined the Nature of every Creature, and found out one which was the most proper for his Purpose, he again returns to Paradise; and, to avoid Discovery, sinks by Night with a River that ran under the Garden, and rises up again through a Fountain that issued from it by the Tree of Life. The Poet, who, as we have before taken Notice, speaks as little as possible in his own Person, and, after the Example of *Homer*, fills every Part of his Work with Manners and Characters, introduces a Soliloquy of this infernal Agent, who was thus restless in the Destruction of Man. He is then describ'd as gliding through the Garden under the Resemblance of a Mist, in order to find out that Creature in which he design'd to tempt our first Parents. This Description has something in it very poetical and surprizing. [179–84]

The Author afterwards gives us a Description of the Morning, which is wonderfully suitable to a Divine Poem, and peculiar to that first Season of Nature: He represents the Earth before it was curst as a great Altar breathing out its Incense from all Parts, and sending up a pleasant Savour to the Nostrils of its Creator; to which he adds a noble Idea of *Adam* and *Eve*, as offering their Morning Worship, and filling up the Universal Consort of Praise and Adoration. [192–9]

The Dispute which follows between our two first Parents is represented with great Art: It proceeds from a Difference of Judgment, not of Passion, and is managed with Reason, not with Heat: It is such a Dispute as we may suppose might have happened in *Paradise*, had Man continued happy and innocent. There is a great Delicacy in the Moralities which are interspersed in *Adam*'s Discourse, and which the most ordinary Reader cannot but take Notice of. That Force of Love which the Father of Mankind so finely describes in the Eighth Book, and which I inserted in my last *Saturday*'s Paper, shews it self here in many beautiful Instances: As in those fond Regards he casts towards *Eve* at her parting from him. [397–401]

In his Impatience and Amusement during her Absence. [838–44]

But particularly in that passionate Speech, where seeing her irrecoverably lost, he resolves to perish with her rather than to live without her. [904–16]

The Beginning of this Speech, and the Preparation to it are animated with the same Spirit as the Conclusion, which I have here quoted.

The several Wiles which are put in Practice by the Tempter, when he found *Eve* separated from her Husband, the many pleasing Images of Nature which are intermixt in this Part of the Story, with its gradual and regular Progress to the fatal Catastrophe, are so very remarkable, that it would be superfluous to point out their respective Beauties.

I have avoided mentioning any particular Similitudes in my Remarks on this great Work, because I have given a general Account of them in my Paper on the First Book. There is one, however, in this Part of the Poem which I shall here quote, as it is not only very beautiful, but the closest of any in the whole Poem; I mean that where the Serpent is describ'd as rolling forward in all his Pride, animated by the evil Spirit, and conducting *Eve* to her Destruction, while *Adam* was at too great a Distance from her to give her his Assistance. These several Particulars are all of them wrought into the following Similitude. [633–42]

That secret Intoxication of Pleasure, with all those transient Flushings of Guilt and Joy which the Poet represents in our first Parents upon their eating the forbidden Fruit, to those Flaggings of Spirit, Damps of Sorrow, and mutual Accusations which succeed it, are conceiv'd with a wonderful Imagination, and described in very natural Sentiments.

When *Dido* in the Fourth *Aeneid* yielded to that fatal Temptation which ruin'd her, *Virgil* tells us the Earth trembled, the Heavens were filled with Flashes of Lightning, and the Nymphs howled upon the Mountain Tops. *Milton*, in the same poetical Spirit, has described all Nature as disturbed upon *Eve*'s eating the forbidden Fruit. [780–4]

Upon *Adam*'s falling into the same Guilt, the whole Creation appears a second time in Convulsions. [997–1003]

As all Nature suffer'd by the Guilt of our first Parents, these Symptoms of Trouble and Consternation are wonderfully imagined, not only as Prodigies, but as Marks of her sympathizing in the Fall of Man.

Adam's Converse with *Eve*, after having eaten the forbidden Fruit, is an exact Copy of that between *Jupiter* and *Juno* in the Fourteenth *Iliad*. *Juno* there approaches *Jupiter* with the Girdle which she had received from *Venus*; upon which he tells her, that she appeared more charming and desirable than she had ever done before, even when their Loves were at the highest. The Poet afterwards describes them as reposing on a Summet of Mount *Ida*, which produced under them a Bed of Flowers, the *Lotos*, the *Crocus*, and the *Hyacinth*; and concludes his Description with their falling asleep.

Let the Reader compare this with the following Passage in *Milton*, which begins with *Adam*'s Speech to *Eve*. [1029–45]

As no Poet seems ever to have studied *Homer* more, or to have more resembled him in the Greatness of Genius than *Milton*, I think I should have given but a very imperfect Account of his Beauties, if I had not observed the most remarkable Passages which look like Parallels in these two great Authors. I might, in the Course of these Criticisms, have taken Notice of many particular Lines and Expressions which are translated from the *Greek* Poet; but as I thought this would have appeared too minute and over-curious, I have purposely omitted them. The greater Incidents, however, are not only set off by being shown in the same Light with several of the same Nature in *Homer*, but by that Means may be also guarded against the Cavils of the Tasteless or Ignorant.

Spectator, No. 357

The tenth Book of *Paradise Lost* has a greater Variety of Persons in it than any other in the whole Poem. The Author upon the winding up of his Action introduces all those who had any Concern in it, and shews with great Beauty the Influence which it had upon each of them. It is like the last Act of a well written Tragedy, in which all who had a Part in it are generally drawn up before the Audience, and represented under those Circumstances in which the Determination of the Action places them.

I shall therefore consider this Book under four Heads, in relation to the Celestial, the Infernal, the Human, and the Imaginary Persons, who have their respective Parts allotted in it.

To begin with the Celestial Persons: The Guardian Angels of *Paradise* are described as returning to Heaven upon the Fall of Man, in order to approve their Vigilance; their Arrival, their Manner of Reception, with the Sorrow which appeared in themselves, and in those Spirits who are said to Rejoice at the Conversion of a Sinner, are very finely laid together in the following Lines. [17–33]

The same Divine Person, who in the foregoing Parts of this Poem interceded for our first Parents before their Fall, overthrew the Rebel Angels, and created the World, is now represented as descending to *Paradise*, and pronouncing Sentence upon the three Offenders. The cool of the Evening, being a Circumstance with which Holy Writ introduces this great Scene, it is Poetically described by our Author, who has also kept religiously to the Form of Words, in which the three several Sentences were passed upon *Adam*, *Eve*, and the Serpent. He has rather chosen to neglect the Numerousness of his Verse, than to deviate from those Speeches which are recorded on this great Occasion. The Guilt and Confusion of our first Parents standing naked before their

Judge, is touched with great Beauty. Upon the Arrival of *Sin* and *Death* into the Works of the Creation, the Almighty is again introduced as speaking to his Angels that surrounded him. [616-8]

The following Passage is formed upon that glorious Image in Holy Writ, which compares the Voice of an innumerable Host of Angels, uttering Hallelujahs, to the Voice of mighty Thunderings, or of many Waters. [641-5]

Though the Author in the whole Course of his Poem, and particularly in the Book we are now examining, has infinite Allusions to Places of Scripture, I have only taken Notice in my Remarks of such as are of a Poetical Nature, and which are woven with great Beauty into the Body of the Fable. Of this kind is that Passage in the present Book, where describing *Sin* and *Death* as marching through the Works of Nature, he adds,

> Behind her Death
> Close following pace for pace, not mounted yet
> On his pale Horse. [588-90]

Which alludes to that Passage in Scripture so wonderfully Poetical, and terrifying to the Imagination. [Rev. vi.8] Under this first Head of Celestial Persons we must likewise take Notice of the Command which the Angels received, to produce the several Changes in Nature, and sully the Beauty of the Creation. Accordingly they are represented as infecting the Stars and Planets with malignant Influences, weakning the Light of the Sun, bringing down the Winter into the milder Regions of Nature, planting Winds and Storms in several Quarters of the Sky, storing the Clouds with Thunder, and in short, perverting the whole Frame of the Universe to the Condition of its Criminal Inhabitants. As this is a noble Incident in the Poem, the Following Lines, in which we see the Angels heaving up the Earth, and placing it in a different Posture to the Sun from what it had before the Fall of Man, is conceived with that sublime Imagination which was so peculiar to this great Author. [668-71]

We are in the second Place, to consider the Infernal Agents under the View which *Milton* has given us of them in this Book. It is observed by those who would set forth the Greatness of *Virgil's* Plan, that he conducts his Reader thro' all the Parts of the Earth which were discovered in his Time. *Asia, Africk,* and *Europe* are the several Scenes of his Fable. The Plan of *Milton's* Poem is of an infinitely greater Extent, and fills the Mind with many more astonishing Circumstances. *Satan,* having surrounded the Earth seven times, departs at length from *Paradise*. We then see him steering his Course among the Constellations, and after having traversed the whole Creation, pursuing his Voyage thro' the *Chaos*, and entering into his own infernal Dominions.

His first Appearance in the Assembly of Fallen Angels, is work'd up with Circumstances which give a delightful Surprize to the Reader; but there is no Incident in the whole Poem which does this more than the Transformation of the whole Audience, that follows the Account their Leader gives them of his Expedition. The gradual Change of *Satan* himself is described after *Ovid*'s Manner, and may vie with any of those celebrated Transformations which are looked upon as the most Beautiful Parts in that Poet's Works. *Milton* never fails of improving his own Hints, and bestowing the last finishing Touches to every Incident which is admitted into his Poem. The unexpected Hiss which rises in this Episode, the Dimensions and Bulk of *Satan* so much superior to those of the Infernal Spirits who lay under the same Transformation, with the annual Change which they are supposed to suffer, are Instances of this Kind. The Beauty of the Diction is very remarkable in this whole Episode, as I have observed in the Sixth Paper of these my Remarks the great Judgment with which it was contrived.

The Parts of *Adam* and *Eve*, or the Humane Persons, come next under our Consideration. *Milton*'s Art is no where more shewn than in his conducting the Parts of these our first Parents. The Representation he gives of them, without falsifying the Story, is wonderfully contrived to influence the Reader with Pity and Compassion towards them. Though *Adam* involves the whole Species in Misery, his Crime proceeds from a Weakness which every Man is inclined to pardon and commiserate, as it seems rather the Frailty of Humane Nature, than of the Person who offended. Every one is apt to excuse a Fault which he himself might have fallen into. It was the Excess of Love for *Eve* that ruin'd *Adam* and his Posterity. I need not add, that the Author is Justify'd in this Particular by many of the Fathers, and the most Orthodox Writers. *Milton* has by this means filled a great part of his Poem with that kind of Writing which the *French* Criticks call the *Tender*, and which is in a particular manner engaging to all sorts of Readers.

Adam and *Eve*, in the Book we are now considering, are likewise drawn with such Sentiments as do not only interest the Reader in their Afflictions, but raise in him the most melting Passions of Humanity and Commiseration. When *Adam* sees the several Changes in Nature produced about him, he appears in a Disorder of Mind suitable to one who had forfeited both his Innocence and his Happiness; he is filled with Horror, Remorse, Despair; in the Anguish of his Heart he expostulates with his Creator for having given him an unasked Existence. [743–50]

He immediately after recovers from his Presumption, owns his Doom to be just, and begs that the Death which is threatned him may be inflicted on him. [771–82]

This whole Speech is full of the like Emotion, and varied with all those Sentiments which we may suppose natural to a Mind so broken and disturb'd. I must not omit that generous Concern which our first Father shews in it for his Posterity, and which is so proper to affect the Reader. [723–31, 817–25]

Who can afterwards behold the Father of Mankind extended upon the Earth, uttering his Midnight Complaints, bewailing his Existence, and wishing for Death, without sympathizing with him in his Distress? [845–53]

The Part of *Eve* in this Book is no less passionate, and apt to sway the Reader in her Favour. She is presented with great Tenderness as approaching *Adam*, but is spurn'd from him with a Spirit of Upbraiding and Indignation conformable to the Nature of Man, whose Passions had now gained the Dominion over him. The following Passage wherein she is described as renewing her Addresses to him, with the whole Speech that follows it, have something in them exquisitely moving and pathetick. [909–24].

Adam's Reconcilement to her is work'd up in the same Spirit of Tenderness. *Eve* afterwards proposes to her Husband, in the Blindness of her despair, that to prevent their Guilt from descending upon Posterity they should resolve to live Childless; or, if that could not be done, they should seek their own Deaths by violent Methods. As those Sentiments naturally engage the Reader to regard the Mother of Mankind with more than ordinary Commiseration, they likewise contain a very fine Moral. The Resolution of dying to end our Miseries, does not shew such a degree of Magnanimity as a Resolution to bear them and submit to the Dispensations of Providence. Our Author has therefore, with great Delicacy, represented *Eve* as entertaining this Thought, and *Adam* as disapproving it.

We are, in the last Place, to consider the Imaginary Persons, or *Death* and *Sin*, who act a large Part in this Book. Such beautiful extended Allegories are certainly some of the finest Compositions of Genius; but, as I have before observed, are not agreeable to the Nature of an Heroic Poem. This of *Sin* and *Death* is very exquisite in its Kind, if not considered as a Part of such a Work. The Truths contained in it are so clear and open, that I shall not lose Time in explaining them; but shall only observe, that a Reader who knows the Strength of the *English* Tongue, will be amazed to think how the Poet could find such apt Words and Phrases to describe the Actions of those two imaginary Persons, and particularly in that Part where *Death* is exhibited as forming a Bridge over the *Chaos*; a Work suitable to the Genius of *Milton*.

Since the Subject I am upon gives me an Opportunity of speaking more at large of such Shadowy and Imaginary Persons as may be introduced into Heroic Poems, I shall beg Leave to explain my self in a Matter which is curious in its Kind, and which none of the Criticks have treated of. It is certain *Homer* and *Virgil* are full of imaginary Persons, who are very beautiful in Poetry when they are just shewn without being engaged in any Series of Action. *Homer* indeed represents *Sleep* as a Person, and ascribes a short Part to him in his *Iliad*; but we must consider that tho' we now regard such a Person as entirely shadowy and unsubstantial, the Heathens made Statues of him, placed him in their Temples, and looked upon him as a real Deity. When *Homer* makes use of other such Allegorical Persons, it is only in short Expressions, which convey an ordinary Thought to the Mind in the most pleasing Manner, and may rather be looked upon as Poetical Phrases than Allegorical Descriptions. Instead of telling us that Men naturally fly when they are terrified, he introduces the Persons of *Flight* and *Fear*, who, he tells us, are inseparable Companions. Instead of saying that the Time was come when *Apollo* ought to have received his Recompence, he tells us that the *Hours* brought him his Reward. Instead of describing the Effects which *Minerva's Aegis* produced in Battel, he tells us that the Brims of it were encompassed by *Terrour, Rout, Discord, Fury, Pursuit, Massacre,* and *Death*. In the same Figure of speaking, he represents *Victory* as following *Diomedes; Discord* as the Mother of Funerals and Mourning; *Venus* as dressed by the *Graces*; *Bellona* as wearing Terrour and Consternation like a Garment. I might give several other Instances out of *Homer*, as well as a great many out of *Virgil. Milton* has likewise very often made use of the same way of Speaking, as where he tells us, that *Victory* sat on the Right Hand of the Messiah when he marched forth against the Rebel Angels; that at the rising of the Sun the *Hours* unbarr'd the Gates of Light; that *Discord* was the Daughter of *Sin*. Of the same Nature are those Expressions, where describing the Singing of the Nightingale, he adds, *Silence was pleased*; and upon the Messiah's bidding Peace to the *Chaos, Confusion heard his*

Voice. I might add innumerable Instances of our Poet's writing in this beautiful Figure. It is plain that these I have mentioned, in which Persons of an imaginary Nature are introduced, are such short Allegories as are not designed to be taken in the literal Sense, but only to convey particular Circumstances to the Reader after an unusual and entertaining Manner. But when such Persons are introduced as principal Actors, and engaged in a Series of Adventures, they take too much upon them, and are by no means proper for an Heroic Poem, which ought to appear credible in its principal Parts. I cannot forbear therefore thinking that *Sin* and *Death* are as improper Agents in a Work of this Nature, as *Strength* and *Necessity* in one of the Tragedies of *Eschylus*, who represented those two Persons nailing down *Prometheus* to a Rock, for which he has been justly censured by the greatest Criticks. I do not know any imaginary Person made use of in a more sublime manner of Thinking than that in one of the Prophets, who describing God as descending from Heaven, and visiting the Sins of Mankind, adds that dreadful Circumstance, *Before him went the Pestilence* [Habakkuk iii. 5]. It is certain this imaginary Person might have been described in all her purple Spots. The *Fever* might have marched before her, *Pain* might have stood at her Right Hand, *Phrenzy* on her Left, and *Death* in her Rear. She might have been introduced as gliding down from the Tail of a Comet, or darted upon the Earth in a Flash of Lightning: She might have tainted the Atmosphere with her Breath; the very Glaring of her Eyes might have scattered Infection. But I believe every Reader will think, that in such sublime Writings the mentioning of her as it is done in Scripture, has something in it more just, as well as great, than all that the most fanciful Poet could have bestowed upon her in the Richness of his Imagination.

Spectator, No. 363

Milton has shewn a wonderful Art in describing that Variety of Passions which arise in our first Parents upon the Breach of the Commandment that had been given them. We see them gradually passing from the Triumph of their Guilt thro' Remorse, Shame, Despair, Contrition, Prayer, and Hope, to a perfect and compleat Repentance. At the End of the Tenth Book they are represented as prostrating themselves upon the Ground, and watering the Earth with their Tears: To which the Poet joins this beautiful Circumstance, that they offer'd up their penitential Prayers on the very Place where their Judge appeared to them when he pronounced their Sentence. [X, 1098–1102]

There is a Beauty of the same kind in a Tragedy of *Sophocles*, where *Oedipus*, after having put out his own Eyes, instead of breaking his Neck from the Palace Battlements (which furnishes so elegant an Entertainment for our *English* Audience) desires that he may be conducted to Mount *Cithaeron*, in order to end his Life in that very Place where he was exposed in his Infancy, and where he should then have died, had the Will of his Parents been executed.

As the Author never fails to give a poetical Turn to his Sentiments, he describes in the Beginning of this Book the Acceptance which these their Prayers met with, in a short Allegory form'd upon that beautiful Passage in Holy Writ; [Rev. viii.3–4; *PL*, XI, 14–20]

We have the same Thought expressed a second Time in the Intercession of the Messiah, which is conceived in very emphatick Sentiments and Expressions.

Among the poetical Parts of Scripture which *Milton* has so finely wrought into this Part of his Narration, I must not omit that wherein *Ezekial* speaking of the Angels who appeared to him in a Vision, adds, that *every one had four faces,* and that *their whole bodies, and their backs, and their hands, and their wings were full of eyes round about.* [127–30]

The assembling of all the Angels of Heaven to hear the solemn Decree passed upon Man, is represented in very lively Ideas. The Almighty is here describ'd as remembring Mercy in the Midst of Judgment, and commanding *Michael* to deliver his Message in the mildest Terms, lest the Spirit of Man, which was already broken with the Sense of his Guilt and Misery, should fail before him. [108–11]

The Conference of *Adam* and *Eve* is full of moving Sentiments. Upon their going abroad after the melancholy Night which they had passed together, they discover the Lion and the Eagle pursuing each of them their Prey towards the Eastern Gates of *Paradise*. There is a double Beauty in this Incident, not only as it presents great and just Omens, which are always agreeable in Poetry, but as it expresses that Enmity which was now produced in the Animal Creation. The Poet to shew the like Changes in Nature, as well as to grace his Fable with a noble Prodigy, represents the Sun in an Eclipse. This particular Incident has likewise a fine Effect upon the Imagination of the Reader, in regard to what follows; for at the same Time that the Sun is under an Eclipse, a bright Cloud descends in the western Quarter of the Heavens, filled with a Host of Angels, and more luminous than the Sun it self. The whole Theatre of Nature is darkned, that this glorious Machine may appear in all its Lustre and Magnificence. [203–11]

I need not observe how properly this Author, who always suits his Parts to the Actors whom he introduces, has employed *Michael* in the Expulsion of our first Parents from *Paradise*. The Archangel on this Occasion neither appears in his proper Shape, nor in that familiar Manner with which *Raphael* the sociable Spirit entertained the Father of Mankind before the Fall. His Person, his Port, and Behaviour are suitable to a Spirit of the highest Rank, and exquisitely describ'd in the following Passage. [238-50]

Eve's Complaint upon hearing that she was to be removed from the Garden of *Paradise* is wonderfully Beautiful: The Sentiments are not only proper to the Subject, but have something in them particularly soft and Womanish. [269-85]

Adam's Speech abounds with Thoughts which are equally moving, but of a more masculine and elevated Turn. Nothing can be conceived more sublime and poetical than the following Passage in it. [315-33]

The Angel afterwards leads *Adam* to the highest Mount of *Paradise*, and lays before him a whole Hemisphere, as a proper Stage for those Visions which were to be represented on it. I have before observed how the Plan of *Milton*'s Poem is in many particulars greater than that of the *Iliad* or *Aeneid*. *Virgil*'s Hero, in the last of these Poems, is entertained with a sight of all those who are to descend from him; but tho' that Episode is justly admired as one of the noblest Designs in the whole *Aeneid*, every one must allow that this of *Milton* is of a much higher Nature. *Adam*'s Vision is not confined to any particular Tribe of Mankind, but extends to the whole Species.

In this great Review which *Adam* takes of all his Sons and Daughters, the first Objects he is presented with exhibit to him the Story of *Cain* and *Abel*, which is drawn together with much Closeness and Propriety of Expression. That Curiosity and natural Horror which arises in *Adam* at the Sight of the first dying Man, is touched with great Beauty. [462-5]

The second Vision sets before him the Image of Death in a great Variety of Appearances. The Angel, to give him a general Idea of those Effects which his Guilt had brought upon his Posterity, places before him a large Hospital or Lazer-House, fill'd with Persons lying under all kinds of mortal Diseases. How finely has the Poet told us that the sick Persons languished under lingring and incurable Distempers, by an apt and judicious use of such imaginary Beings as those I mentioned in my last *Saturday*'s Paper. [489-93]

The Passion which likewise rises in *Adam* on this occasion is very natural. [494–7]

The Discourse between the Angel and *Adam* which follows, abounds with noble Morals.

As there is nothing more delightful in Poetry than a Contrast and Opposition of Incidents, the Author, after this melancholy Prospect of Death and Sickness, raises up a Scene of Mirth, Love and Jollity. The secret Pleasure that steals into *Adam's* Heart as he is intent upon this Vision, is imagined with great Delicacy. I must not omit the Description of the loose female Troupe, who seduced the Sons of God as they are called in Scripture. [614–25]

The next Vision is of a quite contrary Nature, and filled with the Horrors of War. *Adam* at the Sight of it melts into Tears, and breaks out in that passionate Speech. [675–80]

Milton, to keep up an agreeable Variety in his Visions, after having raised in the Mind of his Reader the several Ideas of Terror which are conformable to the Description of War, passes on to those softer Images of Triumphs and Festivals, in that Vision of Lewdness and Luxury which ushers in the Flood.

As it is Visible that the Poet had his Eye upon *Ovid's* Account of the universal Deluge, the Reader may observe with how much Judgment he has avoided everything that is redundant or puerile in the *Latin* Poet. We do not here see the Wolf swimming among the Sheep, nor any of those wanton Imaginations which *Seneca* found fault with, as unbecoming the great Catastrophe of Nature. If our Poet has imitated that Verse in which *Ovid* tells us that there was nothing but Sea, and that this Sea had no Shoar to it, he has not set the Thought in such a Light as to incur the Censure which Criticks have passed upon it. The latter part of that Verse in *Ovid* is idle and superfluous, but just and beautiful in *Milton*.

> Jamque mare & tellus nullum discrimen habebant.
> Nil nisi pontus erat: deerant quoque littora ponto.
>
> —Ovid [*Meta.*, I, 291–2]

> Sea cover'd Sea,
> Sea without Shore . . .   —Milton [749–50] . . . .

In *Milton* the former part of the Description does not forestall the latter. How much more great and solemn on this Occasion is that which follows in our *English* Poet,

And in their Palaces
Where luxury late reign'd, Sea Monsters whelp'd
And stabl'd . . .   [750–2]

than that in *Ovid*, where we are told that the Sea-Calfs lay in those
Places where the Goats were used to browze? The Reader may find
several other parallel Passages in the *Latin* and *English* Description of the
Deluge, wherein our Poet has visibly the Advantage. The Sky's being
over-charged with Clouds, the descending of the Rains, the rising of
the Seas, and the appearance of the Rainbow, are such Descriptions as
every one must take Notice of. The Circumstance relating to *Paradise*
is so finely imagined and suitable to the Opinions of many learned
Authors, that I cannot forbear giving it a Place in this Paper. [829–35]

The Transition which the Poet makes from the Vision of the Deluge,
to the Concern it occasioned in *Adam*, is exquisitely graceful, and copied
after *Virgil*, though the first Thought it introduces is rather in the
Spirit of *Ovid*. [754–61]

I have been the more particular in my Quotations out of the
Eleventh Book of *Paradise Lost*, because it is not generally reckoned
among the most shining Books of this Poem; for which Reason the
Reader might be apt to overlook those many Passages in it which
deserve our Admiration. The Eleventh and Twelfth are indeed built
upon that single Circumstance of the Removal of our first Parents from
Paradise; but though this is not in it self so great a Subject as that in most
of the foregoing Books, it is extended and diversified with so many
surprizing Incidents and pleasing Episodes, that these two last Books
can by no means be looked upon as unequal Parts of this Divine Poem.
I must further add, that had not *Milton* represented our first Parents as
driven out of *Paradise*, his Fall of Man would not have been compleat,
and consequently his Action would have been imperfect.

Spectator, No. 369

Milton, after having represented in Vision the History of Mankind to
the first great Period of Nature, dispatches the remaining Part of it in
Narration. He has devised a very handsome Reason for the Angel's
proceeding with *Adam* after this manner; though doubtless the true
Reason was the Difficulty which the Poet would have found to have
shadowed out so mix'd and complicated a Story in visible Objects. I
could wish, however, that the Author had done it, whatever Pains it
might have cost him. To give my Opinion freely, I think that the

exhibiting part of the History of Mankind in Vision, and part in Narrative, is as if an History-Painter should put in Colours one Half of his Subject, and write down the remaining part of it. If *Milton's* Poem flags any where, it is in this Narration, where in some Places the Author has been so attentive to his Divinity, that he has neglected his Poetry. The Narration, however, rises very happily on several Occasions, where the Subject is capable of Poetical Ornaments, as particularly in the Confusion which he describes among the Builders of Babel, and in his short Sketch of the Plagues of *Aegypt*. The Storm of Hail and Fire, with the Darkness that overspread the Land for three Days, are described with great Strength. The beautiful Passage which follows, is raised upon noble Hints in Scripture. [190-9]

The *River-Dragon* is an Allusion to the Crocodile, which inhabits the *Nile*, from whence *Aegypt* derives her Plenty. This Allusion is taken from that sublime Passage in *Ezekiel*; [Ezek. xxix.3]. *Milton* has given us another very noble and poetical Image in the same Description, which is copied almost Word for Word out of the History of *Moses*. [206-14]

As the principal Design of this *Episode* was to give *Adam* an Idea of the Holy Person, who was to reinstate Humane Nature in that Happiness and Perfection from which it had fallen, the Poet confines himself to the Line of *Abraham*, from whence the *Messiah* was to descend. The Angel is described as seeing the Patriarch actually travelling towards the *Land of Promise*, which gives a particular Liveliness to this Part of the Narration. [128-40]

As *Virgil's* Vision in the sixth *Aeneid* probably gave *Milton* the Hint of this whole *Episode*, the last Line is a Translation of that Verse, where *Anchises* mentions the Names of Places, which they were to bear hereafter. [*Aeneid*, VI, 777]

The Poet has very finely represented the Joy and Gladness of Heart which rises in *Adam* upon his Discovery of the *Messiah*. As he sees his Day at a Distance through Types and Shadows, he rejoices in it; but when he finds the Redemption of Man compleated, and *Paradise* again renewed, he breaks forth in Rapture and Transport. [469-70 ff.]

I have hinted in my Sixth Paper on *Milton*, that an Heroick Poem, according to the Opinion of the best Criticks, ought to end happily, and leave the Mind of the Reader, after having conducted it through many Doubts and Fears, Sorrows and Disquietudes, in a state of Tranquility and Satisfaction. *Milton's* Fable, which had so many other Qualifications to recommend it, was deficient in this Particular. It is here therefore, that the Poet has shewn a most exquisite Judgment, as well as the finest Invention, by finding out a Method to supply the natural Defect in his Subject. Accordingly he leaves the Adversary of Mankind, in the last View which he gives us of him, under the lowest State of Mortification and Disappointment. We see him chewing Ashes, grovelling in the Dust, and loaden with supernumerary Pains and Torments. On the contrary, our two first Parents are comforted by Dreams and Visions, cheared with promises of Salvation, and, in a manner, raised to a greater Happiness than that which they had forfeited: In short, *Satan* is represented miserable in the Height of his Triumphs, and *Adam* Triumphant in the Height of Misery.

Milton's Poem ends very nobly. The last Speeches of *Adam* and the Arch-Angel are full of Moral and Instructive Sentiments. The Sleep that fell upon *Eve*, and the Effects it had in quieting the Disorders of her Mind, produces the same kind of Consolation in the Reader, who cannot peruse the last beautiful Speech which is ascribed to the Mother of Mankind, without a secret Pleasure and Satisfaction. [610–23]

The following Lines, which conclude the Poem, rise in a most glorious Blaze of Poetical Images and Expressions.

Heliodorus in his *Aethiopicks* acquaints us, that the Motion of the Gods differs from that of Mortals, as the former do not stir their Feet, nor proceed Step by Step, but slide o'er the Surface of the Earth by an uniform Swimming of the whole Body. The Reader may observe with how Poetical a Description *Milton* has attributed the same kind of Motion to the Angels who were to take possession of *Paradise*. [624–34]

The Author helped his Invention in the following Passage, by reflecting on the Behaviour of the Angel, who, in Holy Writ, has the Conduct of *Lot* and his Family. The Circumstances drawn from that Relation are very gracefully made use of on this Occasion. [637–41]

The Scene which our first Parents are surprized with upon their looking back on *Paradise*, wonderfully strikes the Reader's Imagination, as nothing can be more natural than the Tears they shed on that Occasion. [641–7]

If I might presume to offer at the smallest Alteration in this Divine Work, I should think the Poem would end better with the Passage here quoted, than with the two Verses which follow. [648–9]

These two Verses, though they have their Beauty, fall very much below the foregoing Passage, and renew in the Mind of the Reader that Anguish which was pretty well laid by that Consideration. [646–7]

The Number of Books in *Paradise Lost* is equal to those of the *Aeneid*. Our Author in his First Edition had divided his Poem into ten Books, but afterwards broke the Seventh and the Eleventh each of them into two different Books, by the Help of some small Additions. This second Division was made with great Judgment, as any one may see who will be at the pains of examining it. It was not done for the sake of such a Chimerical Beauty as that of resembling *Virgil* in this Particular, but for the more just and regular Disposition of this great Work.

Those who have read *Bossu*, and many of the Criticks who have written since his Time, will not pardon me if I do not find out the particular Moral which is inculcated in *Paradise Lost*. Though I can by no means think with the last-mentioned *French* Author, that an Epic Writer first of all pitches upon a certain Moral, as the Ground-Work and Foundation of his Poem, and afterwards finds out a Story to it: I am, however, of Opinion, that no just Heroic Poem ever was, or can be made from whence one great Moral may not be deduced. That which reigns in *Milton* is the most universal and most useful that can be imagined: it is in short this, that *Obedience to the Will of God makes Men happy, and that Disobedience makes them miserable*. This is visibly the Moral of the principal Fable which turns upon *Adam* and *Eve*, who continued in *Paradise* while they kept the Command that was given them, and were driven out of it as soon as they had transgressed. This is likewise the Moral of the principal Episode, which shews us how an innumerable Multitude of Angels fell from their State of Bliss, and were cast into Hell upon their Disobedience. Besides this great Moral, which may be looked upon as the Soul of the Fable, there are an Infinity of Under Morals which are to be drawn from the several Parts of the Poem, and which makes this Work more useful and instructive than any other Poem in any Language.

Those who have Criticised on the *Odissey*, the *Iliad*, and *Aeneid*, have taken a great deal of Pains to fix the Number of Months or Days contained in the Action of each of those Poems. If any one thinks it worth his while to examine this Particular in *Milton*, he will find that from *Adam*'s first Appearance in the Fourth Book, to his Expulsion from *Paradise* in the Twelfth, the Author reckons ten Days. As for that Part of the Action which is described in the three first Books, as it does not pass within the Regions of Nature, I have before observed that it is not subject to any Calculations of Time.

I have now finished my Observations on a Work which does an Honour to the *English* Nation. I have taken a general View of it under those four Heads, the Fable, the Characters, the Sentiments, and the Language, and made each of them the Subject of a particular Paper. I have in the next place spoken of the Censures which our Author may incur under each of these Heads, which I have confined to two Papers, though I might have enlarged the Number, if I had been disposed to dwell on so ungrateful a Subject. I believe, however, that the severest Reader will not find any little Fault in Heroic Poetry, which this Author has fallen into, that does not come under one of those Heads among which I have distributed his several Blemishes. After having thus treated at large of *Paradise Lost,* I could not think it sufficient to have celebrated this Poem in the whole, without descending to Particulars. I have therefore bestowed a Paper upon each Book, and endeavoured not only to prove that the Poem is beautiful in general, but to point out its particular Beauties, and to determine wherein they consist. I have endeavoured to shew how some Passages are beautifull by being Sublime, others by being Soft, others by being Natural; which of them are recommended by the Passion, which by the Moral, which by the Sentiment, and which by the Expression. I have likewise endeavoured to shew how the Genius of the Poet shines by a happy Invention, a distant Allusion, or a judicious Imitation; how he has copied or improved *Homer* or *Virgil,* and raised his own Imaginations by the Use which he has made of several Poetical Passages in Scripture. I might have inserted also several Passages of *Tasso,* which our Author has imitated; but as I do not look upon *Tasso* to be a sufficient Voucher, I would not perplex my Reader with such Quotations, as might do more Honour to the *Italian* than the *English* Poet. In short, I have endeavoured to particularize those innumerable Kinds of Beauty, which it would be tedious to recapitulate, but which are essential to Poetry, and which may be met with in the Works of this great Author. Had I thought, at my first engaging in this Design, that it would have led me to so great a Length, I believe I should never have entred upon it; but the kind Reception which it has met with among those whose Judgments I have a Value for, as well as the uncommon Demand which my Bookseller tells me has been made for these particular Discourses, give me no Reason to repent of the pains I have been at in composing them.

64. Addison on imagination and *Paradise Lost*

1712

Extract from Joseph Addison, *Spectator*, No. 417 (28 June 1712).

If I were to name a poet that is a perfect master in all these arts of working on the imagination, I think Milton may pass for one: and if his *Paradise Lost* falls short of the *Aeneid* or *Iliad* in this respect, it proceeds rather from the fault of the language in which it is written than from any defect of genius in the author. So divine a poem in English is like a stately palace built of brick, where one may see architecture in as great a perfection as in one of marble, though the materials are of a coarser nature. But to consider it only as it regards our present subject: what can be conceived greater than the battle of angels, the majesty of Messiah, the stature and behaviour of Satan and his peers? What more beautiful than pandemonium, paradise, heaven, angels, Adam and Eve? What more strange than the creation of the world, the several metamorphoses of the fallen angels, and the surprising adventures their leader meets with in his search after paradise? No other subject could have furnished a poet with scenes so proper to strike the imagination, as no other poet could have painted those scenes in more strong and lively colours.

65. Welsted on Milton's sublimity

1712

Extract from Leonard Welsted, 'Remarks on Longinus' (1712). John Nichols, ed., *The Works of Leonard Welsted* (1787), 405.

An aesthetician, Leonard Welsted (1688–1747), both praises and criticizes Milton. His main point of objection revolves around Milton's language and style, which he finds inconsistent with the classicism demanded by Milton's genre and aim.

Welsted has been talking of the majesty that Homer gives to his gods.

For a parallel to this quotation, I refer you to the several descriptions of the Messiah in Milton, viz. that of his coming to drive out the rebellious angels; his triumphant return; his riding into chaos; his ascending in jubilee; and others; where you will find all the beauty, energy, and sublimeness, Longinus himself could have wished for.

It is undoubtedly true of Milton, that no man ever had a genius so happily formed for the Sublime. He found one only theme capable enough to employ his thoughts; but he could find no language copious enough to express them.

> His vigorous and active mind was hurl'd
> Beyond the flaming limits of this world,
> Into the mighty space.

When I view him thus, in his most exalted flights, piercing beyond the boundaries of the universe, he appears to me as a vast comet, that for want of room is ready to burst its orb and grow eccentric. . . .

66. Ellwood on the composition of the epics

1714

Extract from Thomas Ellwood, *The History of the Life of Thomas Ellwood* (1714), 233–4.

A founder of the Friends, Ellwood (1639–1713) answered and raised questions in his narrative concerning the composition of *Paradise Lost* and *Paradise Regain'd*. Perhaps these remarks can be read to mean that Milton did not *begin* the brief epic some time after 1665 without denial of any part of Ellwood's report.

Some little time before I went to *Alesbury* Prison, I was desired by my quondam Master *Milton* to take an House for him, in the Neighbourhood where I dwelt, that he might get out of the City, for the Safety of himself and his family, the *Pestilence* then growing hot in *London*. I took a pretty Box for him in *Giles-Chalfont*, a Mile from me; to which I gave him notice: and intended to have waited on him, and seen him well settled in it; but was prevented by that Imprisonment.

But now being released, and returned Home, I soon made a Visit to him, to welcome him into the Country.

After some common Discourses had passed between us, he called for a Manuscript of his; which being brought and delivered to me, bidding me take it home with me, and read it at my Leisure: and when I had so done, return it to him, with my Judgment thereupon.

When I came home, and had set my self to read it, I found it was that Excellent POEM, which he entituled PARADISE LOST. After I had, with the best Attention, read it through, I made him another Visit, and returned him his book, with due Acknowledgement of the Favour he had done me, in Communicating it to me. He asked me how I liked it, and what I thought of it; which I modestly, but freely told him: and after some further Discourse about it, I pleasantly said to him, Thou hast said much here of *Paradise lost*; but what hast thou to say of *Paradise found*? He made me no Answer, but sate some time in a Muse: then brake of that Discourse, and fell upon another Subject.

After the Sickness was over, and the City well cleansed and become safely habitable again, he returned thither. And when afterwards I went to wait on him there (which I seldom failed of doing, whenever my Occasions drew me to *London*) he shewed me his Second POEM, called PARADISE REGAINED; and in a pleasant Tone said to me, *This is owing to you: for you put it into my Head, by the Question you put to me at* Chalfont; *which before I had not thought of.* But from this Digression I return to the Family I then lived in.

67. Eusden on reading Addison

1714

Lawrence Eusden, 'On Reading the Critique on Milton, in the *Spectator*'. Sir Richard Steele, ed., *Poetical Miscellany* (1714), 196–7.

The Poet-Laureate Lawrence Eusden (1688–1730) presents another good example of Milton's prestige among practising poets.

Look here, ye Pedants, who deserve that Name,
And lewdly ravish the great Critick's Fame,
In cloudless Beams of Light true Judgment plays,
How mild the Censure, how refin'd the Praise!
Beauties ye pass, and Blemishes ye cull,
Profoundly read, and Eminently dull.
Tho' Lynnets sing, yet Owls feel no delight;
For they the best can Judge, who best can write.
O! had great *Milton* but surviv'd to hear
His Numbers try'd, by such a tuneful Ear,
How would he all thy just Remarks commend?
The more the Critick own the more the Friend.
But did he know once your Immortal Strain,
Th' exalted Pleasure would encrease to Pain:
He would not blush for Faults he rarely knew,
But blush for Glories, thus excell'd by you.

68. Hughes on the allegory of sin and death

1715

Extract from John Hughes, 'An Essay on Allegorical Poetry', in *The Works of Mr. Edmund Spenser* (1715), I, xxix–xxx, xxxix.

John Hughes (1677–1720) was a poet whose work was well enough known and read in his own time, though today he is forgotten.

Thus, when it is said, That *Death is the Offspring of Sin,* this is a Metaphor, to signify that the former is produc'd by the latter, as a Child is brought into the Word by its Parent. Again, to compare Death to a meager and ghastly Apparition, starting out of the Ground, moving towards the Spectator with a menacing Air, and shaking in his Hand a bloody Dart, is a Representation of the Terrors which attend that great Enemy to Human Nature. But let the Reader observe, in *Milton's Paradise Lost,* with what exquisite Fancy and Skill this common Metaphor and Simile, and the Moral contain'd in them are extended and wrought up into one of the most beautiful Allegories in our Language. . . . There is another Copy of the *Circe,* in the Dramatick way, in a Mask, by our famous *Milton*: the whole Plan of which is Allegorical, and is written with a very Poetical Spirit on the same Moral, tho with different Characters.

69. Blackmore on epic poetry

1716

Extract from Sir Richard Blackmore, 'An Essay on the Nature
and Constitution of Epick Poetry', *Essays Upon Several Subjects*
(1716), I, iv–v (Preface) and 51–2.

Physician, critic, poet, Sir Richard Blackmore, who died in 1729,
imitated Milton's epic style in *Prince Arthur* and *King Arthur*. The
remarks in his essay should be read as those of both an imitator
and a student of aesthetics.

It must be acknowledg'd, that till about forty Years ago, *Great Britain*
was barren of Critical Learning, tho' fertile in excellent Writers; and in
particular, had so little Taste of Epick Poetry, and were so unacquainted
with the essential Properties and peculiar Beauties of it, that *Paradise
Lost*, an admirable Work of that kind, publish'd by Mr. *Milton*, the
great Ornament of his Age and Country, lay many Years unspoken of,
and entirely disregarded, till at length it happen'd, that some Persons of
greater Delicacy and Judgment found out the Merit of that excellent
Poem; and, by communicating their Sentiments to their Friends, propagated the Esteem of the Author, who soon acquir'd universal
Applause. This Curiosity spreading among Persons of Poetical Genius
and Critical Taste, and animated by the Treatise of *Bossu* on Epick
Poetry, which about this Time was brought over from *France*, the finer
Spirits of the Age began to enquire into the Nature and Qualities of it,
and enter'd much farther into this Subject, than the Grammarians and
Commentators had done before; who only hover'd on the Surface,
but never ventur'd into the Depths of Heroick Poetry. . . .

If this arguing be allow'd, then the Criticks will have no occasion
to exercise their Sagacity, in finding out the Hero of *Milton*'s Poem; for
then it will be evident, that it must have been *Adam* himself. Nothing
could have tempted learned Men to have search'd after any other Hero,
but the Prepossession under which they lay, that the chief Person of the

Poem ought always to be active, and in the end prosperous: But by what has been alledg'd I imagine, that Prejudice may be remov'd; and under this view that celebrated Poem will appear more regular and perfect than it has hitherto been allow'd to be. Another Reason why they are not willing to allow *Adam* to be the Hero of the Poem is this, That they believe the Idea of a Hero implies illustrious Vertue as well as military Fortitude; but this Error is occasion'd, by confounding the Notions of a Moral and a Poetical Hero; the first is always a Person of regular and vertuous Manners, but the other may be a flagitious, unjust, and cruel Man; nothing being requir'd in his Character, but that he should be pertinent and necessary in the Fable; that is, that he should eminently serve to bring about the principal End, whence some useful and instructive Moral shall arise: But more of this afterwards.

70. Atterbury on Milton

1717

Extract from Francis Atterbury, Letter to Pope (8 November 1717). George Sherburn, ed., *The Correspondence of Alexander Pope* (1956), i, 452.

The unfortunate Bishop of Rochester, Francis Atterbury (1662–1730), who was executed for his championing of the rights of the clergy, often discussed literary matters with his friend Pope. He also wrote an interesting (anonymous) preface to *The Second Part of Mr. Waller's Poems* in 1690. which adds to the frequent comparison between Waller and Milton.

I return you your Milton, which, upon Collating I find, to be both *Revised,* and *Augmented* in several places, as the Title page of my third Edition pretends to be. When I see you next, I will shew you the several Passages alter'd, and added by the Author, beside that you mention'd to me. I protest to you, this last Perusal of him has given me such new degrees (I will not say, of Pleasure, but) admiration and Astonishment, that I look upon the Sublimity of Homer, and the Majesty of Virgil, with some what less reverence than I used to doe. I challenge you with all your Partiality, to shew me in the first of these, any thing Equal to the Allegory of Sin, and Death, either as to the Greatness, and Justness of the Invention, or the Height and Beauty of the Colouring.

71. Gildon on heroic poetry

1718

Extract from Charles Gildon, *The Complete Art of Poetry* (1718),
i, 269.

If indeed nothing distinguish'd an Heroic Poet from others, but his
manner or sort of Verse, as GERALD VOSSIUS has very weakly determin'd, the Number would be vastly encreas'd, by admitting all into
that Rank who have written in Heroic Verse. But since the Distinction of Authors is rather from their Subject, their Design, their Fable,
their Diction or Language, it is plain that among the Antients we find
only HOMER and VIRGIL, and among the Moderns, not one; unless
we should allow TORQUATO TASSO, and MILTON. The latter indeed
has equall'd, if not excell'd the *Greek* and *Latin* Poets in many Things;
and I must so far agree with the Gentleman, who in the *Spectator* made
his Remarks on his Poem of PARADICE LOST, that if it fail in some
Particulars through the necessity of the Subject, our blind Bard has
discover'd in other Things a Genius worthy of the Fraternity of HOMER
and VIRGIL.

72. Dennis on Milton's reputation

1719

Extract from John Dennis, 'To Judas Iscariot, Esq., On the Degeneracy of the Publick Taste', from *Letters to Steele and Booth* (1719). E. N. Hooker, ed., *The Critical Works of John Dennis* (1939), ii, 169–71.

Nor can I believe that several who pretend to be passionate Admirers of *Milton*, would treat him if living in any other manner [that is, they would declare against his faults and damn him] for the following Reasons.

Because they are so fond of nothing as of that soft and effeminate Rhyme, which makes the very Reverse of the Harmony, and of the manly, and powerful, and noble Enthusiasm of *Milton*. . . . The great Qualities of *Milton* were not generally known among his Countrymen till the *Paradise Lost* had been publish'd more than thirty Years. But when that admirable Poet was among the Italians, the Greatness of his Genius was known to them in the very Bloom of his Youth, even thirty Years before that incomparable Poem was writ, witness the Epigram of *Selvaggi*, an *Italian* Poet, of which *Dryden*'s Epigram which is under *Milton*'s Picture is nothing but a Paraphrase. . . .

Thus, you see, the *Italians*, by his juvenile Essays, discover'd the great and growing Genius of *Milton*, whereas his Countrymen knew very little of him, even thirty Years after he had publish'd among them the noblest Poem in the World.

73: Gildon on Milton's immortality

1721

Extract from Charles Gildon, *The Laws of Poetry* (1721), 34.

The last and greatest of all that I shall much insist upon, is the immortal *Milton*, who, without the help of encouragement from the state, or any particular great and powerful man, equal'd the greatest Poets of antiquity, who had the happiness of enjoying all the encouragement of *Greece* and *Rome*; but then *Milton* was likewise master of an independent fortune, which, tho' not considerable in it self, was yet sufficient to answer all his demands and desires, and to give him that happy tranquillity and ease which 'tis absolutely necessary a Poet should enjoy, to make him capable of producing works truly perfect and admirable.

74. Dennis on *Paradise Lost*

1721–2

John Dennis, 'Letters on Milton and Wycherley', *The Proposals for Printing By Subscription . . . Miscellaneous Tracts* (1721–1722). E. N. Hooker, ed., *The Critical Works of John Dennis* (1939), ii, 221–30.

The following item gives an epitome of Dennis's attitude toward Milton, aesthetics, and particularly *Paradise Lost.*

'Dr. S' is George Sewell, a medical practitioner.

Observations on the Paradise Lost of Milton
To Dr. S——

LETTER I

Sir,

I was no sooner determin'd within my self to make some Observations on the *Paradise Lost* of *Milton*, than I resolv'd to direct them to you, because you know the Truth of some Facts which I shall be oblig'd to relate, and because I have observ'd in you a better Taste of the greater Poetry, than in most of those with whom I have lately convers'd; which having premis'd, I shall without more Preamble enter upon the Subject of which I design to treat.

I believe, Sir, that I have told you more than once, that I, who have all my Life-time had the highest Esteem for the great Genius's of the Ancients, and especially for *Homer* and *Virgil*, and who admire them now more than ever, have yet for these last Thirty Years admir'd *Milton* above them all for one thing, and that is for having carried away the Prize of Sublimity from both Ancients and Moderns: And in most of the Treatises which I have publish'd for Thirty Years, even in those in which I have been unhappily engag'd to detect and to blame the Errors of some of my Contemporaries, I have not been able to forbear pointing at several of the matchless Beauties of *Milton*. In the *Remarks on Prince* Arthur, I cited at large the sublime Description of *Satan* in the first Book of that Poem; and the Speech of that fallen Arch-Angel in the fourth, which begins with that noble Apostrophe to the Sun.

In the *Advancement and Reformation of modern Poetry,* which was publish'd in 1700, I shew'd the vast Advantage which *Milton* had over *Ovid,* and ev'n *Virgil* himself, in his Description of *Chaos* and the Creation.

In the *Grounds of Criticism in Poetry,* which Book was publish'd in 1704, you know very well, Sir, that I cited at large the Description of the Descent of *Raphael* in the fifth Book, and the glorious Hymn to the Creator in the same Book, and likewise the divine Colloquy between God and *Adam* in the eighth Book.

Some Persons, who long since the Publication of the foremention'd Treatises began to write Notes on the *Paradise Lost,* have made particular mention of the same Beauties which I had mark'd out before, without making any mention of me. Tho' you know very well, Sir, that I can bring unquestionable Proof that those Persons had read the foremention'd Treatises, and read them with Applause; but I should not be in the least concern'd at the treating me so unfairly and ungenerously, if they had done Justice to *Milton,* thro' the Course of their Criticisms, of which they have grossly fail'd in the following Respects.

I. They have not allow'd that *Milton* in the Sublimity of his Thoughts surpass'd both Ancients and Moderns.

II. In their Observations which they have made on the *Paradise Lost,* they have insisted too much upon things in which *Milton* has Equals, instead of dwelling intirely on that Sublimity which is his distinguishing and Characteristick Quality, and which sets him above Mankind.

III. In citing Passages from him which are truly sublime, they have often fail'd of setting his Sublimity in a true Light, and of shewing it to all its Advantage.

IV. In those Passages whose Sublimity they have set in a true Light, they have not observ'd, to the Honour of *Milton,* and our Country, that the Thoughts and Images are Original, and the genuine Offspring of *Milton*'s transcendent Genius.

V. They have not shewn how *Milton*'s Sublimity is distinguish'd from that of all other Poets in this Respect, that where he has excell'd all other Poets in what he has exprest, he has left ten times more to be understood than what he has exprest, which is the surest and noblest Mark, and the most transporting Effect of Sublimity.

To shew that they who have writ Observations on the *Paradise Lost,* have not done Justice to *Milton*, with regard to the five foremention'd Articles, is the Design and Subject of the Letters I intend to send you, which shall rather be frequent than long, my Design being to amuse and entertain you, and not to fatigue and tire you.

Decem. 9, 1721.   *I am,* &c.

LETTER II

Sir,

I affirmed in my last that the Persons who had writ Comments upon the *Paradise Lost* of *Milton*, had not done Justice to the great Author in several Respects which are there particulariz'd. And,

First and principally in this, that they have not acknowledg'd that he has born away the Prize of Sublimity from both Ancients and Moderns.

What I asserted in my former, I shall endeavour to prove in this, but on this Condition, that you will give me your Opinion of what I write to you, with the Frankness and that Unreservedness which is due to our Friends, whenever they consult us, and depend upon our Judgment and our Sincerity.

Of all the Commentators on the *Paradise Lost,* Mr. *Addison* was certainly the most ingenious, if he was not the most learned, but he has not given *Milton* his full Due, either thro' want of Discernment, or want of Impartiality. In the 17th Page of the small Edition of his Notes upon the *Paradise Lost,* he has these Words of the Author:

Milton's chief Talent, and indeed his distinguishing Excellence, lies in the Sublimity of his Thoughts. There are others of the Moderns who rival him in every other part of Poetry; but in the Greatness of his Sentiments he triumphs over all the Poets both Moderns and Ancients, *Homer* only excepted.

But as when a Man departs from Truth, which is the only bond of Union and Agreement, both of our Sentiments with those of others, and of our Sentiments with themselves, he is ready immediately to differ from, and to grow inconsistent with himself; Mr. *Addison*, who expresly here either equals or prefers *Homer* for the Greatness of his Sentiments before *Milton*, contradicts himself at least no less than twice in the Course of his Observations; for says he, in the 7*th Page* of the foresaid Edition, *There is an indisputable and unquestion'd Magnificence in every part of* Paradise Lost, *and indeed a much greater than could have been form'd upon any* Pagan *System.* Now if there is a greater Magnificence in every Part of *Milton*'s Poem, there is by Consequence a greater Sublimity than there is in the *Iliads*, which was form'd upon a *Pagan* System.

Again in the 92d Page of the foresaid Edition, Mr. *Addison*, speaking of the Excellence of *Milton*'s Performance in the Sixth Book of his Poem, delivers himself thus:

> *Milton*'s Genius, which was so great in it self, and so strengthened by all the helps of Learning, appears in this Book every way equal to his Subject, which is the most sublime that could enter into the Thoughts of a Poet.

Now, Sir, if *Milton*'s Subject is the most sublime that could enter into the Thoughts of a Poet, and his Genius is every way equal to his Subject; it follows that *Milton* is more exalted than any Poet who has not a Subject so elevated, and consequently than *Homer*, or any other Poet ancient or modern.

But as in the 91st Page of the foresaid Comment, Mr. *Addison* takes a great deal of Pains to shew the Greatness of one particular Passage of *Homer*, and to describe it, after *Longinus*, in all those chosen Circumstances, which may make it appear to be noble and exalted, which Pains he has not taken with any other Passage, we may reasonably conclude that he believ'd this to be the most lofty of any that are in the Works of *Homer*, as indeed it really is: Now as there is a Passage in the 6th Book of *Paradise Lost,* which was produced upon a parallel Occasion, let us see if we cannot find by comparing them, for the Honour of our Country, that the Passage of our *Briton* is as much superior to that of the *Grecian*, as the Angels of the one are more potent than the other's Gods, or as the *Empyrean* Heaven is more exalted than *Ossa, Pelion* or *Olympus*.

In order to this, Sir, give me leave to lay before you the Words which Mr. *Addison* makes use of to set forth the masterly Strokes of *Homer*. After he has told us, that there is no question, but that *Milton* had heated his Imagination with the Fight of the Gods in *Homer*, before he enter'd upon the Engagement of the Angels (of which, by the way, I do not believe one Syllable; I would sooner believe the greatest Absurdities of the *Alcoran*) he is pleas'd to add what follows:

> *Homer* there gives us a Scene of Men, Heroes, and Gods, mix'd together in Battle. *Mars* animates the contending Armies, and lifts up his Voice in such a manner, that it is heard distinctly amidst all the Shouts and Confusion of the Fight. *Jupiter* at the same time thunders over their Heads, while *Neptune* raises

such a Tempest, that the whole Field of Battle and all the Tops of the Mountains shake about them. The Poet tells us, that *Pluto* himself, whose Habitation was in the very Center of the Earth, was so affrighted at the Shock, that he leapt from his Throne. *Homer* afterwards describes *Vulcan* as pouring down a Storm of Fire upon the River *Xanthus*, and *Minerva* as throwing a Rock at *Mars*, who he tells us cover'd seven Acres in his fall.

With these imaginary *ne plus ultra's* had Mr. *Addison* so fill'd his Capacity, that when ten thousand greater Beauties are before his Eyes, he stops short of them, and never in the least discerns them, as you will see immediately; for thus he goes on:

As *Homer* has introduc'd into his Battle of the Gods every thing that is great and terrible in Nature, *Milton* has fill'd his Fight of good and bad Angels with all the like Circumstances of Horror. The Shout of Armies, the Rattling of brazen Chariots, the hurling of Rocks and Mountains, the Earthquake, the Fire, the Thunder, are all of them employ'd to lift up the Reader's Imagination, and give him a suitable Idea of so great an Action. With what Art doth the Poet represent the whole Body of the Earth trembling, even before it was created.

Thus with this very pretty trifling Remark does Mr. *Addison* stop short, within the very touch of one of the vastest and the sublimest Beauties that ever was inspir'd by the God of Verse, or by *Milton*'s Godlike Genius; when the very next Lines, the very next Words, strike and astonish us with such wonderful Ideas, as are able to lift up the Reader's Imagination to a thousand times a greater Heighth than either the Shout of Armies, the Rattling of brazen Chariots, the hurling of Rocks and Mountains, the Earthquake, the Fire, or the Thunder. But that these Beauties may be seen in all their Lustre, and in all their Glory, give me leave to set the whole Passage before you. [VI, 203-23]

But now, Sir, if Millions of fierce encountring Angels fought on either Side, and the very least, the very weakest of so many Millions had Power to rend this Globe of Earth and Ocean from its Axle, and whirl it with its dependent Atmosphere thro' the Æthereal Regions, what must be the unutterable, the inconceivable Effect of so many Millions furiously contending against each other, and each of them exerting all his might for Victory? When

> Each on himself relied,
> As only on his Arm the Moment lay
> Of Victory.   [VI, 238-40]

These are amazing, these are astonishing Ideas, worthy of the great Original Fight, the Battle of the *Empyrean*.

But now, Sir, if the least, if the weakest of so many Millions so fought on either Side, had Strength to remove this Globe of Earth with its dependent Elements, what could not the greatest of them, what could not *Lucifer*, what could not the Prince of the Arch-angels, *Michael*'s next to Almighty Arm do? The following Lines, and our own Reflections on them, may a little help to inform us.

> Long time in even Scale
> The Battle hung, till Satan, who that Day
> Prodigious Pow'r had shewn, and met in Arms
> No Equal, ranging through the dire Attack
> Of fighting Seraphim confus'd, at length
> Saw where the Sword of *Michael* smote and fell'd
> Squadrons at once.   [VI, 245–51]

But now, Sir, of whom were these Squadrons? Why,

> Squadrons of those the least of whom could wield
> These Elements, and arm him with the Force
> Of all their Regions.   [VI, 221–3]

What must the Power of that Arch-angel be, who with one Stroke of his Sword could fell whole Squadrons of those,

> The least of whom could wield these Elements,
> And arm him with the Force of all their Regions?

But let us proceed to the Combat of the two Arch-angels, and we shall see something more in a Passage that is wonderfully sublime, and worthy the Mouth of the Angel who relates it. [VI, 296–310]

Now who were these that retir'd with so much Speed, and could not bear the very Wind of the Weapons of the two Arch-angels, and were threatned with Destruction by their very Motion? Why, this Angelick Throng were the same whom the Angel mention'd above;

> The least of whom could wield these Elements,
> And arm him with the Force of all their Regions.

So that we find, computing by just Proportion, that *Michael* the Prince of the Arch-angels, or *Lucifer* before his Fall, had Might enough to confound and destroy in a Moment the whole Dominion of the Sun, to crush all the Planetary Worlds depending on him, and whirling them through the immense Regions of the Sky, to scatter and disperse them in empty infinite Space. These, Sir, are vast, these are prodigious Conceptions; and the Poet was so sensible that his Genius, though mighty as ever was that of a Mortal, and seeming to be inspir'd by that very Angel whom he introduces relating this; he was so sensible that his Genius sunk under his vast Conceptions, that when he compares the two contending Arch-angels to two Planetary Worlds broke loose, and crushing and confounding each other, and sees this Image so vast in itself, and yet so little answering to his vaster Idea, he finds himself oblig'd to express himself as follows. [VI, 307–15]

The Conflict of two Worlds crushing and confounding each other, appear'd but trivial and light to him, to express his Idea of the Combat of the two Arch-angels; and therefore he says, that he's oblig'd *to set forth Great things by Small*.

What immediately follows accounts for all this, and is transcendently Sublime.

> Together both with *next to Almighty Arm*
> Uplifted, imminent, one Stroke they aim'd,
> That might determine, and not need repeat
> As not of Power at once. [VI, 316–9]

That Expression *with next to Almighty Arm,* includes more than the Thoughts of the greatest Reader can ever comprehend; which recalls to my Remembrance, that noble, that wonderful Image, which the Poet gives of *Satan*, in the second Book of this exalted Poem.

> The Stygian Council thus dissolv'd, and forth
> In order came the grand infernal Peers,
> Midst came their might Paramount, and seem'd
> Alone th' Antagonist of Heav'n. [II, 506–9]

I defy any one to name any thing so sublime in *Homer*, as the latter End of this Passage above.

I am sensible, that this Letter runs into too great a Length, and 'tis high time to conclude it. I have endeavour'd to prove in it, that there is a Sublimity in *Milton*'s Battle of Angels, infinitely superiour to that which is in the Battle of *Homer*'s Gods and Heroes in the twentieth Iliad: And as I have set sublime Beauties before you, of which neither Mr. *Addison*, nor my Lord *Roscommon*, have taken the least Notice, so in my next I shall make an Objection which has not been yet made. If I have any where pass'd the Bounds of the Epistolary or the Didactic

Stile, you will have the Goodness to consider, that it was next to impossible to resist the violent Emotions which the Greatness of the Subject rais'd in me.

Jan. 20. 1722   *I am, Sir,*
                                                   Yours, &c.

LETTER III

Sir,
As in my last I endeavour'd to shew Beauties in *Milton*, which no one had taken Notice of before me, and greater Beauties than any which I believe had been taken Notice of: I shall in this lay before you an Objection, which no one that I know of has made against those very Machines of *Milton*, from the Force and Power of which those sublime Beauties were drawn.

Most of the Machines then in *Paradise Lost*, have the appearance of something that is inconsistent and contradictory, for in them the Poet seems to confound Body and Mind, Spirit and Matter. At the latter End of the first Book we find this Passage,

> Thus incorporeal Spirits to smallest Forms
> Reduce their Shapes immense. [I, 789-90]

Now Form and Shape suppose Extension, and Extension implies Matter. Besides, he has given them solid Arms and Armour, which can be employ'd by Body only, as Helmet, Spear, Shield, Sword, and has shewn both his good and his bad Angels Cap-a-pee in Armour.

To which all the Answer that can reasonably be made is, That both the good and the bad Angels, though in themselves pure Spirits and uncompounded Essences, yet on occasion, either voluntarily assume Bodies, or by superiour Power and divine Command are oblig'd to assume them. And that this was *Milton's* Notion of the thing, the following Verses in the first Book incline us to believe. [I, 423-31]

This is the best Answer I can give to the Objection I have made, and if you are not satisfy'd with it, I desire you would send me your own; for it concerns us to invalidate the most important Objection that can be made to the greatest of our *English* Poets, and perhaps against most of the Machines which are employ'd in the Christian Poetry. And here let me deplore one Unhappiness that attends our modern Poetry: For tho' the Machines with which the Christian Religion supplies us, must be allow'd to be greater, more wonderful, and more terrible, than any which the Pagan Religion affords us, they are less delightful: For that which comes nearest to humane Nature, must in Poetry be most delightful to it; but the Gods and Goddesses of the *Grecian* and *Roman* Poetry, being feign'd to have manifest Bodies, and apparent humane Shapes, and the agreeable Distinction of Sexes, come incomparably nearer to humane Nature, than the Machines of the Christian Poetry, and are therefore more delightful to it; and likewise for the following Reason, because we have, beyond all Comparison, more clear and distinct Ideas of them, than we have of the Christian Machines.

Jan. 24. 1722.   *I am, Yours,*

POSTSCRIPT

I am sorry, that while I was writing what is above, it was not in my Thoughts to acquaint you, that there seems to me to be a vast Difference between some of the Machines of *Milton* and others, with regard to their Justness. When the good Angels, first *Raphael*, and afterwards *Michael*, were feigned by the Poet to be commanded by God to appear before our first Parents, it was very justly suppos'd by him that they assum'd Bodies, and that they appear'd to them in some Form that came near to humane Shape, because it is impossible that any thing but Body can be the true Object of humane Sight, and because every Body that appears, must appear in some certain Shape or Form; and *Milton* could know of no Shape that had more Dignity than the humane. But with all the Veneration that I have for this great Poet, I cannot help thinking, that when in the first and second Books of his Poem, which yet are transcendently Sublime, he describes the fall'n Angels in Shapes that come near to humane, and describes them as having three of the five Animal Senses, *viz.* seeing, hearing and feeling; when he paints them after this manner, communing only one with another in their own infernal Regions, immediately after their Fall; and yet acquaints us at the same time that they are incorporeal Beings, and pure and un-compounded Essences; methinks his Paintings, as to that Point, are not so easily to be justified. I know indeed very well, that *Cowley* in the first Book of his *Davideis*, and *Tasso* have formally and expresly declar'd, as *Milton* has expresly and formally done, that those evil Spirits are incorporeal Beings, and pure and uncompounded Essences; they leave the Reader's Imagination free to fancy, that those fall'n Angels have Bodies; and as they assert no Notions that may be taken

241

to be inconsistent, they have avoided the giving their Readers the occasion of believing, that there is in their Descriptions of those fall'n Angels any real Contradiction, or the trouble of shewing, that what is thought to be a real Contradiction, has but the false Appearance of one.

75. Atterbury on the 'Original MS.', and *Samson Agonistes*

1722

Extract from Francis Atterbury, Letter to Pope (15 June 1722).
George Sherburn, ed., *The Correspondence of Alexander Pope*
(1956), ii, 124.

I long to see the Original M.S. of Milton; but don't know how to come
at it, without your repeated assistance, I shall have superstition enough
to Collate it with my printed Book if Tonson will allow me the use of
it for a few days. There was a time when his Uncle would have leap'd
at such an opportunity of Obliging me, but then I was a Retainer to the
Muses, and he did know but he might have got something by me.

I hope you won't utterly forget what pass'd in the Coach about
Sampson Agonistes. I shan't press you as to time: but sometime or other,
I wish you would review, and polish that Piece, if upon a new Perusal
of it (which I desire You to make) you think as I do, that it is Written
in the very Spirit of the Ancients, it deserves your care and is capable of
being improv'd, with little trouble, into a perfect Model and Standard
of Tragic Poetry, always allowing for its being a Story taken out of the
Bible which is an Objection that at this time of day, I know is not to be
got over.

76. Welsted on Milton's language

1724

Extract from Leonard Welsted, 'A Dissertation concerning the Perfection of the *English* Language, the State of Poetry, etc.', *Epistles, Odes, &c.* (1724), ix.

Nor does any thing, I conceive, require greater Skill or Delicacy, than to improve a Language by introducing foreign Treasures into it; the Words, so introduced, ought to be such, as, in a manner, naturalize themselves; that is, they ought to fall into the Idiom, and suit with the Genius of the Tongue, they are brought into, so luckily, as almost to seem, originally, of its own Growth; otherwise, the Attempt will end in nothing but an uncouth unnatural Jargon, like the Phrase and Stile of *Milton*, which is a second *Babel*, or Confusion of all Languages; a Fault, that can never be enough regretted in that immortal Poet, and which if he had wanted, he had perhaps wanted a Superior.

77. Fenton on *Paradise Lost*

1725

Extract from Elijah Fenton, 'Life of John Milton', *Paradise Lost* (1725).

A literary figure in his own day, Elijah Fenton wrote a repeatedly printed *Life* of Milton, which prefaced his edition of *Paradise Lost*. Fenton edited other poems; his texts were also frequently republished, for they attempt to 'correct' the errors of the early editions. The *Life* is drawn from previous biographical accounts, with Fenton's own appreciations and criticisms of the poems clearly stated.

We come now to take a survey of him in that point of view in which he will be looked on by all succeeding ages with equal delight and admiration. An interval of above twenty years had elapsed since he wrote the mask of Comus, L'Allegro, Il Penseroso, and Lycidas; all in such an exquisite strain, that tho' he had left no other monuments of his genius behind him, his name had been immortal. But neither the infirmities of age and constitution, nor the vicissitudes of fortune, could depress the vigour of his mind, or divert it from executing a design he had long conceived of writing an heroic poem. The fall of man was a subject which he had some years before fixed on for a tragedy, which he intended to form by the models of antiquity; and some, not without probability, say, the play opened with that speech in the fourth book of *Paradise Lost*, v. 32, which is addressed by Satan to the sun. Were it material, I believe, I could produce other passages which more plainly appear to have been originally intended for the scene: but whatever truth there may be in this report, it is certain that he did not begin to mold his subject in the form which it bears now, before he had concluded his controversy with Salmasius and More; when he had wholly lost the use of his eyes, and was forced to employ in the office of an amanuensis any friend who accidentally paid him a visit. Yet under all these discouragements, and . . . various interruptions, in the year 1669 he published his *Paradise Lost*; the noblest poem, next to those of Homer and Virgil, that ever the wit of man produced in any age or nation. Need I mention any other evidence of its inestimable worth, than that the finest geniuses who have succeeded him, have ever esteemed it a merit to relish and illustrate its beauties? whilst the critic, who gazed with so much wanton malice on the nakedness of Shakespeare when he slept, after having formally declared war against it, wanted courage to make his attack; flushed though he was with his conquests over Julius Caesar and the Moor; which insolence his muse, like the other assassins of Caesar, severely revenged on herself; and, not only after her triumph, became her own executioner. Nor is it unworthy of our observation, that though, perhaps, no one of our English poets hath excited so many admirers to imitate his manner, yet I think never any was known to aspire to emulation: even the late ingenious Mr. Philips, who, in the colours of stile, came the nearest of all copiers to resemble the great original, made his distant advances with a filial reverence; and restrained his ambition within the same bounds which Lucretius prescribed to his own imitation. . . .

And now, perhaps, it may pass for fiction, what with great veracity I affirm to be fact, that Milton, after having, with much difficulty, prevailed to have this divine poem licensed for the press, could sell the copy for no more than fifteen pounds: the payment of which valuable consideration depended on the sale of three numerous impressions. So unreasonably may personal prejudice affect the most excellent performances!

About two years after, together with *Samson Agonistes* (a tragedy not unworthy the Grecian stage when Athens was in her glory) he published *Paradise Regained*. But, *Oh, what a falling off was there*! Of which I shall say no more, than that there is scarcely a more remarkable instance of the frailty of human reason than our Author gave, in preferring this poem to *Paradise Lost*; nor a more instructive caution to the best writers, to be very diffident in deciding the merit of their own productions.

78. Burnet's Notice

After 1700

Extract from Gilbert Burnet, *History of His Own Time* (1725), i, 265–6.

Gilbert Burnet (1643–1715), Bishop of Salisbury, presents a brief contemporary opinion of Milton. The manuscript of the *History* was put in order and seen through the press by the bishop's son, Sir Thomas Burnet, who is sometimes therefore given as author.

John Goodwin and *Milton* did also escape all censure, to the surprise of all people. . . . *Milton* had appeared so boldly, tho' with much wit and great purity and elegancy of style, against *Salmasius* and others, upon that argument of the putting the King to death, and had discovered such violence against the late King and all the Royal family, and against Monarchy, that it was thought a strange omission if he was forgot, and an odd strain of clemency, if it was intended he should be forgiven. He was not excepted out of the act of indemnity. And afterwards he came out of his concealment, and lived many years much visited by all strangers, and much admired by all at home for the poems he writ, tho' he was then blind; chiefly that of *Paradise Lost*, in which there is a nobleness both of contrivance and execution, that, tho' he affected to write in blank verse without rhyme, and made many new and rough words, yet it was esteemed the beautifullest and perfectest poem that ever was writ, at least in our language.

79. Voltaire on Milton

1727

François-Marie Arouet de Voltaire, 'Milton', from *An Essay Upon the Civil Wars of France . . . And also Upon the Epick Poetry of the European Nations From Homer to Milton* (1727), 102–21.

François-Marie Arouet de Voltaire (1694–1778) revised the present essay to a more adverse criticism of Milton. His suggestion that Andreini's drama lay in the background of *Paradise Lost* has been both attacked and seriously considered over the years. The play is an analogue of the Adam and Eve story, but that is all. Originally published in English, the essay sought to examine French incompetency in epical writing by contrast with Milton's English achievement.

Milton is the last in *Europe* who wrote an *Epick* Poem, for I wave those whose Attempts have been unsuccessful, my Intention being not to descant on the many who have contended for the Prize, but to speak only of the very few who have gain'd it in their respective Countries.

Milton, as he was travelling through *Italy* in his Youth, saw at *Florence* a Comedy call'd *Adamo*, writ by one *Andreino* a Player, and dedicated to *Mary de Medicis* Queen of *France*. The Subject of the play was the *Fall of Man*; the Actors, God, the Devils, the Angels, *Adam*, *Eve*, the Serpent, Death and the Seven mortal Sins. That Topick so improper for a Drama, but so suitable to the absurd Genius of the *Italian* Stage, (as it was at the Time) was handled in a Manner intirely conformable to the Extravagance of the Design. The Scene opens with a Chorus of Angels, and a Cherubim thus speaks for the Rest. 'Let the Rainbow be the Fiddlestick of the Fiddle of the Heavens, let the Planets be the Notes of our Musick, let Time beat carefully the Measure, and the Winds make the Sharps, &c.' Thus the Play begins, and every Scene rises above the last in Profusion of Impertinence.

Milton pierc'd through the Absurdity of that Performance to the hidden Majesty of the Subject, which being altogether unfit for the

Stage, yet might be (for the Genius of *Milton*, and for his only) the Foundation of an *Epick* Poem.

He took from that ridiculous Trifle the first Hint of the noblest Work, which human Imagination hath ever attempted, and which he executed more than twenty Years after.

In the like Manner *Pythagoras* ow'd the Invention of Musik to the Noise of the Hammer of a Blacksmith. And thus in our Days, Sir *Isaak Newton* walking in his Gardens had the first Thought of his System of Gravitation, upon seeing an Apple falling from a Tree.

If the Difference of Genius between Nation and Nation, ever appear'd in its full Light, 'tis in *Milton*'s Paradise lost.

The *French* answer with a scornful Smile, when they are told there is in *England* an *Epick* Poem, the Subject whereof is the Devil fighting against God, and *Adam* and *Eve* eating an Apple at the Persuasion of a Snake. As that Topick hath afforded nothing among them, but some lively Lampoons, for which that Nation is so famous; they cannot imagine it possible to build an *Epick* Poem upon the Subject of their Ballads. And indeed such an Error ought to be excused; for if we consider with what Freedom the politest Part of Mankind throughout all *Europe*, both Catholicks and Protestants, are wont to ridicule in Conversation those consecrated Histories; nay if those who have the highest Respect for the Mysteries of the Christian Religion, and who are struck with Awe at some Parts of it, yet cannot forbear now and then making free with the *Devil*, the *Serpent*, the Frailty of our first Parents, the Rib which *Adam* was robb'd of, and the like; it seems a very hard Task for a profane Poet to endeavour to remove those Shadows of Ridicule, to reconcile together what is Divine and what looks absurd, and to command a Respect that the sacred Writers could hardly obtain from our frivolous Minds.

What *Milton* so boldly undertook, he perform'd with a superior Strength of Judgment, and with an Imagination productive of Beauties not dream'd of before him. The Meaness (if there is any) of some Parts of the Subject is lost in the Immensity of the Poetical Invention. There is something above the reach of human Forces to have attempted the Creation *without* Bombast, to have describ'd the Gluttony and Curiosity of a Woman without Flatness, to have brought Probability and Reason amidst the Hurry of imaginary Things belonging to another World, and as far remote from the Limits of our Notions as they are from our Earth; in short to force the Reader to say, 'If God, if the Angels, if Satan would speak, I believe they would speak as they do in *Milton*.'

249

I have often admir'd how barren the Subject appears, and fruitful it grows under his Hands.

The *Paradise Lost*, is the only Poem wherein are to be found in a perfect Degree that Uniformity which satisfies the Mind and that Variety which pleases the Imagination. All its Episodes being necessary Lines which aim at the Centre of a perfect Circle. Where is the Nation who would not be pleas'd with the Interview of *Adam* and the *Angel*? With the Mountain of Vision, with the bold Strokes which make up the Relentless, undaunted and sly Character of Satan? But above all with that sublime Wisdom which *Milton* exerts, whenever he dares to describe God, and to make him speak? He seems indeed to draw the Picture of the Almighty, as like as human Nature can reach to, through the moral Dust in which we are clouded.

The *Heathens* always, the *Jews* often, and our Christian Priests sometimes, represent God as a tyrant infinitely powerful. But the God of *Milton* is always a Creator, a Father, and a Judge; nor is his Vengeance jarring with his Mercy, nor his Predeterminations repugnant to the Liberty of Man. These are the Pictures which lift up indeed the Soul of the Reader. *Milton* in that Point as well as in many others is as far above the ancient Poets as the Christian Religion is above the *Heathen* Fables.

But he hath especially an undisputable Claim to the unanimous Admiration of Mankind, when he descends from those high Flights to the natural Description of human Things. It is observable that in all other Poems Love is represented as a Vice, in *Milton* only 'tis a Virtue. The Pictures he draws of it, are naked as the Persons he speaks of, and as venerable. He removes with a chaste Hand the Veil which covers every where else the enjoyments of that Passion. There is Softness, Tenderness and Warmth without Lasciviousness; the Poet transports himself and us, into that State of Innocent Happiness in which *Adam* and *Eve* continued for a short Time: He soars not above human, but above corrupt Nature, and as there is no Instance of such Love, there is none of such Poetry.

How then it came to pass that the *Paradise Lost* had been so long neglected, (nay, almost unknown) in *England*, (till the Lord *Sommers* in some Measure *taught Mankind to admire it*,) is a Thing which I cannot reconcile, *neither* with the Temper, *nor* with the Genius of the *English* Nation. The Duke of *Buckingham* in his Art of Poetry gives the Preference to Spencer. It is reported in the Life of the Lord *Rochester*, that he had not Notion of a better Poet than Cowley.

Mr. *Dryden*'s Judgment on *Milton* is still more unaccountable. He hath bestow'd some Verses upon him, in which he puts him upon a Level with, any above, *Virgil* and *Homer*:

> *The Force of Nature could not further go,*
> *To make a third she join'd the former two.*

The same Mr. *Dryden* in his Preface upon his Translation of the *Aeneid*, ranks *Milton* with *Chapellain* and *Lemoine* the most impertinent Poets who ever scribbled. How he could extol him so much in his Verses, and debase him so low in his Prose is a Riddle which, being a Foreigner, I cannot understand.

In short one would be apt to think that *Milton* has not obtained his true Reputation till Mr. *Adisson* the best critick as well as the best Writer of his Age, pointed out the most hidden Beauties of the *Paradise Lost*, and settled for ever its Reputation.

It is an easy and a pleasing Task to take Notice of the many Beauties of *Milton*, which I call universal: But 'tis a ticklish Undertaking to point out what would be reputed a Fault in any other Country.

I am very far from thinking that one Nation ought to judge of its Productions by the Standard of another, nor do I presume that the *French* (for Example) who have no *Epick* Poets, have any Right to give Laws on *Epick* Poetry.

But I fancy many *English* Readers, who are acquainted with the *French* language, will not be displeas'd to have some Notion of the Taste of that Country: And I hope they are too just either to submit to it, or despise it barely upon the Score of its being foreign to them.

Would each Nation attend a little more than they do, to the Taste and the Manners of their respective Neighbours, perhaps a general good Taste might diffuse itself through all *Europe* from such an intercourse of Learning, and from that useful Exchange of Observations. The *English* stage, for Example, might be clear'd of mangled Carcasses and the Style of their tragick Authors, come down from their forced Metaphorical Bombast to a nearer Imitation of Nature. The *French* would learn from the *English* to animate their Tragedies with more Action, and would contract now and then their long Speeches into shorter and warmer Sentiments.

The *Spaniards* would introduce in their Plays more Pictures of human Life, more Characters and Manners, and not puzzle themselves always in the Entanglements of confus'd Adventures, more romantick than natural. The *Italian* in Point of Tragedy, would catch the Flame from

EIGHTEENTH-CENTURY COMMENT TO 1732

the *English*, and all the Rest from the *French*. In Point of Comedy, they would learn from Mr. *Congreve* and some other Authors, to prefer Wit and Humour to Buffoonery.

To proceed in that View, I'll venture to say that none of the *French* Criticks could like the Excursions which *Milton* makes sometimes beyond the strict Limits of his Subject. They lay down for a Rule that an Author himself ought never to appear in his Poem; and his own Thoughts, his own Sentiments must be spoken by the Actors he introduces. Many judicious Men in *England* comply with that Opinion, and Mr *Adisson* favours it. I beg Leave in this Place to hazard a Reflexion of my own, which I submit to the Reader's Judgment.

Milton breaks the Thread of his Narration in two Manners. The first consists of two or three kinds of Prologues, which he premises at the Beginning of some Books. In one Place he expatiates upon his own Blindness; in another he compares his Subject and prefers it to that of the *Iliad*, and to the common Topicks of War, which were thought before him the only Subject fit for *Epick* Poetry; and he adds that he hopes to soar as high as all his Predecessors, unless the cold Climate of *England damps his Wings.*

His other Way of interrupting his Narration, is by some Observations which he intersperses now and then upon some great Incident, or some interesting Circumstance. Of that Kind is his Digression on Love in the fourth Book: [IV, 744–750].

As to the first of these two Heads, I cannot but own that an Author is generally guilty of an impardonable Self-love, when he lays aside his Subject to descant on his own Person; but that human Frailty is to be forgiven in *Milton*; nay, I am pleas'd with it. He gratifies the Curiosity, it raises in me about his Person, when I admire the Author, I desire to know something of the Man, and he whom all Readers would be glad to know, is allow'd to speak of himself. But this however is a very dangerous Example for a Genius of an inferior Order, and is only to be justified by Success.

As to the second Point, I am so far from looking on that Liberty as a Fault, that I think it to be a great Beauty. For if Morality is the aim of Poetry, I do not apprehend why the Poet should be forbidden to intersperse his Descriptions with moral Sentences and useful Reflexions, provided he scatters them with a sparing Hand, and in proper Places either when he wants Personages to utter those Thoughts, or when their Character does not permit them to speak in the Behalf of Virtue.

'Tis strange that *Homer* is commended by the Criticks for his comparing *Ajax* to an Ass pelted away with Stones by some Children, *Ulysses* to a Pudding, the Council-board of *Priam* to Grasshoppers: 'Tis strange, I say, that they defend so clamourously those Similies, tho' never so foreign to the Purpose, and will not allow the natural Reflexions, the noble Digressions of *Milton* tho' never so closely link'd to the Subject.

I will not dwell upon some small Errors of *Milton*, which are obvious to every Reader, I mean some few Contradictions, and those frequent Glances at the *Heathen* Mythology, which Fault by the by is so much the more unexcusable in him, by his having premis'd in his first Book that those Divinities were but Devils worshipp'd under different Names, which ought to have been a sufficient Caution to him not to speak of the Rape of *Proserpine*, of the Wedding of *Juno* and *Jupiter*, &c., as Matters of Fact.

I lay aside likewise his preposterous and aukward Jests, his Puns, his too familiar Expressions so inconsistent with the Elevation of his Genius, and of his Subject.

To come to more essential Points and more *liable* to be debated. I dare affirm that the Contrivance of the *Pandaemonium* would have been entirely disapprov'd of by Critics like Boyleau, Racine, &c.

That Seat built for the Parliament of the Devils, seems very preposterous: Since Satan hath summon'd them altogether, and harangu'd them just before in the ample Field. The Council was necessary; but where it was to be held, 'twas very indifferent. The Poet seems to delight in building his *Pandaemonium* in *Doric* Order with Freeze and Cornice, and a Roof of Gold. Such a Contrivance favours more of the wild Fancy of our Father *le Moine* than of the serious Spirit of *Milton*. But when afterwards the Devils turn dwarfs to fill their Places in the House, as if it was impracticable to build a Room large enough to contain them in their natural Size; it is an idle Story which would match the most extravagant Tales. And to crown all, Satan and the chief Lords preserving their own monstrous Forms, while the Rabble of the Devils shrink into Pigmees, heightens the Ridicule of the whole Contrivance to an unexpressible Degree. Methinks the true Criterion for discerning what is really ridiculous in an *Epick* Poem, is to examine if the same Thing would not fit exactly the Mock heroick. Then I dare say that nothing is so adapted to that ludicrous way of Writing, as the Metamorphosis of the Devils into Dwarfs.

The Fiction of *Death* and *Sin* seems to have in it some great Beauties and many gross Defects. In order to canvass this Matter with Order.

We must first lay down that such shadowy Beings, as *Death, Sin, Chaos*, are intolerable, when they are not allegorical. For Fiction is nothing but Truth in Disguise. It must be granted too, that an Allegory must be short, decent, and noble. For an Allegory carried too far or too low, is like a beautiful Woman who wears always a Mask. An Allegory is a long Metaphor; and to speak too long in Metaphor's must be tiresom, because unnatural. This being premis'd, I must say that in general those Fictions, those imaginary Beings, are more agreeable to the Nature of *Milton*'s Poem, than to any other; because he hath but two natural Persons for his Actors; I mean *Adam* and *Eve*. A great Part of the Action lies in imaginary Worlds, and must *of course* admit of imaginary Beings.

Then *Sin* springing out of the Head of Satan, seems a beautiful Allegory of Pride, which is look'd upon as the first Offence committed against God. But I question if *Satan*, getting his Daughter with Child, is an Invention to be approv'd of. I am afraid that Fiction is but a meer Quibble; for if Sin was of a masculine Gender in *English, as it is in all the other Languages*, that whole Affair Drops, and the Fiction vanishes away. But suppose we are not so nice, and we allow Satan to be in Love with *Sin, because this Word is made feminine in* English (as Death passes also for masculine) what a horrid and loathsome Idea does *Milton* present to the Mind, in this Fiction? *Sin* brings forth Death, this Monster inflam'd with Lust and Rage, lies with his Mother, as she had done with her Father. From that new Commerce, springs a Swarm of Serpents, which creep in and out of their Mother's Womb, and gnaw and tear the Bowels they are born from.

Let such a Picture be never so beautifully drawn, let the Allegory be never so obvious, and so clear, still it will be intolerable, on the Account of its Foulness. That Complication of Horrors, that Mixture of Incest, that Heap of Monsters, that Loathsomeness so far fetch'd, cannot but shock a Reader of delicate Taste.

But what is more intolerable, there are Parts in that Fiction, which bearing no Allegory at all, have no Manner of Excuse. There is no Meaning in the Communication between Death and Sin, 'tis distasteful without any Purpose; or if any Allegory lies under it, the filthy Abomination of the Thing is certainly more obvious than the Allegory.

I see with Admiration, *Sin*, the *Portress* of Hell, opening the Gates of the Abiss, but unable to shut them again: that is really beautiful, because 'tis true. But what signifies Satan and Death quarrelling together, grinning at one another, and ready to fight?

The Fiction of *Chaos*, *Night* and *Discord*, is rather a Picture, than an Allegory; and, for ought I know, deserves to be approv'd, because it strikes the Reader with Awe, not with Horror.

I know the Bridge built by Death and Sin, would be dislik'd in *France*. The nice Criticks of that Country would urge against that Fiction, that it seems too common, and that it is useless; for Men's Souls want no paved Way, to be thrown into Hell, after their Separation from the Body.

They would laugh justly at the Paradise of Fools, at the Hermits, Fryars, Cowles, Beads, Indulgencies, Bulls, Reliques, toss'd by the Winds, at St *Peter's* waiting with his Keys at the Wicket of Heaven. And surely the most passionate Admirers of *Milton*, could not vindicate those low, comical Imaginations, which belong by Right to *Ariosto*.

Now the sublimest of all the Fictions calls me to examine it. I mean the War in Heaven. The Earl of *Roscommon*, and Mr. *Addison* (whose Judgment seems either to guide, or to justify the Opinion of his Countrymen) admire chiefly that Part of the Poem. They bestow all the Skill of their Criticism, and the Strength of their Eloquence, to set off that favourite Part. I may affirm, that the very Things they admire, would not be tolerated by the *French* Criticks. The Reader will perhaps see with Pleasure, *in what consists so strange a Difference* and what is the Ground of it.

First, they would assert, that a War in Heaven being an imaginary Thing, which lies out of the Reach of our Nature, should be contracted in two or three Pages, rather than lengthen'd out into two Books; because we are naturally impatient of removing from us the Objects which are not adapted to our Senses.

According to that Rule, they would maintain, that 'tis an idle Task to give the Reader the full Character of the Leaders of that War, and to describe *Raphael*, *Michael*, *Abdiel*, *Moloch*, and *Nisroth*, as *Homer* paints *Ajax*, *Diomede* and *Hector*.

For what avails it to draw at length the Picture of these Beings, so utterly Strangers to the Reader, that he cannot be affected any Way towards them; by the same Reason, the long Speeches of these imaginary Warriors, either before the Battle, or in the Middle of the Action, their mutual Insults, seem an unjudicious Imitation of *Homer*.

The aforesaid Criticks would not bear with the Angels plucking up the Mountains, with their Woods, their Waters, and their Rocks, and flinging them on the Heads of their Enemies. Such a Contrivance (they would say) is the more puerile, the more it aims at Greatness. Angels arm'd with Mountains in Heaven, resemble too much the Dipsodes in *Rabelais*, who wore an Armour of *Portland* Stone six Foot thick.

The Artillery seems of the same Kind, yet more trifling, because more useless.

To what Purpose are these Engines brought in? Since they cannot wound the Enemies, but only remove them from their Places, and make them tumble down: Indeed (if the Expression may be forgiven) 'tis to play at Nine-Pins. And the very Thing which is so dreadfully great on Earth, becomes very low and ridiculous in Heaven.

I cannot omit here, the visible Contradiction which reigns in that Episode. God sends his faithful Angels to fight, to conquer and to punish the Rebels. Go (says he, to *Michael* and *Gabriel*). [VI, 51-5]

How does it come to pass, after such a positive Order, that the Battle hangs doubtful? And why did God the Father command *Gabriel* and *Raphael*, to do what he executes afterwards by his Son only.

I leave it to the Readers, to pronounce, if these Observations are right, or ill-grounded, and if they are carried to far. But in case these Exceptions are just, the severest Critick must however confess there are Perfections enough in *Milton*, to attone for all his Defects.

I must beg leave to conclude this Article on *Milton*, with two Observations.

His Hero (I mean *Adam*, his first Personage) is unhappy. That demonstrates against all the Criticks, that a very good Poem may end unfortunately, in Spight of all their pretended Rules. Secondly, The *Paradise-Lost* ends compleatly. The Thread of the Fable is spun out to the last. *Milton* and *Tasso* have been careful of not stopping short and abruptly. The one does not abandon *Adam* and *Eve*, till they are driven out of *Eden*. The other does not conclude, before *Jerusalem* is taken. *Homer* and *Virgil* took a contrary Way, the *Iliad* ends with the Death of *Hector*, the *Aeneid* with that of *Turnus*: The Tribe of Commentators have upon that enacted a Law, that a House ought never to be finish'd, because *Homer* and *Virgil* did not compleat their own; but if *Homer* had taken *Troy*, and *Virgil* married *Lavinia* to *Aeneas*, the Criticks would have laid down a Rule just the contrary.

80. Lyttleton on Milton

1728

Extract from George Lord Lyttleton, Letter 1 to his father, Sir
Thomas Lyttleton (4 February 1728). George E. Ayscough, ed.,
The Works of George Lord Lyttleton (1776), iii, 206–7.

Lord Lyttleton (1709–1773) was a prolific and important letter-
writer when the epistolary genre was a primary vehicle for literary
criticism. His imaginative *Dialogues* pave the way for such later
works as Landor's *Imaginary Conversations.*

I am glad that you are pleased with my Persian Letters, and criticism
upon Voltaire; but, with submission to your judgement, I do not see
how what I have said of Milton can destroy all poetical licence. That
term indeed has been so much abused, and the liberty it allows has been
pleaded in defence of such extravagant fictions, that one would almost
wish there were no such words. But yet this is no reason why good
authors may not raise and animate their works with flights and sallies
of imagination, provided they are cautious of restraining them within
the bounds of justness and propriety; for nothing can license a poet to
offend against Truth and Reason, which are as much the rules of the
sublime as less exalted poetry. We meet with a thousand instances of
the true nobleness of thought in Milton, where the liberty you contend
for is made use of, and yet nature very strictly observed. It would be
endless to point out the beauties of this kind in the *Paradise Lost*, where
the boldness of his genius appears without shocking us with the least
impropriety: we are surprized, we are warmed, we are transported; but
we are not hurried out of our senses, or forced to believe impossibilities.
The sixth book is, I fear, in many places, an exception to this rule;
the *poetica licentia* is stretched too far, and *the just* is sacrificed to *the
wonderful.* . . .

81. Salmon on Abdiel

1728

Extract from Nathaniel Salmon, *The History of Hertfordshire* (1728), 185.

The use of Abdiel as illustrative example by antiquarian and historian Nathaniel Salmon (1675–1742) is one of the clearest pieces of evidence of the widespread knowledge and significance of Milton.

Mr. *Clerk*, who purchased of Mr. *Barrington*, left *William* his eldest Son Heir. *William* left *George*, and *George William*. This last mentioned Gentleman lived in those Times when Estates and Integrity were at variance, and was *True as the Dial to the Sun*. He was one of those that had a Title to *Milton*'s Character of a Cavalier, as I take it, under the Person of a Recusant Angel [Abdiel, V, 896–907].

This Reading may require a little Comment to support it. The chief Difficulty lies in imagining this zealous *Antisalmatian* could dress up a Malignant in so amiable Colours. Let it be considered, that Poetical Fury hath chiefly in view an inimitable Piece: That Rocks, Tempests, Vulcanos, are all agreeable Sights from a masterly Hand. The Happiness of the Occasion, goes a great Way in the Happiness of the Description. This Protestor in a Convention of Rebel Angels, must lose some of the Beauties, unless we suppose him a Cavalier in Masque. Where else is the Propriety of keeping Ground against Numbers, and standing a general Apostate Sneer? The Scripture Account of the Defection makes not the Lapsed so much as a Majority; and if we suppose this but a select Detachment or Capitulum of infernal Dignitaries with but a single Negative, what Notion must we have of Angelic Perfection, to admit *Abdiel* could think himself alone? That he should not be countenanced by Legions of those, who could not be won or driven from their Habitations? That the Sun of the Morning should, with the Splendor of his Appearance, absorb and efface entirely the innate Principle of Honour and Integrity in Angelic Minds? I see no

258

Absurdity in believing *Milton* furnished with a true Poetical *Apathia*, to chuse a Subject proper for the finest Drawing: That he had indeed so far debased his glorious Talents, and sunk his Mind from that superior Habitation, in which over-generous Nature had cantoned it, by a mercenary Application to the dirtiest of Work; that he had arrived at as thorough an Aversion to an upright Angel, as an upright Man; that keeping up to the Dignity of his Subject was his only Aim; that if he had but Scope for a Performance that should be admired, even by those that detested his Memory, he could as *Virgil* or *Michael Angelo* draw indifferently a *Vulcan* or a *Venus*.

82. Dennis on Milton's poetical fire

1729

Extract from John Dennis, 'Remarks Upon Several Passages in the Preliminaries to the *Dunciad*' (1729). E. N. Hooker, ed., *The Critical Works of John Dennis* (1939), ii, 367–8.

But now let us come to *Milton*, in whom, if we will believe this little Gentleman, *the poetical Fire glows like a Furnace, kept up to an uncommon Fierceness by the Force of Art*. Now, I dare engage that there are not Two Persons in the World who understand what the little Gentleman says there, and I do really believe that there is not one. What? is the Transcendency of *Milton*'s Genius, which has been admir'd by all the capable World, reduced to Art? Pray, how is the Fire of *Homer* and *Virgil* kept up? for they seem to me to have vastly more of the poetical Art than *Milton*. Indeed *Milton* had more Felicity than they, which threw him upon the Subject of *Paradise Lost*; a Subject which often furnish'd him with the greatest Ideas, which supply'd him with the greatest Spirit. But to shew that it was rather Felicity than Art or Skill, that determin'd him to the Choice, he was by no means so happy in the Choice of *Paradise Regain'd*, a Subject that could supply him neither with the Ideas nor with the Spirit. For Pride and Ambition, Rage and Revenge, and Fury, furnish'd quite another sort of Spirit, than Patience, Resignation, Humility, Meekness, Long-suffering, and the rest of those quiet divine Virtues that adorn the Christian Scheme. Besides, *Milton*'s Fire is so very far from being kept always up by Art, that for near a sixth Part of the Poem it's set down for want of Art. For this Poem is so order'd, that the Subject of the Eleventh and Twelfth Books could by no means supply him with the great Ideas, nor consequently with the great Spirit, which the First, Second, and Sixth had done before; and several Parts of the other Books likewise.

83. Clarke on defects in *Paradise Lost*

1731

Extract from John Clarke, *An Essay Upon Study* (1731), edition of 1737, 194–203.

Clarke (1687–1734), a schoolmaster and classical scholar, indicates his vocations in this excerpt from *Essay on Study*. His criticisms of Milton try to correct what he apparently feels is an untoward (and false) hold that Milton has on readers.

Milton, for Sublimity of Invention, has none I know of to equal him but *Homer*: Tho' there are, in my Opinion, some fundamental Flaws, in the Plan of his Poem, proceeding from a Defect of Judgment in the Author; which because they have not, I believe, been taken Notice of by others, I shall here offer to the Consideration of the Criticks.

1. The Poem is founded upon a very absurd Supposition, that has not the least Appearance of Probability; but on the contrary, seems utterly impossible, *viz*. The Rebellion of Angels against God, with a Design to dethrone him; a Design that could never enter into the Thoughts of any created Being, especially of exalted Knowledge, as the Fallen Angels are every where represented by the Poet. This therefore is contrary to a Rule, as sacred as any in Poetry besides. . . . For the Thing here supposed by the Poet, is so far from being *proximum vero*, that it is at as wide a Distance from it, as Impossibility itself can set it; and an Impossibility apparent and visible to the last Degree. This is to the Tune of,

Humano capiti Cervicem jungere Equinam,

to join Stupidity, carried in Supposition to the utmost Excess, to a Height meerly imaginary, and in Nature impossible, with the most elevated intellectual Powers; such as the Poet up and down intimates those of the Fallen Angels to be. Which, in my Mind, is just as ridiculous, as it would be to represent a Man as a Mathematician of the first Rank, but yet uncapable of counting to Twenty. This therefore seems an unpardonable Flaw.

261

2. The next is a Sequel of the former, and what some perhaps will think, may be more properly reckoned a Part of it, than a distinct Fault, viz. the introducing the Rebel Angels blaspheming. This is making them talk in Character, it's true; but if that was sufficient to justify the Poet, then might the vilest Piece of Stuff, that ever appeared upon a Stage, *the Beggars Opera* be defended; because all the Wretches that act in that *Nauseous Farce*, setting aside their unseasonable Singing, act and talk in a Manner suitable to their Characters. But Characters so shockingly vicious, should, in my Mind, be very sparingly introduced into Works of Invention of any Kind; and where they are, it ought ever to be done in a Way proper to heighten, and not lessen our Abhorrence of them, by making them too familiar to the Mind: Which is the Fault of *Paradise Lost*, as well as the sorry Performance mentioned above. The Reading of Blasphemy indeed naturally raises Horror in Religious Minds, but then that in the Case before us, proceeds from the Nature of the Thing only; and not from any Art or Contrivance of the Poet. He makes the wicked Angels pour forth one blasphemous Harangue after another, without any Interruption or Correction, or any ill Consequence redounding therefrom to the Blasphemers in the Sequel of the Poem; so that his Conduct in this Matter, has a Tendency to take off very much from that Abhorrence, the Mind naturally has of Blasphemy. Swearing and Cursing are allowed, I presume, by all Persons of any Taste, too grating to Virtuous Ears, to be at all used in Poetry, or upon the Stage; but Blasphemy is still worse, and therefore is not to be born with by any Means; as being not consistent with the Reverence due to the Great God, and naturally tending to the Diminution thereof. The Design of Poetry is to please and entertain the Mind; but Blasphemy, even in the Mouth of Daemons, is so far from answering such an Intention, that it is offensive and shocking to the last Degree, utterly uncapable of being rendered agreeable, by any Management of a Poet; and if it was not so, that would be only a stronger Reason, why it ought to have no Place in Poetry. For my Part, I could never read those Passages in *Milton* I here except against, without Pain, and some Indignation against the Author, for defiling his own Invention, and the Minds of his Readers with such abominable Stuff, as ought to have no Admission into the Thoughts of Men, upon any Pretence whatever.

3. Another Thing hard of Digestion in *Milton*, is the Fight of Angels, which, by common Supposition, are Immaterial Beings; and therefore it looks ridiculous at first Sight, to represent them as cutting, slashing, and stabbing one another. If it should be said in Answer to this, that

they are likewise vulgarly supposed capable of assuming Bodies, which is sufficiently to justify the Poet; I humbly conceive it is not. For to take no Notice of the Absurdity of supporting them capable of receiving Pain by the Wounding of such Bodies, they are likewise supposed capable of laying them aside at Pleasure: Which Power rendered the Use of all Arms, both offensive and defensive, the Poet has supplied them with, perfectly needless and ridiculous; because by suddenly dropping their Vehicles, they could prevent, or immediately deliver themselves from all Pain: And therefore it was needless for any of them to hold up a Shield, to guard off a Stroke; when throwing away his Body at once, was a much better Security against the Mischief apprehended. Our Author was drawn into this Absurdity by *Homer*, who has set his Gods a fighting in the *Iliad*; a Thing not only ridiculous, but profane in him, if he looked upon them as real Beings, and Objects of Worship: But if he did not, as, by the Freedom he affectedly takes up and down to ridicule them, one would think it impossible he should, he was then to be sure a downright Atheist: For he appears not in his Writings to have had the least Apprehension of any other Gods, but such as he drolls upon. His Thoughts as to that Matter go no higher than Jupiter, whom he spares as little as the rest of the Tribe.

4. The Introducing of God, and the Son of God, as Actors in his Poem, and delivering themselves in long Speeches, is, in my Mind, an unpardonable Boldness. A Poet may contrive Scenes of Action, and find Speeches for his Fellow-Mortals of the highest Degree, because if he trips in his Judgment, and does not well suit their Characters, no Harm is done. But shall a Man, a poor short-sighted Creature, dare to bring down the most High into a Scene of Diversion, and assign him his Part of Acting and Speaking, as if he was a proper Judge of what is fit for him to do, and to say, upon any Occasion, wherein, to serve the Ends of his own Vanity, or Amusement, he has a Fancy to introduce Him, Him whose Judgments are a great Deep, and whose Ways are past finding out; and where if the presuming poor Animal steps never so little awry, in applying to him, any Action or Language unsuitable to the Character of his unfathomable Wisdom, it is Blasphemy; however, his Weakness may excuse him from the Guilt of it, in the Eye of his Merciful Creator! Shall Men be less tender of the Honour of him, whose Honour ought to be the End of all their Actions, than *Augustus* was of his own; who gave Charge to the Praetors, Ne *paterentur Nomen suum Commissionibus obsolefieri*? The Emperor judged right, in thinking his Honour would be endangered, from the insipid Praises of silly

Orators and Poets. But how much more difficult is it, to make God act a Part in an Epick Poem, suitable to his Glory, than to celebrate the Praises of a Prince, in a Way that shall not discover the Flaws of his Character, or place it in a disadvantageous Light?

Besides these Faults in the Plan of *Paradise Lost*, there is another observable in that admired Poem, viz. the Negligence of the Author with respect to the Smoothness of his Verse, which is sometimes scarce distinguishable from Prose. Had the Delicious Translator of *Homer* acquitted himself no better in that Respect, he would never have found his Advantage with regard to his Character as a Poet, and other Ways, so much as he has done. If a Man pretends to write Verse, let it be Verse indeed, and not move on here and there with a Roughness scarce allowable in Prose. The Advantage of Smoothness and Glibness in the Numbers of a Poet, is no where more visible than in Mr. *Pope*'s Translation of the Catalogue of the Ships in *Homer*'s *Iliad*; which tho' one of the dryest Subjects in the Poem, is thereby rendered one of the most agreeable.

The Reader will, I hope, be so good as to excuse this long Digression; and the rather, because it is not wholly foreign to the Subject I am upon. The rectifying of Mistakes in the Conduct of a Poet, of *Milton*'s Fame and Authority, is a Means to prevent others from being misled into an Imitation of his Faults, as he was by those of *Homer*, who having foolishly set his Gods together by the Ears, and made Jupiter superintend and direct now and then in the Scene of Action at Troy, our Author must needs do something like it: But being in want of Gods for the Purpose of fighting, he has made the Good and Bad Angels fall to it; and has, with great Imprudence and Irreverence, engaged the Son of God in such a ludicrous Piece of Fiction: Whilst God the Father has much the same Superintendency assigned him in the whole Affair of the Poem, as Jupiter has in the Iliad. Which are Extravagances, *Milton*, it's likely, would never have thought of, had not *Homer* set him a Copy.

Appendices

1632: 'On Shakespear' in Second Folio of Shakespeare's *Works* (see also 1640 and 1664).

1637: 'A Mask'.

1638: 'Lycidas' in *Justa Edovardo King naufrago*.

1640: 'Another on the Same [Hobson]' (see also 1657 and 1658) and *'Hobson's Epitaph' (see also next item, 1657, and 1658) in *Banquet of Jests*. *'Hobson's Epitaph' in *Wit's Recreation*. 'Epitaphium Damonis'. 'On Shakespear' in Shakespeare's *Poems*.

1641: March, *'Postscript' in Smectymnuus, *An Answer to a Booke entituled, An Humble Remonstrance*. May(?), *Of Reformation*. July(?), *Of Prelatical Episcopacy*. July, *Animadversions Upon the Remonstrants Defence, against Smectymnuus*.

1642: February(?), *The Reason of Church Government*. April, *An Apology against a Pamphlet call'd A Modest Confutation*.

1643: August(?), *The Doctrine and Discipline of Divorce* (see also next item and 1645).

1644: February, *The Doctrine and Discipline of Divorce*, second ed., enlarged. June, *Of Education* (see also 1673). August, *The Judgement of Martin Bucer*. November, *Areopagitica*.

1645: March, *Tetrachordon* and *Colasterion*. *The Doctrine and Discipline of Divorce*, third ed. *Poems*, including all those previously printed except for the questionable 'Hobson's Epitaph' (see also 1673).

1648: 'Sonnet 13' in *Choice Psalmes put into Musick for Three Voices*.

1649: February, *The Tenure of Kings and Magistrates* (see also 1650). May, *Observations Upon the Articles of Peace*. October, *Eikonoklastes* (see also 1650).

1650: February, *The Tenure of Kings and Magistrates*, second ed. *Eikonoklastes*, second ed.

1651: February, *Joannis Miltoni Angli Pro Populo Anglicano Defensio* (numerous further editions and reprints).

1654: May, *Joannis Miltoni Angli Pro Populo Anglicano Defensio Secunda*.

1655: August, *Joannis Miltoni Angli pro se Defensio*.

* Authorship uncertain.

1657: 'Another on the Same' and *'Hobson's Epitaph' in *Banquet of Jests*.

1658: 'On the University Carrier', 'Another on the Same', and *'Hobson's Epitaph' in *Wit Restor'd*.

1659: February, *A Treatise of Civil Power*. August, *Considerations Touching the likeliest means to remove Hirelings*.

1660: March, *The Readie and Easie Way to Establish A Free Commonwealth* (see also next item). April(?), *The Readie and Easie Way to Establish A Free Commonwealth*, second ed. April, *Brief Notes Upon a Late Sermon*.

1662: 'Sonnet 17' in *Life and Death of Sir Henry Vane* (see also 1694).

1664: 'On Shakespear' in Third Folio of Shakespeare's *Works*.

1667: August(?), *Paradise Lost* (see also 1674); reissued in 1668 and 1669 with prefatory matter.

1669: June, *Accedence Commenc't Grammar*.

1670: *The History of Britain* (see also 1698).

1671: *Paradise Regain'd* and *Samson Agonistes*.

1672: May(?), *Joannis Miltoni Angli, Artis Logicae Plenior Institutio*.

1673: May(?), *Of True Religion, Haeresie, Schism, Toleration. Poems*, second ed., enlarged, including all minor poems previously printed except the questionable *'Hobson's Epitaph' and 'Sonnet 17'; and including *Of Education*, second ed.

1674: *Paradise Lost*, second ed. May, *Joannis Miltonii Angli, Epitolarum Familiarium Liber Unus* (with college prolusions). July(?), *A Declaration, or Letters Patents*.

1676: October(?), *Literae Pseudo-Senâtus Anglicani* (see also 1682).

1681: April(?), *Mr. John Miltons Character of the Long Parliament*.

1682: February, *A Brief History of Moscovia*. Translations of *Literae Pseudo-Senâtus Anglicani*.

1694: 'Sonnets 15, 16, 17, 22' and *Letters of State*.

1698: *A Letter to a Friend, The Present Means and brief Delineation of a Free Commonwealth*, and additions to *The History of Britain* in *A Complete Collection*.

1825: *Joannis Miltoni Angli De Doctrina Christiana* (two eds., one Latin, one an English translation).

1876: 'Carmina Elegiaca' and 'Ignavus Satrapam dedecet' plus an early prolusion in A. J. Horwood, *A Common-Place Book of John Milton*, Camden Society, N.S., Vol. XVI.

1938: 'Proposalls of certaine expedients for the preventing of a civil war now feared, & the setting of a firme government' in Columbia edition of *Works*, XVIII, pp. 3–7.

(*b*) SELECTED SECONDARY REFERENCES AND
COLLECTIONS SIMILAR TO THE PRESENT VOLUME

Bond, Richmond P. *English Burlesque Poetry, 1700–1750.* Harvard University Press, 1932; reprinted, N.Y., 1964.

Darbishire, Helen, ed. *The Early Lives of Milton.* London, 1932.

Diekhoff, John S. *Milton on Himself.* Oxford University Press, 1939; reprinted, N.Y., 1958. Contains extensive excerpts from Milton's work, dealing with aims, plans, and self-criticism, *passim.*

Dowden, Edward. 'Milton in the Eighteenth Century (1701–1750)'. *Proceedings of the British Academy,* 1908.

Dowling, John, ed. *Testimonies and Criticism Relating to the Life and Works of John Milton.* St. Austell, 1903. A similar collection with some connective discussion and emphasis on nineteenth-century materials.

French, J. Milton, ed. *The Life Records of John Milton.* Rutgers University Press, 1949–58. Five vols. A chronological listing, with notes, of all known documents relating to Milton or discussions of him during his lifetime, and to his immediate relatives before his birth and after his death.

Gillespie, Edgar B. '*Paradise Regained*: A History of the Criticism and an Interpretation.' Unpublished doctoral dissertation, Duke University, 1966.

Good, John W. *Studies in the Milton Tradition.* University of Illinois Press, 1915; Reprinted, N.Y., 1967.

Graham, James J. G., ed. *Autobiography of John Milton.* London, 1872. Prints items dealing with aims and inspiration.

Grewe, Eugene F. 'A History of the Criticism of John Milton's *Comus,* 1637–1941.' Unpublished doctoral dissertation, University of Michigan, 1964.

Havens, Raymond D. *The Influence of Milton on English Poetry.* Harvard University Press, 1922; reprinted, N.Y., 1961. A list of poems, which were influenced by Milton's works, categorized by year and types, is appended.

Keeley, Gracie Lee. 'Milton's Reputation in the Eighteenth Century as Reflected in the *Gentleman's Magazine* and the *Monthly Review.*' Unpublished master's thesis, University of Georgia, 1940.

Mackail, J. W. 'Bentley's Milton.' *Proceedings of the British Academy,* 1924.

Manuel, M. *The Seventeenth-Century Critics and Biographers of Milton.* Trivandrum, India: University of Kerala, 1962.

Moore, C. A. 'Miltoniana (1679–1741).' *Modern Philology,* XXIV (1926–7), 321–39.

Oras, Ants. *Milton's Editors and Commentators From Patrick Hume to Henry John*

Todd (*1695–1801*): *A Study in Critical Views and Methods*. Dorpat Universitet, Acta, XX (1930).

Parker, William Riley. *Milton's Contemporary Reputation*. Ohio State University Press, 1940. Contains a list of printed allusions, dated from 1641 to 1674.

Plunkett, Frank W. 'The Miltonic Tradition in One of Its Phases. The Criticism of Milton as Found in Leading British Magazines of the Pre-Romantic and Romantic Periods (1779–1832).' Doctoral dissertation, Indiana University, 1931, printed in summary form by Arkansas State College Press, 1934.

Robertson, J. G. 'Milton's Fame On The Continent.' *Proceedings of the British Academy*, 1908.

Sherburn, George. *The Early Popularity of Milton's Minor Poems*. University of Chicago, 1920. Originally published in *Modern Philology*, XVII (1919–20), 259–78, 515–40.

Spingarn, J. E., ed. *Critical Essays of the Seventeenth Century*. Oxford, 1908–9; reprinted, Indiana University Press, 1957. Three vols. Essays and remarks, *passim*.

Thorpe, James, ed. *Milton Criticism: Selections from Four Centuries*. New York, 1950; reprinted, London, 1966. Contains Marvell's and Dryden's commendatory poems; excerpts from Dryden, Toland, Dennis; the first six papers on *Paradise Lost* by Addison; and excerpts from Pope, Richardson, Johnson's *Life*, and Thomas Warton. The introduction presents a brief history of Milton criticism.

(*c*) NOTEWORTHY CRITICISM OMITTED IN THIS SELECTION

Samuel Barrow, 'In Paradisum Amissam Summi Poetae Johannis Miltoni', *Paradise Lost*, London, 1674.

Daniel Defoe, *A Review of the State of the British Nation*, Vol. VIII, No. 159, 29 March 1712, 637–40.

Henry Felton, *A Dissertation on Reading the Classics, and Forming a Just Style*, London, 1709. Pages 227–9, 237–8 in Ed. 4, 1730.

Antonio Francini, 'Ode' (in Italian), *Poems*, London, 1645. Prefixed to the Latin poems.

Johann Christoph Gottsched, *Versucheiner critischen Dichtkunst vor die Deutschen*, Leipzig, 1730, pp. 69, 151, 177–8, 312, 547.

Constantin de Magny [pseudonym], *Dissertation Critique sur de Paradise Perdu, Poëme Heroique de Milton*, Paris, 1729.

Danielis G. Morhofi, *Polyhistor sive de Notitia Auctorum et rerum commentarii*, Lubbock, 1688, 304–5.

John Oldmixon, *An Essay on Criticism As It Regards Design, Thought, and Expression, in Prose and Verse*, London, 1728, *passim*.

Edward Phillips, *Theatrum Poetarum*, London, 1675. Preface, 18–28; under 'John Phillips', 114–5.

Edward Phillips, 'Tractatulus de Carmine Dramatico Poetarum Veterum, cui subjungitur Compendiosa Enumeratio Poetarum Recentiorum', appendix to John Buchler, *Sacrarum Profanarumque Phrasium Poeticarum Thesarus*, London, 1669. Page 399 in edition of 1679.

Sir Richard Steele, *The Tatler*, No. 237, 14 October 1710.

Select Index

I

Critics and Critical Works

II

Milton's Works

III

Topics

IV

General

MORGAN COMMUNITY
COLLEGE LIBRARY